Travel and   ment

Other books by Douglas Foster

Managing for Growth
Managing for Profit
Marketing Imperative
Mastering Marketing
Planning for Products and Markets
Successful Management in Developing Countries (vols 1–4)
The Management Quadrille

Travel and Tourism Management

Douglas Foster

MACMILLAN

First published 1985 by
THE MACMILLAN PRESS LTD
Houndmills, Basingstoke, Hampshire RG21 2XS
and London
Companies and representatives
throughout the world

ISBN 0–333–36408–2 hardcover
ISBN 0–333–36409–0 paperback

A catalogue record for this book is available
from the British Library.

Printed in China

10   9   8   7
00   99   98   97   96   95   94

To ELIZABETH

whose encouragement and support and assistance with the preparation of the final manuscript made this book possible

'Travel, in the younger sort, is a part of education; in the elder a part of experience. He that travelleth into a country before he hath some entrance into the language, goeth to school, and not to travel.'

FRANCIS BACON (1561–1626) 'Of travel'

Contents

Preface

Tourism (and travel) encompasses a substantial number of business activities. These include accommodation of all kinds, transport both international and local, numerous entertainment activities and other attractions with various support services. In addition in recent years, new developments such as leisure centres, marinas, sports resorts and new types of tourism such as sea cruises, fly-drive cruises, motoring holidays, coach tours and the like have increased the range of businesses in this 'industry'. Finally, national tourist organisations of various kinds are also involved.

To cover all this in complete detail in a book of manageable length is not possible. So this work concentrates on the major aspects appropriate for the business courses for which it is intended. Those readers wishing to go into more detail on any part of tourism, because they are or will be actively involved in their careers in one sector or other, must study the various specialist books on accommodation, transport, the retail travel trade and so on. This book is intended to be a balanced, general presentation of tourism and travel.

The book is intended for students taking National and Higher National courses on Tourism, business studies and other courses (e.g. HCIMA, etc.) having core or option modules on tourism. It will be appropriate for those taking 'A'-level and equivalents and professional courses in which tourism is featured, or where some people intend to work in the industry. It will help those already working in the industry who wish to improve the professional standards of their work and so enhance their career prospects. Even central and local government civil servants and politicians involved in tourism development and management should find the book of considerable assistance to them.

Woking, 1985   DOUGLAS FOSTER

1

Tourism: its Impact and Motivations

The tourism industry moves people from one region of the world to another on visits of a few weeks to destinations outside the area where the holiday tourist or business traveller normally lives and works. It is also concerned with the activities of these people at the resorts or destinations.

For the holiday or leisure tourist (hereafter referred to as *tourist* unless qualified for a specific reason) the industry may also be described as a 'dream machine'. It realises a dream or fantasy for one brief moment in the tourist's otherwise toilsome life. For the business traveller, the industry is an important provider of travel and other services vital for the execution of business on an international scale. With modern holiday tourism, the tourists are often encapsulated in their *package tour* from start to finish. However the greater sophistication of recent years allows tourists to be more adventurous and escape this encapsulation as often as they wish. The individual no longer has to rely on the all-inclusive package but can choose from an ever widening range of non-inclusive arrangements (discussed in later chapters). The choice depends on the degree of independence and adventurousness shown by individuals and their ability to pay for these holidays. The main motivating factors that brought about the rapid expansion of tourism from the 1950s onwards, for people from the northern hemisphere are listed in Table 1.1. The prime motivation was the search for the sun.

This mass movement of people required substantial investment in transportation facilities. Without good and efficient transport systems, mass tourism is impossible. However, technological developments did not always reduce the relatively high cost of mobility. In some instances (e.g. Concorde) they appear to have increased it in money terms. While the world's economic recession of the late 1970s and early 1980s saw some cutback in investment and mass unemployment reduced the ability of many people to travel long distances, demand for tourism has remained fairly stable, even if some growth rates decreased. (For example, in 1983 some nine million people from the United Kingdom went on holiday, mainly abroad. This compares with four and a half million in 1977.) The industry responded to these adverse economic trends by making various economies in the packages offered. Less expensive, lower grade hotels have been used. The number of airlines serving a country or resort and the number of flights per week have been reduced. Unnecessary, luxurious trimmings have been removed. These and other economies have been applied to provide acceptable holidays at prices the consumer can still afford. In addition, in 1984, several major British tour operators introduced substantial price reductions and a 'price war' between them ensued.

Tourism allows people who might otherwise not have the chance, to sample a little of the joys and excitement of other 'worlds', countries or cultures. The fact that some holidays may prove almost as harsh realities for people as their normal lives, does not seem to matter too much! They may only insist on greater 'safety', realised by sticking to familiar things. They travel by their national airlines with compatriots, are guided and wet-nursed by couriers from their own countries, stay in cosmopolitan hotels which hardly reflect local culture and eat familiar foods obtainable in their own homes. This is the average modern 'package tourist'. Happily in response to growing demand for more individuality and adventure, the non-inclusive and 'activity holidays' have been developed. The latter range from voyages to Antarctica, trekking in the

Table 1.1   Tourism: motivational factors

Recreational/pleasure
1   Rest – to escape from daily routine
2   For an enjoyable time
3   To obtain an adventurous or romantic experience

Cultural and educational
1   To see other countries – the people and culture
2   To see places of special interest – historical sites, museums, art galleries, etc.
3   To visit places featured in current events
4   To attend special events including concerts, exhibitions
5   To learn more about one's hobbies and other interests

Ethnic
1   To visit the family's country of origin
2   To see places visited by relatives or friends
3   To see unusual or quaint cultures/customs in remote regions

Miscellaneous
1   Sporting events
2   Change of weather or climate
3   Adventure
4   Sociological – to get to know other parts of the world
5   Business/conference/congress travel

foothills of the Himalayas, journeys up the Amazon and safari into jungles and deserts. However for the average tourist, holidays still represent the brief realisation of a dream. The industry could do well to remember this, for without contravening the advertising laws which apply, their consumer advertising could be more effectively devised to increase sales, whilst minimising disappointment because reality did not match consumers' expectations.

Tourism today is a phenomenom of the post-Second World War period when the word 'tour' entered into common usage in the English language. However it has been used from the eighteenth century to describe special journeys made by wealthy people (i.e. the 'Grand Tour', dating from 1748) or orchestra, theatre and opera companies. Those who could afford to travel did so individually or in family or friendship groups. The word then implied involvement in a certain amount of adventure. The travellers really mixed with the local people and societies of the lands through which they travelled. There were real cultural exchanges and cross-fertilisation of ideas as a result.

Now tourism has grown in importance to such an extent that many Third World (or developing) countries cannot balance their international trading accounts without their considerable earnings from tourism. With this growth has developed some still unanswered questions. Are the assumptions of twenty-five years ago still valid? Does tourism really benefit the host countries to the extent originally imagined? Or does it help to destroy the culture and ecology of host nations? As mass tourism advances so wildlife and Nature retreat? For example, the need to develop the infra- and superstructure for mass tourism, linked with the growing need to expand resources through increased extraction of mineral and other raw materials, can destroy natural habitats such as the tropical rain forests of the world, so vital for the continuation of all life forms. Reasonably content but unsophisticated societies become discontented and hanker after the (unnecessary?) 'luxuries' which the tourist demands?

The development of international airlines, hotel groups, tour operators and travel agents have ensured that substantial proportions of tourism expenditure remain in, or are remitted back to the home countries of the tourists. Is it in the interest of developing countries to leap, in one go, from an agriculturally based economy to a service economy dependent on a seasonal business such as tourism? Does too rapid development of tourism inhibit real, balanced growth in other more stable activities? The over-development of resorts can do harm, as several extant examples testify mutely. These and other questions, discussed more fully in other sections of the book, need more detailed study if balanced and beneficial tourism development is to be achieved.

1.1 Concepts and definitions

Mankind's basic, primitive motives are fear, lust, love and greed but there is also the need for stimulation through change, excitement and novelty by doing something different. Travel and tourism can provide that stimulation physically while music, art and literature stimulate the senses. Many tourism products are designed to achieve both forms of stimulation. Travelling away from familiar locations provides diversity and can be pleasantly exciting. Excursions to concerts, art galleries and other cultural attractions stimulate the senses. In a few words, tourism allows people to escape from their normal, humdrum lives. As Mark Twain said, 'Even heaven can be boring after a while'.

The human animal needs change if it is to operate at optimum levels. Travel provides that change. However the level of satisfaction achieved from tourism depends on the age, health, energy, background and expectations of the individual. The younger and better educated travel more than the elderly and less educated, provided the time and money are available. So what may be a satisfying challenge to one may be an energy-sapping frustration to another. What may be fun at twenty or thirty years of age may be too overpowering at fifty or sixty! So attitudes to tourism vary considerably and can do so even within the same age group.

At the present time also there is the increased search for the exotic or unusual holiday. However, at the end of each day, most travellers prefer to return to a base (hotel or whatever) that provides the familiar and so represents safety (witness the cosmopolitan, modern 'lodges' provided for safari groups). Even for the sophisticated person there is a limit to the 'local colour' they can take.

1.1.1 Concepts
Tourism is an activity involving a complex mixture of material and psychological elements. The material ones are accommodation, transportation, the attractions and entertainments available. The psychological factors include a wide spectrum of attitudes and expectations as mentioned earlier and as illustrated in Table 1.1. These attitudes and expectations range

from pure escapism to fulfilment of a dream or fantasy, or rest, recreation, educational and other social interests. All are usually subjectively assessed and evaluated by the tourists themselves. This poses problems for the tour operator who somehow, must find reliable ways of quantifying these 'values'. Otherwise the pattern and nature of demand cannot be estimated accurately, when they cannot be certain of giving their customers what they want.

Tourism often involves travellers in activities which may vary only minimally from their normal behaviour patterns when at home. Yet these activities must be presented to potential customers as something 'different' if interest in them is to be created. On the other hand, tourists' activities can differ greatly from those of the nationals of the host countries and can be the cause of friction between the different nationals. The tour operator should try to minimise the possibility of this discord.

Further, the cost of travel and tourism is usually paid from the residue of the consumer's net discretionary income, a very small fraction of their gross income. Thus in the 1950s tourism was low down on most people's list of priorities, being desirable but not essential. Demand had to be created through persuading consumers to buy this exotic product. By the 1960s tourism had been accorded greater significance and demand grew substantially. By the early 1980s, the world's economic recession once again forced many people to accord a lower degree of essentiality to holidays especially with the high rates of inflation and unemployment prevalent at the time. Thus demand for tourism products can fluctuate considerably and be unstable according to the economic conditions prevailing at the time.

Purchasing decisions on holidays in the affluent 1960s were sometimes of the 'impulse' type. People had the money so the impact of tour brochures did lead to some 'snap buys'. Gradually as consumers became more sophisticated, experienced and less affluent, decisions became based on careful consideration of what was on offer from competing tour operators. Potential customers now seek much more information about these offerings. In recent years, major disappointments, doubtful conduct and claims by some operators and some bankruptcies of smaller firms have led to greater caution being shown by consumers. A more professional approach to its business by the tourism industry is now essential. It is claimed that the majority of holidaymakers now give as much consideration to their decisions on holidays as they do for the purchase of a new car. They may also stick with the one tour operator who has proved satisfactory and has a good image for dependability.

1.1.2 *Definitions*

The Committee of Statistical Experts of the League of Nations in 1937 first defined 'foreign tourist' as 'any person visiting a country, other than that in which he actually resides, for a period of at least twenty-four hours'. Persons staying for less than twenty-four hours were to be treated as 'excursionists'. Within this definition, tourists would be those travelling for pleasure, domestic reasons, health, business purposes, conferences, meetings, diplomatic and religious purposes plus arrivals on sea cruises even if they stay for less than twenty-four hours. Persons not to be considered as 'tourists' were those not stopping in a country, those arriving to take up residence, residents of frontier zones, those who live in one country and cross over to another to work (for example, Spanish workers who used to cross to Gibraltar daily), students and young persons attending school or universities and people with or without work permits arriving to take up occupations or any business activities in a country. Subsequently, members of armed services stationed in another country, whether by treaty or agreement or not, were also not counted as tourists.

Figure 1.1 illustrates the various purposes of travel and the basic differences between tourists and excursionists. It shows also some more recent modifications to practice in that nationals of a country resident abroad are now considered to be tourists when visiting their own country provided they stay for at least twenty-four hours. In recent years, common practice is to use the word 'tourist' to describe all who travel for holiday, leisure, recreational, cultural, ethnic, educational and sporting purposes. The term 'business traveller' then refers to all who travel for business purposes, or to attend meetings, conferences, congresses and exhibitions to do with business affairs. This concept is used in this book unless otherwise qualified. It is

Figure 1.1 Classification of travellers and purpose of travel

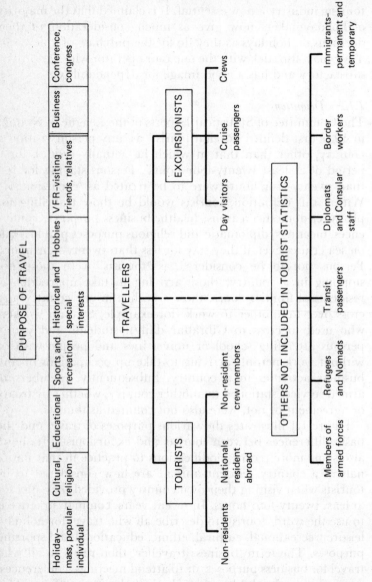

argued also that passengers from sea cruises should more correctly be considered by the industry (if not official statistics) as excursionists since their needs and expectations are more in line with the excursionist than with the tourist or business traveller. However, non-resident crews (usually air crew) staying in a country for twenty-four hours or more are also counted as tourists. All crew staying for less than this qualifying time are excursionists!

The purposes of a visit or journey are usually as defined by the United Nations Conference in Rome in 1963, on international travel and tourism. It also defined 'visitors' (or travellers) as 'any person visiting a country other than that of their normal residence other than for following a remunerated occupation within the country visited'. This Rome conference accepted the definitions proposed to it by the International Union of Official Travel Organisations (IUOTO) but it was not until 1968 that this was approved by the United Nations Statistical Commission. (IUOTO has now been replaced by the World Tourism Organisation – WTO).

At a further meeting of the UN Statistical Commission in New York during April–May 1965 it was pointed out that with the absence of frontier formalities between certain countries (for example Scandinavian and EEC nations) it was impossible to collect data according to the 1963 Rome definitions. Further, since it is possible to obtain a permit to reside or work in a country after having crossed a frontier, it was decided to exclude certain categories from tourism statistics (see Figure 1.1). In analysing international tourism it is important to separate the sectors comprising these movements since they are likely to have different characteristics. Their growth is also likely to be influenced by quite different factors. For example, the growing internationalisation of business has led to a greater number of foreign nationals residing and working in countries other than that of their origins or normal places of residence. However until a better system can be devised, the general definition of the League of Nations (1937) is still used for statistical purposes.

It is also necessary to distinguish between two further classifications. First, *international tourism* refers to visitors of all kinds who go to foreign countries for their vacations or for business purposes. It also covers those nationals of a country going abroad (outflows) and foreign visitors coming into that country (inflows). Second, *domestic tourism* refers to local nationals and residents of a country who travel to other parts of that country for their holidays.

In 1960 the International Monetary Fund (IMF) also made recommendations on methods for calculating travel receipts and payments as a basis for estimating the travel element of a country's balance of payments. These were as follows:

(a) travel covers expenditures in a compiling country by all foreign visitors (credits) and expenditures abroad by all residents visiting foreign countries (debits);

(b) travel should cover all expenditures (in a country) that is incidental to travel (for example, transport and the purchases of goods other than for business purposes). However, payment to foreign carriers (other than local transportation) should be recorded separately and not be included under the heading of 'travel';

(c) the five categories of persons whose expenditures should be included under travel receipts and expenditures were defined as tourists, business travellers, students, government officials and others;

(d) to be excluded were expenditures by crews of international carriers, military personnel, migrant workers, diplomats and other personnel of foreign governments.

1.1.3 Statistics

Statistics defining the *volume* of tourism to any country must measure the number of visitors entering that country, the length of their stay or the number of days or nights spent in the country. Usual practice is to measure the number of arrivals and the length of their visits. About forty countries obtain this information and data from registrations at the various types of accommodation. About sixty countries record them at the points of entry on the frontier.

Accommodation records are useful if the legal enforcement of detailed registration procedures are operated efficiently for all types of accommodation. This is especially useful when recording at frontiers is not possible (for example, as between member nations of the EEC) or when open frontiers are maintained as between Canada and the United States of America. However it is not always practical to cover all types of accommodation (for example, private homes, small boarding houses, camping sites or when casual camping off official sites takes place). So official volume statistics compiled by this method rarely cover all traffic. Sometimes this method may be supplemented by household surveys in countries of origin when the outward traffic of residents to destinations abroad may be measured. However, correlating these two different sources of data is not always easy to do.

Frontier statistics are obtained either from immigration or custom control points and are accurate when stringent control methods are used. For example, in the United Kingdom and USA, the use of landing or entry cards and forms completed by visitors is very effective. But as the freedom of movement across frontiers increases (e.g. the EEC) it becomes more difficult to obtain accurate data by this method.

For *expenditure statistics*, foreign travel expenditures are divided into those in the countries visited and fare payments to international carriers. The traditional method for measuring expenditures in a country is by use of bank records and foreign exchange controls. With the increasing flow of tourists and the reduction of foreign exchange controls (again as between members of the EEC where the free movement of capital is an important plank of the Treaty of Rome) this method becomes unreliable. Considerable amounts of currency can be exchanged in many countries by residents, particularly foreign residents, which may not be for the purpose of impending travel.

With inclusive tours especially, a substantial proportion of travel payments are made in the countries of residence. Further, transactions by international organisations including carriers, are often based on net payments. Then when foreign exchange controls are enforced, bank records will understate foreign visitors' expenditures by the degree of smuggling (of currency) that takes place. They overstate the position when currency allocated for travel is in fact used for capital expenditures (such as the down-payment on holiday villas) in the countries visited.

An alternative method is to estimate visitors' expenditures from surveys of hotels, travel agents and other recipients of tourist expenditures, for example, those who sell other services to tourists. The problem is that the last category find it difficult to separate tourists from other receipts so even this method can be unreliable. A more reliable approach is to use sample surveys of departing tourists which seek information on their expenditures during their visit, usually at their points of departure or subsequently. These surveys are related to traffic flows which are representative of total visits to a country. The information obtained is cross-checked against other sources, hotels (for hotel tariffs and expenditures), tour operators (for details on inclusive tours), and fares lists and passenger manifests of carriers. The same problems also arise when attempting to assess expenditures by business travellers. Obtaining the necessary information from their employers can however provide more reliable data.

1.2   Significance of tourism

It was in 1620 that Thomas Mun wrote in his *England's Treasure by Foreign Trade* that the one item H.M.'s Customs were unable to bring into their accounts was the expenses of travellers. In the intervening 360 years, travel and tourism has grown from a minor fiscal nuisance and an activity limited to the privileged rich, including traders, into its present-day industry having major economic and social significance. While in the nineteenth century the roots of modern tourism can be perceived when the rich travelled for private purposes (trade, leisure, recreation, culture), today ordinary people of most walks of life may travel for any of the purposes shown in Table 1.1. The economic significance can be gauged by the fact that by 1972 world expenditure on tourism exceeded £8 billion (£8000 million) and by 1982 was in excess of £10 billion (at rates of exchange current in those years).

The social significance stems from the greater appreciation of other cultures, institutions, ways of life and social structures which travel and tourism are said to facilitate. This is very true for the individual travellers who must enter into the very fabric of life of the countries visited to achieve their purpose. It is arguable if it is nearly as true for today's average tourist on a packaged holiday. The former must move around and live amongst the local nationals and be involved in various exchanges (business, cultural and social) with them. The latter is carefully cocooned in a group, usually of their compatriots and stays in an hotel which tries to provide the food and atmosphere of their home country. Any trips outside are usually by carefully escorted çoach or train. The contact and exchange with local people is often limited to ordering food and drink and buying souvenirs. Only in the case of 'special interest tours' might there be any cultural exchange. Even here this may take the form of carefully escorted group trips to a concert, the opera or museums and art galleries. In every case the courier might be a national of the home country or one so versed in the language and culture of that country that little cultural exchange is effected.

However, in theory, bringing together people of different countries and backgrounds does have political and educational significance as well as the economic and social aspects mentioned below. The degree achieved depends on the opportunities offered to tourists to meet freely with nationals of the host countries and the ability to converse in the relevant languages. In the ideal situation, tourism enhances awareness, knowledge and ultimately understanding between nationals, balancing in part the bias that a simple study of politics and utterances by politicians might give. The Twenty-first United Nations General Assembly designated 1967 as the International Tourist Year. It set the seal on the importance of tourism when it passed the following resolution unanimously: 'tourism is a basic and most desirable human activity deserving the praise and encouragement of all people and all governments'. Today tourism also has significance in furthering technological changes, in promoting religious understanding and sporting activities.

1.2.1 *Economic and social significance*
Another indicator of the growing economic significance of tourism is the growth that has taken place in the number of tourist trips being taken. WTO in its *Economic Review of World*

Tourism showed that in 1982 total world tourism arrivals exceeded 2.6 billion (2600 million), a 4 per cent increase on 1981. Domestic tourism totalled 2.3 billion while international tourism arrivals were 365 million. The latter figure compares with 280 million in 1975. The international arrivals generated tourism receipts in excess of $106 billion ($106,000 million) representing an increase of 12 per cent on 1981. (In the UK the industry's total turnover was £8 billion of which foreign earnings were about £4 billion.) This shows that tourism is a major contributor to world trade. Its foreign earnings are double the world value for exports of non-ferrous metals and minerals and greater than the value of international trade in iron and steel.

While the world recession in the early 1980s slowed down the rate of growth in tourism, when the developed world recovers from the recession, further expansion in growth is expected. According to the WTO also, governments' role in the tourism sector is expected to increase (see also Section 1.5.3). This will be particularly so in developing countries as they realise the important contribution that tourism plays in the broadening and growth of their economy. This greater involvement will extend into the vocational training of persons in the industry and in the planning, development and promotion of tourism.

More flexible use of accommodation and diversification in tourism equipment, infrastructure and superstructure are foreseen (the last two are discussed in Chapter 6). Further, changes in the international regulation of air transport and technological developments in this important contributor to tourism are anticipated. Trends in the design and development of resorts will also require a new approach to the identification and planning of new resorts, particularly in developing countries. Similar developments in the revitalisation of existing resorts in most countries is expected (see also Section 1.5).

Without question tourism affects the economy of the host country. An increase in expenditure by foreign tourists will raise national income. However an increase in expenditure on tourism abroad lowers national income. Thus the net income generated in a country by tourism will vary directly with the expenditure of foreign visitors in the host country and inversely with expenditures abroad by the nationals of the host nation.

Expenditure on imports has a similar effect on a nation's income as expenditure on tourism abroad. Therefore imports for tourism purposes further reduce the net income from tourism and the tourism economic multiplier (see Section 1.3). Since with developing countries many tourists needs can be supplied only by imports, the economic effect of tourism on the economy will have a lesser effect than at first imagined.

Further, the benefits and costs are not distributed evenly. What may be a benefit to one group of a community may be a cost to another. Hotel and restaurant operators benefit from tourism but the local nationals not in these activities suffer costs measured in terms of over-crowding, noise and pollution. In some cases immigrants may be used to serve the tourism industry and this is a cost to the community since they increase the demand for medical services, water and sewerage systems, roads, transportation, schools and in some instances, other welfare services and funds. A new airport may be fine for expanding tourism but if the country is poor (developing) many local nationals cannot afford to use it. This applies also to new luxury hotels and restaurants.

The economic impact of tourism is not just the tangible effects of tourism development and structural changes in a specific region. It leads also to an increase in population (both permanent and temporary). Tourism is thus a dynamic agent of change and many individuals and organisations, large and small, are affected by it. The nature and scale of tourism also varies by time and place. Figure 1.2 is a simple illustration of this. It shows the basic economic and social impacts for the three stages of development: I – undeveloped; II – developing and III – developed. The pyramid represents the relative volume of business obtainable.

The economic impact of tourism has a disproportionate or lesser effect on the host community because of the multiplier effect (see Sections 1.3.4 and 1.3.5) which spreads the benefits far beyond the resort. A simple consideration of the expenditures in that location overstates the benefits believed to accrue there. However the economic impact can be divided into three stages. First there is a *direct expenditure* by tourists on the goods and services provided by hotels, restaurants and other tourist facilities in the region. Next is the *indirect expenditure* due to the resultant

Figure 1.2 Economic and social impact of tourism

STAGE	TYPE OF TOURIST	ECONOMIC IMPACT	SOCIAL IMPACT ON LOCAL NATIONALS
I Undeveloped	New or non-existent; a few explorers (individuals)	Minimum	Euphoric
II Developing	Seekers of the off-beat or unusual individuals and groups	Moderate	Apathetic
III Developed	Mass or popular tourists (large groups)	Substantial	Very apathetic or antagonistic

business transactions arising from the first stage. Finally there is the *induced expenditure* due to the re-spending of income by local nationals employed in or benefiting from, the tourism expenditures in their regions.

So the consideration of the economic impact on an area needs analyses of the creation of new employment, effects on all related business activities as well as tourist expenditures, the indirect business activities affected by such expenditures, any new taxes generated and other facilities required by tourists entering the region. The multiplier effect shows how the spread of spending by tourists beyond the initial recipients maintains the economic viability of a region and the enterprises that might otherwise fail.

The social impact can also be estimated via the effect of tourism expenditures on the increasing income of the area and the rising incomes of those involved in all the business activities in the region. The standard of living and quality of life should increase or improve but does not always! However the creation of dissatisfaction with former standards can have a negative effect. The nature of the new employment must also not be forgotten. Much of it is part-time in nature. Where demand is very seasonal employment may be for only a few weeks in a year. Then the new jobs may employ mainly women who too often are paid lower wages than men. Further, mainly unskilled labour may be needed and this commands much lower wages than that of skilled labour. So the economic and social impacts may not be as great as initial, superficial consideration may suggest.

Then there is the question of public and private *economic and social costs*. Against the economic benefits accruing must be ranged the costs or disadvantages. First, while tourism requires the improvement of the infrastructure of the region, the cost of this must often be carried solely by the host government. This can lead to an increase in taxation for the local nationals and trigger inflationary pressures. Then if tourist demand is seasonal there is the problem of under-utilisation of the infrastructure reducing the profitability of hotels, restaurants and transport without reducing the need for expenditure on maintenance and repairs. If a considerable number of local houses are bought for second or holiday homes this can raise the general price level for domestic properties. This can create further problems for the local community and lead to considerable resentment.

The social costs can be many. They can range from the destruction of historical and cultural aspects which gave the area its original tourist appeal. Or local culture may become stylised to suit a pattern of tourist-related entertainment. This may soon become a travesty of the real culture (examples are the 'cultural shows' now on offer in many countries). It is also becoming obvious that such stylisation does not secure all the economic and social benefits for residents of developing countries. Much of this expenditure may be remitted abroad to the home countries of the organisers of such shows. So, in total, the economic, social and environmental problems created by tourism, if not properly controlled, can counterbalance any of the oft-claimed benefits accruing to the host country.

The main beneficiaries of tourism are obviously those enterprises involved in supplying tourist needs (e.g. tour operators, travel agents, hotels, restaurants, souvenir shops, camping sites). Some of them (e.g. souvenir shops, camping sites and some restaurants and entertainment providers) are entirely or almost entirely dependent on demand from tourists for their profitable existence. Several others (banks, local transport and general retailers) rely partly on tourism but exist in the main to serve the local resident population. They all share a common interest even though the difficulty of definition does not allow the application of the traditional concept of what is an industry. However the industry can be classified into first, primary tourist enterprises who are wholly or chiefly dependent on the tourists for their income and second, those who are partly dependent on tourists.

1.2.2 *Other significances for developing countries*

While the comments in the previous sub-section also apply to developing (or Third World) countries in varying degrees, some other points need consideration. First, should tourism be encouraged and expanded and will there be net benefits for the country or region? For many nations these considerations may be academic. The country may have no other options, especially for very poor countries or those with no other resources (other than tourism potential) that could be developed. Second, the main benefits are the provision of jobs, increased income and improved amenities for resident nationals. Compared with other types of economic development increase in tourist traffic and expenditures permit a relatively faster improvement in living standards. Operational skills are simple and can be quickly mastered by people with even moderate education. Higher skills are usually imported at least for a few years thus buying time in which to train local nationals (now demanded by most developing countries). Further, the industry is labour intensive and can absorb substantial amounts of unemployed labour very quickly, whether skilled or unskilled.

Third, in many countries tourism is the major, sometimes only, employer and it has the advantage that employment can be created with relatively low investment in fixed assets per employee. Thus many countries with few or limited exploitable natural resources or exportable products but with a large number of unemployed people, give priority to the development of tourism. In such countries receipts from international tourism account for a high proportion of their total national income. For many others, it is their main source of foreign exchange earnings.

Fourth, Government revenue may also be increased through taxes and import duties on goods and services imported for tourism purposes. Sales or value added taxes may also be levied and income tax receipts will be increased as employment rises and subsequent increases in incomes are taxed. Taxes on the profits of enterprises in tourism also add to the fiscal coffers. Fifth, besides the development in hotels, tourism requires investment in airports, roads, public transport, telecommunications and public utilities. This improvement of the infrastructure and superstructure create long-term benefits for other parts of the economy.

However, they create the costs and other disadvantages discussed earlier. In addition, too rapid development of tourism can contribute to inflation by causing land prices to rise encouraging speculation on land and properties and destruction of agricultural land. It also puts excessive demand on construction and other industries that are suppliers to tourism. Next, this may add to the problems of pollution and danger to the ecology of the country, especially the flora and fauna. Historical, cultural and archaeological sites may also need protection through restrictive legislation. Then since most tourism developments are irreversible, sudden changes in demand may lead to greater unemployment, substantial trading losses and increased social tensions. Facilities cannot often be converted to other uses and the creation of alternative employment takes time and substantial investment. The last may not be possible for many poorer nations. Finally, social disadvantages may arise. The presence of a large number of tourists encourages consumption and behaviour patterns which are often inappropriate for local nationals.

1.2.3.   *Types of tourism*

So it is insufficient to consider only the apparent economic benefits and improvements in the general infra- and super-structure stemming from tourism development. The costs and 'disbenefits' which formerly were not considered must now receive greater attention. These advantages and disadvantages should be considered in economic terms and that of their impact on the environment and culture of the resort area and the geographical region as a whole. If these are to be fully understood so that tourism can be more effectively managed for the mutual benefit of host country and tourists, a better understanding of the different types of tourism is necessary. This will permit better analyses of the motivations and requirements of the different types of tourists.

As indicated by Table 1.1 there are five types of tourism. First is *recreational tourism* which is what most people have in mind when 'tourism' is mentioned. This is where mass- and popular-package tours, involving substantial sized groups, seek mainly sun-sea-sand and fresh air or sporting activities of various kinds. These groups are primarily seeking a change and rest. However, 'rest' is interpreted in different ways by people. For some it is lazing all day on a beach. For others it is seeing as much as possible that is within reach of their holiday base. Some of the smaller groups ('popular tourism') may also be made up of individuals who make use of the cost savings from travelling in a group but on arrival, will follow their own pursuits.

Second is *cultural tourism*. The aim here is to experience new cultural activities. These can be centred on rural, peasant (primitive) areas or be based in towns offering special cultural activities (e.g. folklore, art, music, etc.). Third is *historical tourism*. This involves visits to heritage locations, museums, cathedrals, monastries and so on. Fourth is *ethnic tourism*. This involves contact with unusual or quaint customs in remote areas, visiting the family's country of origin and relatives or friends. Finally there is *environmental tourism* when the higher income groups in particular, are interested in visiting remote or 'pure' environments. Because of their remoteness these journeys involve substantial expenditure. Therefore they are often outside the means of those who normally take mass – or popular – packages.

Thus the lower income groups and a portion of the middle income ones would primarily be interested in recreational tourism. Those with active hobbies and other activities and the necessary income form the main patronage for historical and ethnic tourism with higher income groups also being interested in ethnic tourism. These are very rough divisions of interest and in recent years, people of all income levels, educational backgrounds and job status have shown interest from time to time in all five types of tourism. Nevertheless analyses of the consumers taking these different holidays will give a clear indication of their motivations and needs. This helps those in tourism to plan their offerings with greater precision. (The marketing implications are discussed later in Chapters 7 and 8.)

1.3   The impact of tourism

There are various aspects to consider.

1.3.1   Tourism and employment
The tourism industry is a major provider of employment. Growth in tourism results in an increase in employment. However it is not easy to analyse accurately the extent of employment resulting directly from tourism. First, the people primarily involved in providing services and goods for the

tourists may also be doing the same for non-tourists. For example hotel restaurants will be serving some local nationals as well as the tourists staying at their establishment. Second, those employed in enterprises not specifically intended for tourists (e.g. local transport) will number some of the latter amongst their customers. Third, most official statistics on employment cover employees only and not the self-employed nor employers. The tourism industry being comprised of a large number of small units does in fact have a substantial number of the last two working in it. So any official statistics could understate the total employment in tourism. Fourth, a substantial proportion of employment is seasonal so that the numbers employed vary considerably from one period of the year to another. Finally, those employed in tourism are seldom distinguished in official statistics from others employed in similar activities (e.g. transport, laundry services and entertainment activities).

However in 1982 the EEC estimated that there were some 11 million jobs in the Community that were directly or indirectly related to tourism. Of this about 30 per cent were believed to be concerned with foreign tourists including visitors from other EEC countries, while the balance were involved with domestic tourism. In 1972 it was estimated that some $1\frac{1}{2}$ million people in the UK were employed in tourist-related employment. Despite the recession of the early 1980s in 1984 it was estimated by the British Tourist Authority (BTA) that some $1\frac{1}{2}$ million were still employed in tourist-related businesses. However if the economic circumstances of the world in the rest of the 1980s remain fairly static increases in tourism-related employment in the UK are not expected to be substantial.

Because of the limitations of official and quasi-official statistics and difficulty in defining the industry, it is not possible to make more detailed analyses of employment in tourism other than the general statements above. However it is appreciated that direct employment in tourism is only a part of the total employment, there being a substantial indirect involvement. The latter are those from other sectors of the economy who provide goods and services used by tourists. Further employment arises as incomes derived from direct and indirect employment are spent or re-spent. As stated earlier, for several

countries tourism is a major, or only, source of
Even in the UK, some areas account for as much ¦
of total employment (e.g. in coastal resorts) while
have as much as 10 per cent involved in supplying services ιυι
tourists. The national average is about 7 per cent.

1.3.2 Tourism and conservation

Assessing the impact of tourism on the environment and thus
the need for conservation of the ecology is difficult. Emotional
factors and consideration of private interests also intervene and
the lack of appropriate data, especially of internal (and in
many cases domestic) tourist movements does not help. However the idea of the management of tourism attractions and
their protection from the worst impact of mass tourism started
in the USA in 1872 with the development of Yellowstone
National Park. In the UK in 1883, concern over the destruction of the natural beauty of the Lake District resulted in the
creation of a defence society to protect the area.

Now, several countries have awakened to the need for
planning and control of tourism and the dangers of uncontrolled and too rapid development, not only of tourism.
Conservationists view tourist development and tourists as
threats to the survival of wildlife and treasured landscapes (for
example the problems arising in East Africa and Southeast
Asia). They are far more apprehensive of development than
experts in the industry believe. Those with vested interests in
tourism, whether because they see it as the only salvation for
poor economics or because they stand to gain profit from it,
view conservationists as a threat to the viability of existing
enterprises and future growth. The latter's fears are heightened
because of the large range of destinations.

Conservationists are afraid that those organisations or people investing substantial funds into new tourist facilities, or in
renovating old ones, wanting a quick and substantial return on
their capital, will build large and cheap properties to achieve
this end. Happily in a few countries, including the UK, more
thought is being given to the quality of development. However
some form of control of planning, design and restoration is
essential if the worst aspects of tourism development are not to
destroy the original attraction of the area. Central government

could exercise control of aesthetic matters while local government could consider the commercial advantages and weigh these against the 'social costs' of the project. Such controls could be effected through building restrictions, planning approval, control of the scale of development and the selective award of development grants.

Some countries relatively recently into large-scale tourism development (e.g. Spain since the Second World War) have over-developed their coastal attractions and ended up with a concrete jungle of high-rise hotel blocks. Little of the original beauty remains. Others (e.g. Switzerland and Austria) with a long history of tourist development have managed to expand their tourism facilities without damage to the environment. Singapore, a small island nation, dependent to some extent on tourism has not quite achieved either states. However, despite many postwar hotel developments, high-rise apartment blocks, commercial and industrial buildings, Singapore has still managed to keep some of its limited countryside unspoilt. Bali tottered on the brink of becoming another Costa Brava but realised in time that uncontrolled development would destroy the spiritual atmosphere and other attractions that made the island famous. At the moment, tourist development is restricted to the southern coastline which already has a number of tourist hotels. Some other countries are taking a more cautious view of development. Mauritius and parts of the Kenyan coast have gone for tasteful, single- and two-storey establishments using local materials and designs.

The trend is now to avoid attracting unnecessary large numbers of cheap, package tour groups who spend relatively little in the country. Countries are being more selective in their choice of target markets. They try to attract the higher income groups who spend more when abroad, or people who will have minimal impact on the local population, especially those who will accept or integrate with local customs and culture. Thus they hope to limit those who will only import their own cultures and standards.

Conservation is said to be the wise use of resources. With the countryside this means the safeguarding of visual beauty. This is a subjective concept since landscapes can be natural, man-modified or manmade. In man-modified ones, low level development can allow the retention of many characteristics of natural landscapes. With manmade ones the highly valued landscapes are those that have escaped the impact of modern forestry and intensive farming. Conservation of wildlife involves the concept of the viability and survival of living things (flora and fauna) and of the individual species measured in terms of numbers, successful breeding and quality.

The impact of tourism also varies according to the density of population and its distribution in relation to the greatly valued wildlife and scenery. In compact countries like the UK and other European countries, such areas are within easy reach of densely populated zones. They are subjected to intensive use with frequent visits by the populace. They are under much greater threat from pollution and destruction. In continental sized countries like the USA, Australia, India and Canada, most valued areas are in sparsely populated regions and often some distance from major centres of high population. It requires the organisation of a major holiday to visit them. Because of this and their area they are less under threat than similar regions in Europe.

The adverse impact of tourism involves loss of habitat, disturbance of flora and fauna and their eventual destruction by pollution (including litter) and fire (through careless use of bonfires and empty bottles left on the ground under a blazing sun). Animals and birds are disturbed by excessive traffic and withdraw into more confined areas unable to support their numbers. In desperate attempts to find food, they will destroy the vegetation of their confined habitat. Many die of hunger and the ecological damage is accelerated. Doomsday may then not be far off for that wildlife and region. Too many human feet or vehicle wheels can also destroy a nature reserve and other holiday areas.

These forms of damage are being experienced in widely different parts of the world. These include the safari parks of East Africa, the rain forest of Malaysia and some of the national parks in Britain. Planners and promoters of tourism and tourists themselves, who rarely have training in, or knowledge of ecological matters, often feel they have made every effort to minimise such damage. They are annoyed if they are attacked for not doing enough! Yet many of these adverse effects can be minimised, even removed, with more effective, comprehensive, planning and better management of tourist attractions and flows. The industry has a growing responsibility for finding ways of optimising the benefits of tourism *and* minimising all these 'social costs'. Perhaps this will be achieved by promoting better understanding of the problems to tourists.

Most tour operators do not appear to be interested in conservation. They appear to say and do nothing about it. One excellent exception in Britain is Sunmed Holidays, operated by Redwood Travel Ltd. In their 1984 brochure they give valuable space to stress their support of conservation and to urge their customers to do so also. They ask tourists to think about the effect that successful tourism can have on wildlife. They ask their customers to observe a simple code. This ranges from not buying souvenirs which are, or are made from, parts of wild animals including shells and bits of coral to not digging up wild flowers (which die very quickly anyway) and not eating pickled or cooked wild birds. Sunmed also support the work of the World Wildlife Fund. In the same brochure they reprint a report by this organisation of what happened to a Loggerhead Turtle (an endangered species) that came ashore at Zante to lay her eggs. This process was watched by a large crowd of humans who walked over and crushed other turtles' egg clutches. The turtle was caught and killed by the locals. Her carapace was dried in the sun and then polished. Her mummified flippers and head were reattached and the carcase joined the many others that were for sale in the souvenir shops. The article was titled 'Death of a Turtle'. Perhaps if more tour operators took a leaf out of Sunmed's book, the tide running against conservation would be turned.

1.3.3   Other considerations

Another aspect to be considered is that every resort or region has a specific saturation level which if exceeded will lead to physical discomfort, inability to provide adequate facilities and other discomforts for all. These negate the original attractions of the resort. Some Mediterranean coastal regions are examples. Then potential tourists will consider it not worth the effort to visit such resorts. This *concept of saturation* has only been recognised in recent years with the substantial increase in tourist flows to accessible regions.

The problem arises in four ways. First, the increasing use of land for tourism denies its use for other urgent or important purposes (e.g. schools, hospitals, housing and open spaces). Second, increased tourism traffic places increasing demand and pressure on the urban super- and infrastructure but mainly on transport. Third, the seasonality of demand for labour to service tourism (usually unskilled and semi-skilled) unbalances the structure of local employment. Finally, these three combined, lead to the alienation of the local inhabitants. Thus it is necessary to consider in advance of development, what might be the saturation point for a proposed resort and at what levels of demand the social costs or disbenefits mentioned in the preceding sections become serious.

The intensity of the land problem varies with each region. In sparsely populated areas (e.g. East Africa) it may be a conflict between the needs of the flora and fauna and tourists. In major cities where land is at a premium, there are increasing pressures for more 'green belt' areas to reduce the density of housing or to increase the number of hospitals, schools and other amenities. While new hotels can help the local economy, careful consideration should be given to their location. Should they be in city centres or in the suburbs? In the latter case they can help to turn these communities into more viable commercial possibilities. They can bring new life into a rundown area or lead to the rehabilitation of historic buildings that might otherwise fall into disrepair.

Regarding the employment problem, overdependence on the tourism industry with its relatively low productivity potential, can retard economic growth of the region. This problem is less acute where other economic development is not possible or practical. Further, because tourism is seasonal, labour may be imported from other regions or countries, at least for peak demand periods. Where the imported labour is of a different ethnic group political tensions could arise. The earnings of this imported labour will have only a marginal effect on the economy of the resort as much of this income will be remitted to the workers' home countries.

Inadequate planning and the lack of national and regional policies based on the real capacity of resorts, aggravate the problems. In addition, tourists are intensive users of only part of a region's super- and infrastructure, for example transport, water supply and other utilities. The uneven distribution of resorts hinders the balanced development of these support services. The growth in coach tours and motoring holidays on inadequate roads adds to existing traffic congestion and the exasperation of local residents. So increasing the tourist population, which increases population density at peak periods, means more sharing of limited resources. Both tourists and residents suffer delays and frustration on all fronts. Hence the need to use the concept of resort saturation.

1.3.4 The economic multiplier

In Section 1.2.1, *Economic significance*, it was stated that the total income of a resort or country increased not only by the direct expenditure of tourists. There were also the indirect and induced expenditures resulting from tourism. Because of the recirculation of incomes from this source the total effect on an economy is greater than actual tourist expenditure. This event is called the *multiplier* effect. *Economic multipliers* are used by economists and others to estimate how much extra total income is produced as a result of the initial injection or spending of cash in an economy.

The size of the multiplier depends on how much of the original income is spent and not saved. Other influencing factors include whether tourism leads to increased imports to meet visitors' needs and how much of their income hotels and airlines are allowed to remit to their home countries. Money spent by tourists on imported goods and services increases the income of the region by less than would be the case if it was spent on locally produced items. Thus the initial expenditure by tourists gives only a general indication of the impact of tourism on an economy. Use of the appropriate multiplier gives a better indication of the value of tourism to a host country. Against this must be set the disbenefits or social costs. From research to date, economic multipliers range from 1 to $2\frac{1}{2}$ and are usually around 1 for tourism.

1.3.5 Tourism and economic multipliers

Tourists' expenditures are part of a host country's 'invisible earnings' being an additional inflow of foreign currency. This direct revenue leads to increased turnover in all related businesses. This increases government revenues (taxes) and the income of households with members working in the tourism and other affected industries, especially transport, cultural activities, souvenirs and so on. However as stated, some businesses may remit part of their income abroad. So not all of the total tourist expenditure represents income for local nationals. In addition, hoteliers and others have to spend money on restocking and maintaining the fabric of their establishments and pay all their taxes. So some money will be paid to persons who may not be residents of the region.

The money remaining in a host country is mainly the salaries paid to local nationals, any retained profit and the relatively small amounts spent on souvenirs. In addition there is the money spent on local produce and products, utilities such as water, electricity and local transport, and government dues and taxes. The increased demand for labour and goods may lead to increased employment in related local industries directly (through the employment of extra people) and indirectly (through the increased earnings of those already employed). This could lead to an improvement in the standard of living and increased purchases to satisfy expanding wants. Local industries benefiting from increased sales may have to spend more on purchases of raw materials and components. This will improve the earnings of the suppliers of these items. Thus a further chain of expanded economic activity results.

As the general income of the region and country increases, personal incomes and level of employment will improve. This assumes that the necessary unutilised resources are available. If the country is already at its optimum level of activity, tourism revenue might just start an inflationary spiral with its usual short- and long-term harmful effects. The indirect effects will depend on how much local firms depend on each other for goods and services (the *inter-sector linkages* as it is called). In poor nations these linkages are small and increased imports are necessary. This reduces the benefits from the original inflow of currency due to tourism.

The further income and employment generated is referred to as the *induced effects* of tourism revenue. The sum of the direct and indirect effects is called the *secondary effect* of tourism. The *tourism economic multiplier* is a measure of these total effects of tourism expenditures. There are four models used to identify the 'flows' resulting from the multiplier effect.

First is the *income multiplier model* which demonstrates the relationship between the change in the level of income in the economy for each additional unit of tourism expenditure. The calculations should include the secondary effects from the respending of income in the host country by non-residents. That which is not respent is extracted from the calculations since this portion does not benefit the country.

Next is the *sales or transactions multiplier model* which measures the change in economic activity for each extra unit of sales to tourists. It measures the increase in business turnover or revenue resulting from tourist expenditures. Then there is the *output multiplier model*. This is similar to the previous one but takes into account also, real changes in related inventories in the host country.

Finally there is the *employment multiplier model* which has two variations. The first measures the employment generated by a given amount of tourist spending. The second compares the direct and indirect (or secondary) employment created by additional tourist spending with direct employment only.

The use of multipliers assists those who have to make decisions on tourist developments. Their usefulness depends on the accuracy of data available and how well the models have been defined. Assumptions have to be made and the accuracy and relevance of these determine the soundness of the resultant information. Substantial errors can arise if the assumptions prove unrealistic.

The models are designed to measure the impact of change on economies having some unused resources. The assumption is made that supply is elastic in all sectors of the economy. Then increased demand can be met by increased output. If this is not so, resources will have to be diverted from other sectors of the economy or imports will have to be increased. Multipliers cannot measure the effects of these major changes nor the resultant opportunity costs.

Further, it is assumed that there are no relative changes between suppliers in an economy whether these are due to technological change or because of their inability to supply the additional services or products. Then there is the question of the suitability of the technique for gauging the impact of tourism. Multiplier analysis cannot measure the long-term benefits gained by a host economy from tourism development. Their value will depend on the nature of the economy and the degree to which suppliers to tourism are major suppliers to other sectors of the economy. Yet despite these reservations, used with care, multiplier analyses can be useful methods for measuring the *possible* impact of tourism on the host economy.

1.4 Motivations and determinants

The consumer who travels for vacations and recreation forms the largest sector of the tourism market. Former economic growth and increasing prosperity were the main reasons for the expansion of the industry. However other socio-economic factors helped.

1.4.1 Motivations

Increases in net discretionary incomes, especially of the younger age groups, and improved educational standards increased interest in foreign lands and cultures. So the demand for tourism increased. The occupation of the head of the household, resultant promotion and the increase in the number of wives going to work also affected the growth in demand. For example a person made a company director would strive to take the family, or at least the spouse, on a winter holiday. They become a two-holiday-a-year family. A winter holiday in the Carribean or Far East became a status symbol. A wife's net earnings increased the family income and its ability to buy more or better holidays. On the other hand, the life cycle of the family can have negative effects on demand.

Young couples, whatever their job or income status, with small children may find it difficult to travel abroad. If just starting out on their careers they may not be able to afford holidays abroad, or even at home resorts (except by staying with friends or relatives). The elderly may lack the funds or have the money but not the health or energy to go abroad. (In recent years the special, low-cost two or three month holidays in Spain and elsewhere, in off-peak periods, for the retired, have partly overcome the cost problem.)

Then there has been the development of less expensive holidays catering for the eighteen and twenty-five year olds. These dispensed with some of the frills expected by older people with larger incomes. Indeed, 'roughing it' was often promoted as one of the attractions. Travelling to India by lorry and sleeping under canvas *en route* is an example. Then a large range of 'activity holidays' have been developed. Perhaps the supreme example is the trekking holiday in the foothills of the Himalayas. Contrary to original expectations, it is the over 55- and often 65-year-olds (in good health!) who patronise this particular holiday the most. The development of better and cheaper air transport (measured as the cost per air mile) saw an increase in demand for long-distance holidays. Colour television programmes of remote and unspoilt regions, often transmitted by communication satellites was one of the main motivating factors in this case. The greater internationalisation of business and increased competition have also contributed to the growth in business travel.

However care is needed in applying these general statements to interpretations of tourism statistics; the real cause of certain behaviour patterns by travellers may be different from the apparent, obvious point. Attempting to correlate these factors is also fraught with danger. For example a person from a low income group may have won a scholarship to a university. Would the adult then follow the holiday habits of the family background or the acquired educational one? That is, would an inexpensive holiday on the coast of Spain be taken in July or August or would a holiday in Greece or North Africa, for example, be taken at some other time of the year? Perhaps income, flexibility regarding the timing of vacations and hobbies or special interest would play more significant roles in the decision process? Do people in the upper income groups always take the more expensive, long-distance or 'exotic' holidays? Recently these people have shown more interest in simple, basic holidays if not actually choosing one that is a 'return to nature'. The last may be favoured by persons who tire of the so-called cosmopolitan and sophisticated life. Everyone can have a surfeit of anything!

There are other motivating factors. First, persons with special interest could be keen to extend their knowledge of the appropriate subjects. This can be of such importance to them that even the lower income groups, who normally cannot afford the appropriate tours, will scrimp and save to do so. The author remembers a plumber who did just this to be able to take himself, his wife and two teenage daughters on a *Canberra* cruise in two of the most expensive cabins on that ship, also the carpenter who saved up for a holiday in the USA travelling both ways by *Concorde*. On the other hand, highly paid executives who are sun lovers would accept relatively inexpensive holidays where long hours of sunshine and a good beach (not necessarily a deserted one) are normally assured.

Then there is the subject of visits to relatives and friends. Many thousands have managed somehow to find the money to visit Australia, New Zealand and Canada, for example, to see relatives. Normally they would not consider such long-distance and expensive journeys. Living with the relatives does cut down on the total costs. Finally, escapism plays a part. Tourists seek vacations whose characteristics differ from those of their social or income groups. Or animal lovers will save for safari holidays and so on (see also Table 1.1).

1.4.2 Determinants

So the factors that determine a traveller's choice of destination and accommodation will depend on the purpose of the trip. The vacationist will choose resorts which have the facilities seen to be essential for a 'good' holiday (however they may evaluate what is 'good' as 'poor'!). These are usually resorts with a wide selection of accommodation and attractions. The price must also be acceptable and what they can afford. Whether a seaside, inland or city centre location is chosen depends on what they want to do on holiday. However, they must accept the route and mode of transport of the selected package tour. Thus within cost constraints they have some freedom of choice and their requirements are easily identified. The holiday tourist is said to be satisfying their wanderlust, or sunlust.

Business travellers, those with special interests or hobbies or who are visiting relatives or friends have little choice about where or when they go. They travel as their business or other needs dictate at times prescribed by business considerations and the convenience of the people being visited. However business travellers can choose routes and modes of transport that are faster and more convenient to themselves.

Wanderlust incidentally has been described as the desire to change the known for the unknown, to leave familiar things and seek new experiences. The traveller wishes to see different peoples, cultures and places including historical relics of the past. This applies even if the traveller has made one visit to such destinations but feels that there are still other new experiences or knowledge to be gained from any return. On the other hand, *sunlust* is travel that depends on the resort having long hours of sunshine per day which does not occur in their home areas. Thus persons from colder northern climes seek sun and heat. However, those from the tropics visit Europe and Scandinavia for the relative coolness.

1.4.3 *Effects of increased leisure and improved transport*

Increased leisure time, especially with improved incomes in the developed countries, has led to growing demand for tourism both at home and abroad and the expansion and improvement in associated facilities. Four weeks' paid holiday a year had become almost universal in these countries since the late 1970s despite the economic recession. More people can travel further and stay longer, or take two major holidays, often overseas, thus creating changes in the nature and venues of international tourism. This applies also to domestic tourism but the greatest growth here has been in long weekends or a few days spent in short breaks from work activities. These short breaks are taken in addition to the main international holiday. For the lower income groups, the improvement in domestic facilities has allowed more people to take short-break holidays when previously they may only have been able to take their annual holidays at home and just have one- or two-day excursions to obtain a much needed change from normal circumstances.

The development of the car, associated road networks, the railways (before their decline in the 1950s) and better and more efficient aircraft offering greater comfort and safety all contributed to the better use of increasing leisure time and greater demand for tourism. However it is not only the frequency and speed of transport that is important, but also the cost of it and the other related components of tourism (accommodation and support facilities). Thus prices, frequency, speed and efficiency of transport all play a part. The faster the mode of travel and the lower the prices the more is tourism demand stimulated. More people with limited discretionary incomes or those with limited time for travel, can indulge in tourism, domestic and international.

In addition, the development of bus and coach tours and railway excursions have played a (lesser) part in the growth in demand for tourism but have had their greatest impact on those with limited incomes. Long-distance, international air travel improvements, especially cheaper fares, have increased demand from the higher income groups but also extended possibilities for such holidays to the middle income and less well-off persons (especially the artisans). Finally, promotional and marketing activities have played significant roles in making people more aware of what is available and the wide choice existing today.

By the early 1980s over 65 per cent of the population of the UK were taking annual holidays and over 20 per cent second holidays of four nights or more away from home, in Europe as well as in Britain. In addition, more than another 50 million short holidays, of three nights or less, were being taken away from home. The relative proximity and easy access to resorts is also important to the growth of both short holidays and day trips. In the UK nearly three-quarters of the population can reach another part of the country in a day trip. So can most residents in other European countries reach major resorts not only in their own country but in neighbouring ones, in a day.

1.4.4 *The tourism decision process*

The process by which people arrive at their decision to buy a certain holiday from the wide selection available is illustrated by Figure 1.3. This is what is called a *descriptive model*. It attempts to illustrate the various influencing factors and the resultant thought processes that follow. It cannot be quantified. Values or 'weights' cannot be assigned to the different factors. These will vary according to the type of potential customer involved. Perhaps in some future time sufficient

Figure 1.3 The travel decision process

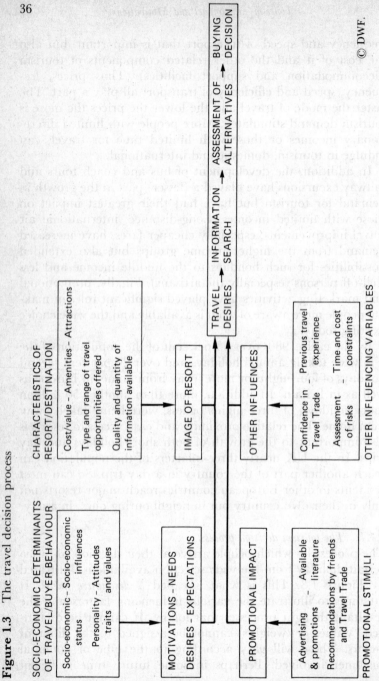

SOCIO-ECONOMIC DETERMINANTS
OF TRAVEL/BUYER BEHAVIOUR

Socio-economic – Socio-economic
status   influences

Personality – Attitudes
traits   and values

MOTIVATIONS – NEEDS

DESIRES – EXPECTATIONS

CHARACTERISTICS OF
RESORT/DESTINATION

Cost/value – Amenities – Attractions

Type and range of travel
opportunities offered

Quality and quantity of
information available

IMAGE OF RESORT

TRAVEL → INFORMATION → ASSESSMENT OF → BUYING
DESIRES   SEARCH   ALTERNATIVES   DECISION

OTHER INFLUENCES

Confidence in – Previous travel
Travel Trade   experience

Assessment – Time and cost
of risks   constraints

OTHER INFLUENCING VARIABLES

PROMOTIONAL IMPACT

Advertising – Available
& promotions   literature

Recommendations by friends
and Travel Trade

PROMOTIONAL STIMULI

© DWF.

research data will be available to permit quantification but not at this moment. Nor can it be used as a predictive tool, forecasting demand for a given destination (or service).

There are four groups of factors that are involved in this decision process. First, there are the socio-economic determinants (the socio-economic status of the person; the resultant influences of this; their personality traits, attitudes and values) which establish the motivations, needs, desires and expectations of the would-be traveller. Second, are the characteristics of the destination (the cost and value of the amenities and attractions offered; type and range of travel opportunities offered; the quality and quantity of the information available on the resort) which influence the image of the resort. Third, are all those factors which provide promotional stimuli and thus promotional impact (advertising; sales promotions; literature on the tours offered; recommendations of friends and the travel trade). Finally, there are the other influencing variables. These include the confidence of the would-be tourist in the travel trade and their own past travel experience. Also important is how they see the risks (health, travel, political) that are involved and the time and cost constraints the decision-maker has to accept. All these create the necessary travel desires and the search for relevant information needed to allow the right decision to be made. With this information the potential customer then has to assess the alternatives possible before arriving at a final decision on which tour/holiday to buy or book. (For other, marketing aspects see Section 8.1.1.)

1.5 Tourism planning and development

This subject is a very large and important one and is extensively covered by numerous books dealing only with this aspect of tourism. Students wishing to go into it extensively should refer to these works. Here only the major points of interest to tourism management will be summarised (see also Chapter 6).

1.5.1 Planning and development difficulties
It is claimed that many tourist development plans are difficult to implement fully as originally conceived. This is because

tourism development is a very sensitive subject with several uncertainties. In addition sufficient attention is not always given to the various problems that arise nor to the integration of tourism into the whole economy of the country concerned.

While planners concentrate on extensive economic, market and resources surveys and estimates of costs and revenues, they give little attention to the following. First, there is the difficulty of proper land control without which, once the plans are known, lead to land speculation. Second, the possible competition from alternative destinations is not taken into sufficient account. Third, the plans are usually not capable of adaptation to meet changing conditions. Then the critical qualitative aspects, such as the socio-economic impacts, pollution, etc., are not evaluated or quantified sufficiently. Finally the components of the tourism industry and their integration into the host country's socio-economic policies or priorities are given insufficient attention.

These problems may be resolved if the interdependency of tourism development and the socio-economic plans of the country are properly considered. Further, consideration must be given to the interdependence between international and domestic tourism and recreation. Finally, it must be realised that the tourist sector is dependent on the various market sectors to be attracted, the resources of the host nation, the existing structure of the industry and the interests of all the participants including the local nationals who will be affected by it.

It is often claimed that tourism destroys the environment so careful planning of tourist projects that takes into account the protection of the environment and ecology of the proposed resort is necessary. Planning must take into account the tourist capacity of a particular site as well as the facilities needed and ways of limiting pressures on resources (which include the local flora and fauna). Then it should be remembered that there is an inverse relationship between the number of visitors and the attractiveness of the original location (for example the Costa Brava of Spain which once was an area of much natural beauty with colourful fishing villages and small towns). Finally, ways must be found to provide the amenities necessary (parks, accommodation, etc.) while maintaining areas of environmental control and conservation.

When considering the policies and intentions of host countries, thought must be given to the image of the country abroad, its relationships with neighbouring states and the priority given to national independence especially when foreign developers submit proposals for major projects. Then there is the question of regional economic development plans. Will the tourism project help or hinder these? Finally the relationship between social tourism and domestic recreation with the major project, and the degree of public funding of the first two should not be forgotten.

It must also be remembered that the development of tourism in communities of different cultural background, standard of living and social structure can lead to a traumatic contact between alien behaviours and personalities. Induced modernisation which may result, creates additional pressures on the host society and can erode traditional cultures that were perhaps the main, original reasons for the attractiveness of the region. The result would be to accelerate the decline of these cultures.

Finally, tourism is very dependent on the development of other sectors of the economy of the host country. Apart from the obvious ones of transportation, accommodation, urban development, telecommunications, health and handicrafts, development in education, industry, agriculture, forestry and public and private finance are also necessary. It is important therefore for a sector of the economy such as tourism, so dependent on these other sectors, to be carefully integrated into a comprehensive development plan at national, regional and resort levels.

Consideration should also be given to the competition existing in international tourism. A resort seldom attracts just one category of tourist. Thus the tourist flows to all resorts will be comprised of a variety of socio-economic groups. While demand is constrained by the income and other limits of each market segment, competition between alternative destinations and tourist products has increased. The intensity of competition depends on the facilities offered at each destination, resources of the destinations, ease of access and the prices charged. This notion of possible demand and competition is of considerable importance throughout the planning of every new tourist project.

1.5.2 Project appraisal: basic considerations

Tourism development involves substantial capital, has long payback periods and is a high risk activity. Thus project appraisal of new tourism ventures should be done carefully and in detail. The basic considerations for such appraisals are summarised in Table 1.2. Further, tourism has certain special characteristics which require other aspects to be studied. These are summarised in Table 1.3.

The main purpose of an appraisal is to check that the estimated return on investment would be in excess of the opportunity costs of the capital needed. Then rewards would be obtained that were in keeping with anticipated risks. Appraisals should also indicate what the long-term viability of the project would be and its contribution to the aims and aspirations of the host government.

Table 1.2 Project appraisal – basic considerations

1	*Economic and social assessment*	of location/site; economic prospects (short- and long-term); legal and social constraints; tax and other fiscal aspects including control of remittance of profits, etc.
2	*Accessibility and transportation*	what is current? what is planned? possibility of further development? costs? official attitudes on how cost may be shared and financed? viability?
3	*Market evaluation*	current demand? trends? possible future demand? ruling market prices? competition? consumer attitudes, etc.? market shares?

4 *Accommodation*	grade and other characteristics – current availability and future needs? rooms available and required? to build or building? food and beverage needs? interlining? conference needs? other related developments and effects on demand? diplomatic needs? government involvement?
5 *Site evaluation*	description, position and general suitability; topography and soil; access to utilities; infrastructure; environmental aspects.
6 *Financial aspects*	project costs; timing; loan terms; operating costs including overheads; return and cash flow; debt/equity ratio; taxes (property, corporation, sales, other); capital and depreciation allowances.
7 *Possible impact on*	economy of resort area and host country; local population, customs and traditions; ecology; national policies and aspirations; land control/speculation; image of developers; pollution; non-tourist sectors of the economy; interdependence of components of tourist infrastructure; international and domestic tourism; foreign currency earnings and expenditures.

© D.W.F.

Thus the backers (governments and financiers) of projects require appraisals to be comprehensive, not just limited to financial aspects and be well researched by competent advisers. Appraisals are now expected to be based on a 'current price' basis (figures adjusted for anticipated rates of inflation over the construction period of the project). Those based on 'constant price' assessments (costs, revenue and profit at some fixed date, usually the opening of the project) are no longer acceptable.

Table 1.3   Tourism project appraisal: special aspects

1   The economic conditions in the tourist-generating areas for the project.
2   The political and social stability of the host country and the tourist-generating areas.
3   Financial stability of host country and its currency.
4   Accessibility (international and local) of the project.
5   Characteristics of the tourist product at the location and the scale, quality and effectiveness of competitive and substitute products.
6   The professional abilities of the 'partners' in the project, their marketing and promotional abilities.
7   Marketing and promotional needs and their availability.
8   Policies and attitudes of established tour operators, travel agents and airlines to the location and host country.

Governments also require estimates on foreign currency earnings by the projects and the net revenues that are likely to accrue. The latter include direct and indirect taxes, airport fees, profit from state participation and import dues on construction materials. Import duties on the consumables required by the project when in operation and anticipated revenues from utilities such as transport should also be included in the estimates. Forecasts are also required on the new employment that would be generated, the direct and indirect benefits to the host country's export trade and any inter-sector linkages and benefits that would result (see also Section 9.3, *Investment appraisal*).

1.5.3   Government involvement

In many countries since the Second World War, governments have shown increasing interest, and have become more involved in, the business of tourism. Involvement ranges from general encouragement to help with promoting tourism to their countries, setting up of National Tourist Organisations (NTOs) and financial and other assistance aimed at improving the tourism super- and infrastructures. In the less developed countries and those with limited resources, governments have made available scarce foreign exchange to permit the import of goods and services needed by the tourism industry. There are many reasons for this.

First, tourism is a foreign currency earner. In the last two decades even developed countries have been keen to increase their net earnings, especially of so-called 'hard currency'. Second, tourism has been a consistent growth activity. Even with the world recession of the late 1970s and early 1980s, the business has not been as badly affected as others. Third, tourism is a source of employment and for many nations, an ever growing one. It is a labour intensive industry and despite its seasonality, can promote national prosperity for host nations. Fourth, it is seen as helping to promote a better or improved image for the host country. For example, Iron Curtain countries promote tourism so that people from the Western nations can see for themselves that their hosts are not as bad as politicians paint them!

Finally some countries have natural advantages over others which they wish to exploit. Examples include the wildlife and coast of Kenya, the scenery of North America and the great range of attractions of India, to mention a few. It is possible that for political, fiscal and economic reasons government involvement in tourism will increase in the future. This can be beneficial but if it becomes restrictive in nature with all kinds of rules and regulations, it will be harmful to the growth of tourism.

1.5.4   *Future policies*

With the growing awareness of the disbenefits of uncontrolled development, those responsible for evolving future policies will have to consider all the relevant points covered in this chapter. It must be remembered that development once made cannot be reversed. Also the rural environment and ecology are vulnerable to all development activities and there is need to take care of the flora and fauna, the raw materials of the basis for tourism in the first place. Whenever there are doubts about the longterm wisdom of any tourist development, it is better not to proceed or at most, conceive a smaller, less harmful project.

Future policies should aim at protecting the ecology and natural resources, remembering that major developments can also cause changes in the weather pattern. It is also necessary to protect and enhance the cultural resources of the region and the integrity of manmade items such as historic towns and buildings, archaeological relics and so on. The policies must lead to better management of the impacts of tourism on host societies, minimising if not removing the damage or social costs that uncontrolled development does bring. This may require legislation as well as controls and incentives. Ecological and heritage conservation planning is needed and project appraisals must evaluate the environmental costs and benefits that would result. Conservation, cultural and educational policies might also be necessary if optimal benefits are to be obtained from tourism.

1.5.5 Problems and solutions for Britain

The basic tourism problem for Britain is similar to that faced by other industries, increasing competition from exotic countries who offer not only unique attractions but also lower costs and prices. The UK resorts no longer enjoy a captive home market and the industry to date has done little to adapt facilities to meet changing demand from home and abroad. If competition from countries new to tourism, who are copying ideas such as activity holidays, is to be contained and Britain keeps her market share, British tourism facilities must adapt far more to the changes than it has done so far.

This problem is made worse by the fact that there is little pressure on the home tourism industry to respond to changing demand. This contrasts with the speed with which package tour operators and the resorts they use respond to these changes. The latter see this as essential if profitable survival is to be sustained. In Britain the industry does not appear to know if they should respond, does not apparently know what to do and feels that it cannot do it on its own. The smallness of the units in British tourism makes it difficult for them to act independently. It requires large groupings of these units to pull off worthwhile changes. The fierce independence of many units, however, makes it difficult to achieve these groupings.

Finally, tourism is increasingly opposed by local residents whose lives, amenities and convenience are disrupted by tourists. Everyone wants tourism to be developed provided it is not in the areas where they live, work and play. On an island like

Britain, these pressures increase the difficulties faced by developers and those who wish to regenerate outdated facilities. The lack of accurate and detailed information on demand and supporting or complimentary facilities needed, complicates the issue.

The type and quality of the leisure tourist product needed must be known by both the providers and those who would use them. This should be matched to the grade of tourist attracted to each resort and the facilities must be compatible. For example, a Grade 1 hotel should not be served by a Grade 3 transport system. Further, enthusiastic supporters of development are often unrealistic on what can be achieved and the time and resources needed and available. The total costs are also often underestimated. Finally, the interests of residents and visitors must be kept in balance, not only that of the tourists. Better control of land usage is unavoidable.

1.5.6 Training for tourism

In the last two decades it has been accepted that all those employed in the tourism industry should be trained for their jobs. For tour operators and travel agents, professionally trained staff will provide more efficient and profitable business with greater customer satisfaction. On the last can be built a growing business with a suitable percentage of repeat business, customers who come back year after year. They have been pleased with the service and products provided. There are now many colleges and universities offering a range of tourism courses.

For hotel and catering staff the purpose of training is not only to make staff more proficient at their work but also to promote a sense of hospitality and friendship towards guests with whom they are in frequent daily contact. It is a specialised form of training and the colleges have developed appropriate courses for this need.

For Third World (developing) countries, problems connected with recruitment and training are not uniform. Each country has to evaluate its own personnel needs and ensure that adequately trained staff are available. Several have done just this. In most cases it is better for training programmes to be arranged locally. These can then be geared to the special needs and characteristics of the nation. For example in Kenya, all staff receive initial training and each year go back for short refresher and development courses. The result is that hotels in that country, arguably, have the most efficient and friendly service of any and these qualities are consistently maintained.

1.6   Case illustrations

The traditional annual holiday at the seaside and even day trips to the coasts of Britain, in the 1980s, have been threatened by changes in consumer demand for the types of holiday that are taken. Other developments have also produced further changes in holiday and recreational activities. The cases below illustrate some of the changes taking place.

1.6.1   Theme parks
Loosely based on the concept developed by Disney in the USA, theme parks are being developed in the UK.

In 1979, Ready Mixed Concrete spent £12½ million (at mid-1970s prices) in reclaiming 500 acres (1250 hectares) of disused gravel pits near Chertsey, Surrey and created Thorpe Park. Since then entrepreneur John Broome spent £20 million converting a similar sized stately home to establish a Disney-style fun park in the setting of an English country garden, known as Alton Towers. Another recent development is the Pleasurewood Hills Theme Park at Lowestoft, Suffolk. This will eventually cover 120 acres (300 hectares).

The most ambitious project, due to be opened in 1985, is the £50 million creation of Britannia Park on a 350 acre (850 hectare) site in Derbyshire. The grandest concept is that of Wonder-world, a development by Group Five Holdings, planned for 1985. It will cover 1000 acres (2500 hectares) in Corby, Northamptonshire, and is expected to cost over £300 million. The English Tourist Board believes the British leisure market could stand the development of more theme parks, especially in the West Country.

1.6.2   Some other developments
Many other less spectacular developments (in money terms

and objectives) have taken place. These range from 'farm tourism' (the Peak Moorlands Farm Holidays formed by a group of fourteen farmers) to the revitalisation of derelict or disused historical sites. With the latter, exhibits (often fully working ones) have been created to show visitors what activities took place in the past and the way of life followed by people then living there. Examples include Morwellham Quay, Devon, an open air museum based on the historic river port of Morwellham on the River Tamar. Other developments include the Afan Valley Project, Cefn Coed Coal and Steam Centre and the Margam Country Park. For activity holidays, various marina, sports centres and complexes have been built in many countries.

1.6.3　Portugal
The tourism industry in Portugal accounts for about 5 per cent of the gross national product (GNP). According to the Bank of Portugal, tourist receipts in 1982 were about 70,000 million escudos (£390 million at £1 = 180 escudos). Despite the importance of tourism there has been a lack of central, coordinated planning. This has resulted in the mushrooming of hotels and holiday homes in a few main tourist centres. However the rest of the country is poorly equipped. Of 300 hotels in Portugal, some 60 per cent are in the four major towns plus Porto and Braga in the north and Faro in the south. In parts of the Algarve, haphazard speculative building has not been supported by development of the rest of the infrastructure. Deluxe hotels have to function in the middle of a wasteland.

Lack of access roads and amenities are coupled with the serious shortage of water. Dry winters in the early 1980s have led to serious scarcity in the summer. Then, over-speculation has meant that several tourist units begun in 1973–5 still remain to be finished in 1984. At Estoril and Cascais on the outskirts of Lisbon, tourist developments have led to a conflict with their role as dormitory towns for Lisbon. Shortage of water and the pollution of the sea have become added problems. The Ministry of Commerce and Tourism has now declared its determination to attack all these problems resolutely.

Assignments

1 Your company, consultants on tourism projects, has been called in by a small, developing country, with limited resources, to advise on the development of a tourist complex. The country has one major town (the capital) and one commercial but small port. It has an airport near the capital that can just handle the large wide-bodied jets but there is little room for safety. There is one good, sealed main road linking the port and capital but the rest of the limited road network is of narrow unsealed roads. There are several small towns and villages and three or four sandy but undeveloped beaches used only by local fishermen. The water supply depends on finding artesian wells but one large reservoir serves the capital. The population is $1\frac{1}{2}$ million.

You have been given the task of making a preliminary report on the resource problems that would affect the size and nature of any tourism project. The people are also rather reserved and guard their customs and way of life very actively. What aspects of the problem do you consider need thorough study? How can the inherent problems be overcome? What type and size of project would you recommend for more detailed consideration?

2 A major country with a sound integrated economy and a reasonably developed tourist industry wishes to expand the latter to earn more foreign currency. It is interested in ensuring that further development should not damage the ecology and wildlife for which it is renowned. It is also keen not to start land speculation. How should it go about tackling this requirement?

3 A large country with traditional holiday resorts – seaside and inland mountain areas – realises that its tourism products are now falling out of favour with both international and domestic tourists. What should it consider if it wishes to revitalise its tourist infrastructure to make its basic amenities once again attractive to tourists? How should it alter its ideas if any upsurge in demand should increase the need for imports and thus adversely affect its foreign exchange earnings?

2

Tourism – the Industry

The development of international travel and tourism came in four stages. First there was the restricted and adventurous travel of the pre-railway era. This required considerable effort on the part of the traveller. Attendant risks were high. Then the coming of the railway, whose basic network was established by 1914, brought substantial expansion of travel. Accommodation became available at termini and wayside stations. The golden age of the ocean liner dawned but soon after came the birth of its eventual destroyer, the commercial aircraft. International travel more or less as we know it today, was established though in Britain, mass package tourism did not begin until 1950.

Before the Second World War motoring was mainly the privilege of the wealthy although the use of motor coaches increased between the wars. *Greyhound* in the USA and *Southdown* and others in Britain were patronised by the middle and lower income groups. These coaches gave good, comfortable services to the main business centres and holiday resorts. The latter were then developing and expanding. After the war, the full 'flowering' (?) of air transport saw the modern travel and mass tourism industry achieve full development. (For a fuller history of tourism see Appendix A.)

Efficient transport systems are vital for mass tourism and extensive business travel. Development of faster and more efficient modes of transport, with the economic growth of the 1950s to 1970s have brought travel and tourism within the reach of many. However the idea has still to be 'sold' to many people. For example in Britain nearly 50 per cent of the people have never stayed in an hotel or motel. Thus considerable expansion is still possible. However if international tourism out of most countries is to grow, people must stop seeing it as expensive and dangerous! Apart from fear, other deterrent factors include fluctuating foreign exchange rates and political uncertainty. These represent hazards which many people do not understand and are not prepared to risk.

The structure of the industry is a hodge-podge of different component parts, often working independently of each other. If they do work together it is usually for some limited purpose. The major components (accommodation, transport, national tourist organisations and the infra- and superstructure of the industry) are dealt with more fully in later chapters. This chapter will discuss them in outline, concentrating on the travel trade (tour operators, travel agents and associated organisations).

2.1 Structure and organisation

The structure and components of the industry are shown in Figure 2.1. In addition there are other enterprises such as coach and rail operators, conference and congress organisers, car hire companies, cruise ships and reservation agencies. Also in recent years automobile associations, travel conglomerates, tourist and trade associations have become active constituents of the business.

The very fragmented nature of the industry results in there being a large number of small organisations in it. In the USA, for example, some 40 per cent of hotels are small enough to have only one paid employee in addition to the owner-proprietor. With travel agents, there are many with only two or three paid employees even in the UK. This fact may be obscured by the existence of 'big names' such as Thomas Cook, American Express and major tour operators such as Thomson Holidays, Cosmos and Global to mention a few.

Opportunities exist for vertical and horizontal integration.

Figure 2.1 The tourism industry

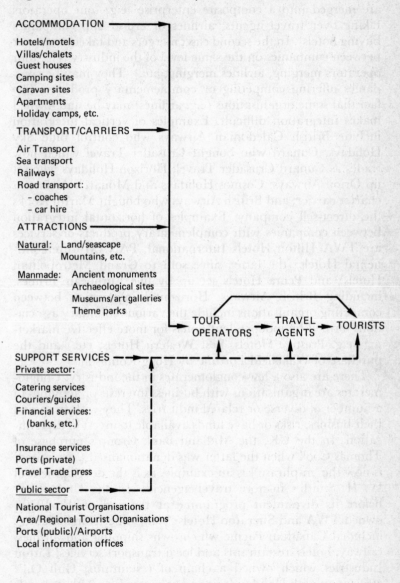

ACCOMMODATION

Hotels/motels
Villas/chalets
Guest houses
Camping sites
Caravan sites
Apartments
Holiday camps, etc.

TRANSPORT/CARRIERS

Air Transport
Sea transport
Railways
Road transport:
  – coaches
  – car hire

ATTRACTIONS

Natural: Land/seascape
          Mountains, etc.

Manmade: Ancient monuments
          Archaeological sites
          Museums/art galleries
          Theme parks

TOUR OPERATORS → TRAVEL AGENTS → TOURISTS

SUPPORT SERVICES

Private sector:

Catering services
Couriers/guides
Financial services:
  (banks, etc.)

Insurance services
Ports (private)
Travel Trade press

Public sector

National Tourist Organisations
Area/Regional Tourist Organisations
Ports (public)/Airports
Local information offices

With the first, organisations at different levels of the industry are merged into a composite enterprise (e.g. tour operators taking over travel agents; airlines or cruise ship companies buying hotels). In the second case, mergers and takeovers occur between companies on the same level of the industry (e.g. tour operators merging, airlines merging, etc.). They may be companies offering competing or complementary products. The fact that some organisations (e.g. airlines) may be state-owned makes integration difficult. Examples of vertical integration include British Caledonian Airways who control Blue Sky Holidays; Cunard who bought Crusader Travel which now trades as Cunard Crusader Travel; Horizon Holidays who set up Orion Airways; Cosmos Holidays and Monarch Airlines a charter carrier; and British Airways who bought Martin Rooks the direct-sell company. Examples of horizontal integration between companies with complementary products or services are TWA–Hilton Hotels International; PANAM–Intercontinental Hotels (the latter since sold to Grand Metropolitan Hotels) and Penta Hotels set up by five European airlines, including British Airways. Horizontal integration between competing organisations include the various voluntary associations formed by independent hotels for more effective marketing (e.g. Prestige Hotels, Best Western Hotels, etc.) and the purchase of Wakefield Fortune by Hogg Robinson.

There are also a few conglomerates in the industry. Conglomerates are organisations with business interests or activities in a number of diverse or related industries. They wish to spread their business risks or have funds available to invest in diversification. In the UK, the Midland Bank Group's purchase of Thomas Cook when the latter was denationalised ('privatised' is now the 'in-phrase') is an example, as is the development of W. H. Smith's in-store travel agencies. In the USA, ITT, before its divestment programme at the end of the 1970s, owned TWA and Sheraton Hotels. Some other conglomerates included Canadian Pacific which owns shipping and airlines, railway, hotels, restaurants and local transport services; Litton Industries which owned a chain of restaurants; Gulf Oil's association with Holiday Inns and of course Esso with its hotels and motels.

In recent years, NTOs or their regional counterparts

(RTOs) have begun to play more active roles in coordinating the activities of related components in the industry (see Section 9.4).

2.1.1 Tour operators and operations

Tour operators buy or reserve in bulk, accommodation, international and local transportation and other services as necessary and combine them into various packages (hence 'package tours'). They then sell these at a single price, individually to consumers and travel agents. Some tour operators make it a condition for dealing with a specific travel agent that the latter will take some stated minimum number of tours from them annually, that is, guarantee a certain volume of business.

Usually tour operators offer a wide range of fully inclusive and 'semi-inclusive' (or 'independent package') tours for the general public. The latter is an attempt to maintain the facade that the tourists taking them are on their own. They are free to do what they like at the resorts but enjoy the benefits of lower costs through making use of group reservations of accommodation and transport. The 'independents' travel with the group, get the same courier and transport services (but may get a better room) and have more choice of menu. They may also make use of the local excursions included in the package or may go off on day trips on their own. They can hire cars, or use other excursions organised by local companies. The tour operator is in effect the wholesaler of the industry or 'bulk purchaser' of tourism products.

Most tour operators will accept direct bookings from individuals. Though they may like to do away with the middlemen (travel agents) and save the commission payable, costs and the desire to obtain national coverage for their sales makes this difficult. However, towards the end of the 1970s some direct-selling organisations (e.g. Vingressor, Tjaereborg, Portland Holidays, Martin Rooks) have operated quite successfully in the UK. Tour operators depend on their brochures to sell the often bewildering array of packages they offer. They need the travel agent to carry suitable stocks of brochures to make them available to the general public.

Some smaller tour operators do however limit their activities to specialist areas or operations (e.g. India, Southeast Asia, safaris and so on). These depend mainly on direct sales, interest being generated by selective advertising. However, they may also use travel agents to boost their selling activities. Direct door-to-door selling of holidays is however not practised in the UK. This is because various consumer protection laws make this difficult if not impossible to do and the British have an aversion to this method of selling.

The larger operators able to make larger block bookings, are in a stronger bargaining position with airlines and hotels. As a result they can obtain much better bulk reservation terms, the benefits of which are usually passed on to the customer in lower prices. They can also command the reservation of better rooms from the hotels they use especially if their advanced bookings are for a substantial number of rooms. In smaller and Third World (developing) countries there may be only one largish tour operator and this is often state-owned.

The inclusive tour was initially organised before the Second World War in the USA. At first these operated out of New York, Chicago and Washington to the coasts of California and Florida and to the islands of the Caribbean and Hawaii. After the war they were expanded to cover destinations in South America, Mexico, Europe and the Middle East and departures from other cities. In the UK they appeared in 1950 for destinations in Europe and the Mediterranean resorts. Scandinavia and West Germany soon followed. Initially they used secondary airlines for the holiday charter business. This was originally intended for special interest or 'affinity groups' such as clubs, congress participants, religious groups and so on. These tours had a specific purpose other than a simple vacation, for example visiting historical sites and monuments, concerts and other artistic performances. In subsequent years they were also open to the general public who helped to fill up the seats which the affinity groups, for which the charter was made, did not require.

Now charter flights can be used for packages offered to everyone. Thus they are alternatives to scheduled flights and are usually slightly cheaper in price. At first they tended to operate at night or other inconvenient times but now charters can be used for any time of departure, most days of the week, according to demand. Package tours using charter flights which offer accommodation and other amenities sold at a single price to everyone are now known as *inclusive tours by charter* or *ITCs*.

During the late 1970s and early 1980s, inflation caused all costs to soar. Although the tourism industry was not as badly affected as home-based industries because the inflation rates of host countries varied and were often less than in Britain, tour prices did rise. Last minute 'surcharges' were imposed. Their unpopularity had resulted in many tour operators guaranteeing there would not be any, provided costs beyond their control did not rise above stated limits. More to the point perhaps, the pressure on consumers' net discretionary incomes was intensified as prices of other items at home rose, with inflation in the 20 per cent plus per annum range. They had less money to spend on holidays. Thus ways had to be found to overcome this problem. The solution was to obtain the lowest rates possible for the transport and accommodation elements of package tours. Another idea was to offer packages which provided the necessary transport but only the very cheapest, basic accommodation possible, to comply with British law on what constitutes a true package, to qualify for the special cheap fares. The accommodation is usually such that no one would use it and it added only a pound or two to the air fare. The idea was that business people and independent travellers would stay at hotels known to them or with friends and relatives. It was a device for getting the lowest return air fare and was attractive for those undertaking long journeys. It was also of interest to people who owned villas or apartments abroad.

The development of inclusive tours, especially ITCs, played a major role in the growth in demand for tourism. By the 1970s the range of tours on offer had expanded from the Mediterranean basin of Europe to America, North and East Africa and even further afield. In particular, interest in Florida grew, especially with time-sharing of villas and apartments. As sterling strengthened against the US dollar, hotel tariffs proved to be good value for money and tours to other parts of the USA enjoyed increasing demand. Even when sterling weakened against the dollar and the initial advantage was eroded, holidays in America continued to be attractive.

The impact of inclusive tours by air on tourism demand can

be judged from figures published in various 'International Passenger Surveys' by the Department of Industry in their *Business Monitor* (M6 – Overseas Travel and Tourism). While in 1963 inclusive tours out of the UK just exceeded 600,000, by 1971 it was nearly 2.5 million. Despite inflation and rising costs, by 1979 the figure had exceeded 3.5 million. (If holidays by sea and independent travellers are included the total was about 7 million.)

National and other scheduled airlines responded with lower fares. Initially these were only available to tour operators and travel agents for combination with accommodation into packages. These tours were designated ITX by the trade. This allowed the airlines to improve their load factors which might otherwise not have exceeded 60 per cent. The tourists occupied seats that would have remained unused.

While this move improved the profitability of the flights concerned, it discriminated against business people and other travellers paying the full fare. Resentment grew as these passengers found themselves sitting next to tourists who had paid much less but enjoyed the same services. The development of Club Class by British Airways and equivalents by other airlines, was an attempt to overcome the problem. Full fare paying passengers travelled Club Class and were supposed to get better service and treatment than tourists in their tourist class (see also Section 2.1.3).

Although the inclusive tour was designed originally to attract people in the middle and lower income groups, they are not confined to the cheaper ('down market') sector of the business. Packages of all kinds now offer a very wide range of products. There are many expensive (semi-inclusive and 'independent') packages which form the 'up-market' sector of the industry. These range from expensive cruises down the Nile, to adventure holidays of all kinds and longer tours (four to six weeks or more) to South America, Australasia and the Pacific Islands to mention only a few. However the mass market is best catered for by ITCs which have allowed millions of people to enjoy holidays abroad. The major British mass market tour operators include Cosmos, Enterprise, Global, Horizon (formerly Horizon Midland, a subsidiary of the collapsed Court

Line/Clarkson group), Intasun, Sovereign, Wings/OSL, Thomson Holidays and Club 18–30.

Brokers on the other hand are enterprises or individuals who make bulk purchases of aircraft seats, usually, but sometimes do the same with accommodation and other support services. By doing so they can achieve lower prices for these items. They then sell individual or small blocks of seats (and accommodation) to travel agents who can make up their own 'packages'. Their mark-up gives them a very acceptable level of profit while offering competitive prices to their customers. Their activities are helpful to the small travel agent who may not be able to command such advantageous prices from direct negotiations with airlines and hotels because of the limited size of their potential business.

2.1.2 Retail agents and operations

Travel agents are the *retailers* of the travel industry. Their role differs from that of retailers in other industries in that they do not usually purchase travel facilities in advance for resale to the customer. When a consumer has decided on the holiday they want the travel agent will approach the tour operator on the customer's behalf. They do the same for other travellers, approaching the carrier and/or hotel the customer wishes to use. In some cases, the travel agent may have a set allocation from tour operators and other principals and they will then call off from these whatever their customer requires. If the sale goes through the travel agent will get an agreed commission from the principles. However, for tours organised by tour operators who are members of the Association of British Travel Agents (ABTA), the agent must also be an ABTA member to get this commission. For carriers with an Air Transport Operator's Licence (ATOL) the agent must also be ATOL approved to earn commission on the sale of aircraft seats. Where agents have made advance block bookings for their own account they can obtain better terms than if they sold tours individually. (Organisations like Thomas Cook and American Express who sell the products of other operators as well as their own package tours are in fact operating both as travel agent and tour operator.)

Excluding those with their own package tours, travel agents generally show little brand loyalty for any particular tour operator's packages. This is the reason why some operators require guarantees of a certain minimum volume of business per season from a travel agent before they will sell their tours through them. While the lack of brand loyalty poses marketing problems for the principals, it should be advantageous to customers if the advice given by the travel agent is impartial (it is not always!). The fact that travel agents do not hold 'inventories' removes a strong incentive experienced by retailers in other industries, the drive to sell the stock in their storeroom, especially if it has already been paid for, that is bought from the supplier.

Travel agents may be classified in various ways. First is according to their location and second, by the type of business in which they specialise. *City centre agencies* are located in or close to the main business and shopping areas of cities or major towns. They are meant to catch business from those who visit and pass through these zones. Because the rent and other costs of these locations are high, they will need a substantial turnover or revenue to show a reasonable trading profit. With the growth of international business travel in the last two decades, these agencies give priority to the development of business accounts. This is especially so if major corporations have head or other offices in the vicinity. Then annual contracts or other agreements can be made between the travel agent and the firms. Big multiple agencies (like Thomas Cook and American Express) usually have branch offices in these locations. Advertising is usually in national media, trade or business magazines and any appropriate local media. (The subject of business travel is covered more fully in Section 3.1.7.)

Next there are *surburban agencies* who serve the residents of dormitory suburbs. Located in the main shopping areas they sell holidays, usually inclusive and semi-inclusive package tours and independent travel facilities. If any firm has its office nearby, the agent may of course try to sell business travel services to it. Demand tends to be seasonal and in off-peak periods they may make tempting 'special offers' or, more usually, will promote strongly any special off-peak offers of their tour operator principals. Advertising is usually concentrated in appropriate local media. If they are part of a multiple agency, they would expect to benefit from any national advertising by their group. They expect also to benefit from the national advertising of the tour operators whose products they sell. Because of the lower costs a high level of turnover as required by city centre locations is not essential. However the seasonality of the business requires them to get the most business they can during peak sales periods. The fact that holidays are being taken more evenly through a year has eased this problem.

County town agencies serve the resident population and business community in their towns. Surveys have shown that this mix of holiday and business travel makes these agencies the more profitable ones. Their function is similar to that of city centre agencies and they are usually bigger than the average suburban agency. They too may have branches in other nearby towns. Their value to business organisations located outside cities and large towns can be considerable if they are able to offer a sound service on business travel.

Business house agencies are intended chiefly to serve the needs of industrial and commercial enterprises but they will also deal with personal holiday needs, particularly from staff of their clients. They are most effective when employing direct marketing to potential client firms. This involves visits by appropriate agency staff to the travel decision-makers in the firms, with supporting direct mail shots, letters and telephone calls (for more details see Chapters 7 and 8). For the casual holiday customer, the agency depends on its name being known and their reputation for handling business travel efficiently. Window and other displays are used also. Advertising is usually in related business journals and the *Financial Times*.

Usually their staff and office costs are higher than those of the other types of agencies. They put further pressure on their profits by extending credit to their clients. However if competition is strong they may not be able to avoid this, especially with firms who drive hard bargains with all their suppliers.

Increasing competition has tended to make all these agencies accept whatever business comes their way but this classification is still reasonably valid. The total volume of business, as stated earlier, has increased and the increase in demand for winter holidays has helped to improve the profitability of the business. Tour operators, carriers and other principals expect the travel agents they deal with to support the promotions of the principals with appropriate local advertising. However, rising costs and agents' commission remaining basically unchanged at about 10 per cent, are increasing the operational cost problems of the agencies.

Some tour operators would like to do without travel agents who are seen by them to be rather expensive post boxes without brand loyalty. These principals believe they can improve their profitability and/or be able to charge lower prices, if they can save the middlemen's commission. In reality, if tour operators wish to achieve nationwide coverage for their products and appeal effectively to their target markets, it is doubtful if they could do this on their own. Even the direct sellers, depending on the expensive business of direct mail have to select target markets (types of consumer) carefully, if costs are to be kept within bounds. Besides increasing postal charges they have to contend with rising printing costs for brochures and leaflets. For maximum impact these publications have to be in several colours and this adds to printing costs. Current practice now relies on advertisements raising requests for brochures, avoiding the cost (and wastage) of unsolicited mass mailings.

However in the late 1970s, prompted by successful direct mail selling in Germany and Scandinavia, Vingressor of Sweden and Tjaereborg of Denmark set up operations in the UK. In addition British Airways had Martin Rooks. The interest in this approach caused Thomson Holidays at the end of the 1970s to set up Portland Holidays. They maintain that with higher prices for packages resulting in more money being paid to travel agents it was cheaper to sell direct to the public even when some of the cost saving is passed on to the consumer in lower prices. At the time of writing, direct selling of tourism products in the UK has not grown as substantially as was originally anticipated.

In 1975 the Universal Federation of Travel Agents' Associations (UFTAA) and the International Air Transport Association (IATA) conducted a worldwide survey of travel agents' costs. While the figures varied from country to country, those quoted in Table 2.1 are representative for most of the major tourist generating countries.

Table 2.1   Travel agents' average costs

Item	Percentage of total costs
Salaries and wages	60
Telephone, cables, stationery	7
Rent, lighting, heating, etc.	7
Advertising and promotions	4
Depreciation, financial expenses	3
Travel and associated expenses	3
Other, not specified above	16

Source: UFTAA, 1975.

Travel agents fall into two groups, those who belong or are members of ABTA and those who are not. Membership imposes some obligations. Agents must abide by ABTA codes of conduct and their records and offices must be open to inspection by ABTA staff. However the Restrictive Practices Court has overturned another condition and agents are free to discount prices and sell non-travel products (referred to in the trade as 'mixed selling'). New minimum standards on staff competence have replaced previous longstanding regulations based on job experience and age. Under the Resale Price Maintenance Act it is illegal for any principal to insist that their products should be sold at only the published prices but individual agreements between individual tour operator and travel agent can include such clauses.

In the United Kingdom there are still no legal licensing requirements so that anyone can set up business as a travel agent. However some countries do have various forms of government licensing and the European Community has been studying this possibility. Tour operators continue to depend on agency agreements with individual travel agents and if there is no such agreement the principal can refuse to pay the agent any commission. Nevertheless hotels and other principals seldom insist on such agreements.

If travel agents wish to sell the products of a tour operator who is a member of ABTA, then the agent must be a member also. This ABTA ruling was challenged by the Office of Fair Trading but upheld in 1982 by the Restrictive Practices Court. So only ABTA travel agents may sell tours by operators who are also members of ABTA and these agents agree not to sell tours by non-ABTA members. This closed shop agreement, introduced in 1965 (called *Operation Stabiliser*), is supposed to offer protection to the traveller. Also, should an ABTA member collapse and go into liquidation, the Association uses the *Common Fund* (created from membership subscriptions) to compensate the customers for lost holidays and ensure their repatriation should they be abroad on holiday when the collapse occurs. When alternative bonding arrangements were introduced for tour operators, to protect customers from operator bankruptcies, etc., this fund became the *Retailers' Fund* and is now used to protect customers affected by the closure or bankruptcy of travel agents.

Formal approval is also necessary from National Coaches, British Rail, shipping and car hire companies and domestic airlines before travel agents can make sales on their behalf which will earn commission. This is normally a formality for agents who are members of ABTA or who are IATA appointed agents.

Travel agents wishing to earn commission for sales on behalf of members of IATA must obtain an IATA licence. Since international travel forms such a substantial proportion of an agency's business, this licence is vital to travel agents wishing to offer the public a full range of services. Approval is granted by the Agency Administration Board of IATA. An Agency Investigation Panel (AIP) comprised of members of IATA vet the security for control of ticket stocks, financial standing, staff qualifications and the ability of the agency to generate business. If these are satisfactory, a Passenger Sales Agency Agreement is issued. The agency is then given a numeric ticket validation code which is stamped on all tickets issued by the agency. This procedure can be lengthy and during it the travel agency is expected to generate suitable business for IATA members without commission.

In the USA, the equivalent organisation to ABTA is the

American Society of Travel Agents (ASTA). Because the USA is a major tourist-generating area for international tourism and travel, membership is not confined to retailers based in the USA. Many principals and agents in other countries are also members. Thus British tour operators have particular interest in the decisions of this organisation.

It is estimated that over 2000 travel agents in the UK are not ABTA members. These include the so-called *bucket shops* (unbonded, unlicensed agents). These are convenient outlets for airlines who have unsold seats which they wish to dump on to the market at short notice. Usually the fares are heavily discounted. This reduces the potential revenue of IATA/ABTA agents and many airlines fought for a change in the rules to allow appointed agents to sell such tickets. In 1981 British Airways was authorised to sell discounted tickets for selected destinations through IATA and ABTA agents. However the growth of sales by 'bucket shops' continue to increase especially as the economic conditions continue to affect airline ticket sales adversely. Many non-ABTA agents who are not bucket shops seem content to sell the products of non-ABTA tour operators.

Whatever type of travel agent is involved, the work of their staff is very similar. The main points are listed in Table 2.2. Most agencies are relatively small organisations and it is not always possible for staff to specialise in one particular area of work. They have to become competent in most of these activities. In addition, senior members of staff have to arrange to protect stocks of tickets and other negotiable documents. They must also develop accounting and marketing skills. Since travel agents also provide ancillary services (obtaining foreign currency and travellers' cheques, passports and visas, and arrange insurance) the knowledge expected of the staff increases the need for professionally trained people to replace untrained, eager amateurs.

The income of agents is not dependent only on the commission earned (usually 9 to 10 per cent) from tour operators and carriers. There is also the commission from the sales of ancillary services. If they have their own package tours there will be the profit from these sales. They should also be able to generate income from the careful short-term investment of

Table 2.2   Travel agents: staff responsibilities

1   Advise clients on – resorts/destinations
                            – carriers (international and local)
                            – accommodation
                            – tour operators and travel organisations (rail, shipping, etc.)
                            – other travel facilities
all on a worldwide basis unless the agent is specialising in a limited area or type of holiday/business travel.

2   Plan itineraries – simple and complex for multi-stopover independent trips.
3   Make necessary reservations for all travel facilities.
4   Calculate airline and other fares accurately and make out/issue travel tickets, accommodation and other vouchers.
5   Maintain and display effectively, stocks of brochures.
6   Maintain accurate records of reservations, sales, etc.
7   Correspond in writing and by telephone and telex with travel principals and customers.
8   Handle customer complaints and negotiate on these with principals on behalf of the customers.

deposits and any pre-payments received from customers. As deposits are now expected some eight or more weeks before departure, with payments to principals due not more than four weeks in advance, a reasonable addition to income is possible given the substantial funds that pass through agency hands.

To summarise, the basic role of the travel agent is to provide a convenient location where potential travellers may first obtain all the information necessary to make buying decisions and then conclude the purchase. It is of no great significance to the customer that the agent does not carry stock but concludes the purchase by a call on a principal's own stock. In the UK in 1984, the retail travel trade was dominated by four big groups. These were Thomas Cook, Hogg Robinson (now including Wakefield Fortune) Pickfords and Lunn/Poly. The major foreign agency is American Express.

However, airlines and major tour operators also have sales

offices in some major centres and a growing number of people prefer to deal direct with principals. In addition, most airlines are capable of planning and organising travel and individual tour arrangements. If the latter is a substantial venture, airlines may also offer special rates resulting in prices which are competitive with anything the travel agent can do. If the places to be visited have been long and well served by the airline their knowledge should exceed that of agency staff. If the agency is many thousands of miles away and the staff have not visited the destination, the travel agent must depend on published information for the advice they give to their potential customers. Misinterpretation of that information is always possible.

2.1.3 Cheap fares
By the 1980s there was a bewildering array of cheap fares and the offers made by airlines and others were subject to various changes, often at short notice. Further, some airlines did not always broadcast all the discounted fares that were available. The most widely known and used is the APEX fare (Advanced Purchase Excursion schedule air fare). They are available for many destinations but for round trips only. They must be booked and paid for about twenty-one days before the flight and involve a minimum stay abroad of seven days. They have what is called an 'open jaw' facility. For example, the passenger can fly to, say, the USA but return from a point in Canada or even the Carribean.

ABC (Advance Booking Charter) fares are, at the moment, only applicable for flights to and from North America, though extension to West Africa may be possible in the future. They cover only return tickets which must show the dates of departure and return. These cannot be altered at a later date and open-ended return tickets are not permitted. Bookings must be made at least twenty-one days before departure to a destination in the USA and thirty days for Canada. Payment is sometimes required three or four months in advance (with dates declared twenty-one days before departure). If there is a subsequent cancellation the whole of the payment may be forfeited.

Minimum-rated package tour fares involve the offer of a

package covering transport and conveyance to and from the airport and the accommodation. The accommodation provided is minimal and may be in rooms without washing facilities or a bed in a dormitory. Sometimes there is no bed and the traveller is expected to take a sleeping bag. Meals are not provided. As mentioned earlier in this chapter, the traveller is not expected to use this accommodation!

Standby fares are much cheaper than normal fares but the intending traveller has to wait, until about half an hour before departure, to see if an unfilled seat is available. Since the number of standby seats may be limited the traveller takes the risk of not being able to get on the flight. Then they have to start all over again with the next flight usually by another airline. It is a cheap way to travel for those who do not have to keep to any schedule. The number of standby seats that can be offered, even in offpeak periods, is usually limited by agreements between competing airlines.

Then there are Late Saver, Early Saver and African Saver fares which British Airways now call just 'Savers' to simplify the situation. Generally there is a Saver fare of some sort to almost every destination. All these are referred to as 'promotional fares' and have various restrictions concerning how far in advance they must be booked and paid for, the minimum and maximum lengths of stay at the destination, no change of route and time of departure (and sometimes return) once the ticket has been bought, no change of airline, no stopovers or limited stopovers for additional payment. Usually, back-tracking is also not permitted. Most of these fares are obtainable through airline ticket offices and IATA agents. These fares are liable to change at short notice but can be purchased twelve months in advance, thus guaranteeing the cost.

There are also consolidation fares on schedule flights. A seat-only tour operator or wholesaler will buy blocks of seats and then sell them to customers at prices cheaper than the cheapest fare available. If the consolidation fare is no cheaper than the APEX normally available, the seller may throw in inducements such as free insurance or free rail travel to the point of departure. 'Knock down' charter fares are also sometimes available for unsold seats on charter flights but this is a volatile market. Finally there are the 'unofficially discounted fares' sold through bucket shops but these are not normally available for domestic, European or North American routes. The main areas served are Asia, the Far East, Australasia, Africa and Latin America and are for simple 'out and return' journeys. By 1984 an Air Travel Advisory Service was established in London to help consumers through this fare jungle to the best fare for their needs.

Cheap fares are subject to considerable changes at any time. This is especially so when competition is severe. The above reports the situation at the time of writing but may have changed by the time this book is published!

2.2 Accommodation

Accommodation is a very important component of tourism products. The type, scale and nature of it available at any destination determine the type and scale of tourism that is possible. The range of accommodation available is listed in Table 4.1. As will be seen from it, accommodation can be split into three categories. First there is the *serviced accommodation* such as hotels, pensions and so on that provide rooms, restaurants or meal service and others such as room service, housekeeping, porterage and so on. Second is the various forms of *self-catering establishments* listed in the table. A third category is those units which may *either be serviced or self-catering*.

Accommodation may also be *classified* according to the number of private bathrooms and bedrooms provided. It can also be *graded* according to the number and size of public rooms, restaurants and other facilities (e.g. car parking space) provided. In the United Kingdom, the Automobile Association's and Royal Automobile Club's 'star rating' are used most commonly. In other countries various descriptions are used such as 'Superluxe', 'de-luxe', 'standard', 'first category', 'second category' and so on.

In Britain the Development of Tourism Act, 1969, made provision for the classification and grading of hotels. This has been resisted by the industry and the British Tourist Authority (BTA) made no attempt to impose it. They preferred instead the system of voluntary registration introduced in 1975. This relies on facts provided by the hoteliers without any control or inspection by an independent body. The AA's and RAC's ratings are dependent on inspections by their staff but the quality of the services and premises are judged subjectively. However the statements by the hoteliers on the nature and extent of the rooms and services and the physical premises provided are checked more objectively. Of the other guides available, the better known include the one published by Egon Ronay and the *Good Hotel Guide*, a companion volume to the *Good Food Guide*.

The many other aspects of accommodation are discussed in Chapter 4.

2.3 Transportation

Another important component of tourism is transport. Without fast, safe, comfortable and convenient public and private transport at reasonable costs, the mass market tourism of today would not be possible. Developments in transportation have had major effects on the growth in demand for tourism and the nature of that demand. People can travel further afield for their holidays today than hitherto. However transport enterprises serving tourists' needs also operate for other markets (local residents, commuters and freight). They are not solely dependent on tourist demand. National airlines, rail services, bus and coach companies also offer normal scheduled services. Many provide a social service which has little to do with tourism, such as the essential commuter services into and out of city centres.

Most transport systems, including their terminals, are capital intensive and may require financial assistance from government sources. They also offer economies of scale by careful planning of the number of daily departures and the carrying capacity of each plane, train, bus or coach. National airlines, for prestige purposes, do load their overheads and operating costs by insisting on having high quality, city centre offices and points of sale.

The fact that transport services supply other markets can be beneficial to tourism since these other demands can improve

the viability of systems that would otherwise be solely dependent on tourism needs. The development of transport systems is
easier if they must also carry mail efficiently and swiftly. Before
the Second World War when long distance travel by sea was
unavoidable, it was better to take a ship carrying Royal Mail as
it was invariably faster. This meant also that the ships were
bigger and better appointed.

Other aspects of transportation are discussed in Chapter 5.

2.4 Other components

Other components of the tourism industry are worthy of at
least brief mention.

2.4.1 Incoming operators

Incoming operators (or 'handling agents') are probably the
least known members of the tourism industry. They handle the
ground arrangements in the United Kingdom for overseas
visitors on behalf of an overseas tour operator, tour organiser,
travel agent or carrier. Ground arrangements cover all aspects
of a tour except the flight into and out of the country. They
will also resolve any problems that may arise about the
outward flight. These operators can influence considerably
where the foreign tourist groups go in Britain and which
attractions they should visit. Most of them are based in London
and can be classified by the type of work in which they
specialise (see Table 2.3).

2.4.2 Conference and congress organisers

Conference and congress business is of importance to the hotel
sector of the industry. It helps to improve the occupancy rate.
Where short or long stays follow or precede the conference,
these make a useful, additional contribution to the tourism
receipts of the host country. This tourism element of conference business falls somewhere between the definitions of 'vacational' and business travel.

While much of the conference business is placed direct by
the enterprise requiring it, where special technical or other
organisational skills and knowledge are required, a conference

Table 2.3   Incoming operators – classification

Companies specialising in conference/congress business

Organisations specialising in business travellers

Enterprises promoting one-off programmes: each arrangement is tailored to suit the requirements of particular tour groups. Those looking after special interest and study tours and incentive travel are included in this classification

Organisations handling activity holiday groups

Companies looking after youth travel groups

'Track operators': organisations operating tours with specified departure times each year, i.e. scheduled tours

Organisations handling arrangement for individual travellers, e.g. driver-guide companies taking tourists by limousine/private car where ever they wish to be taken

London offices of overseas organisations (e.g. banks) with their own travel departments handling their own executives and VIP clients

London office of overseas parent travel companies: these are responsible for carrying out the operations planned or created by the parent company

organiser may be used. The special expertise can range from the provision of multi-screen, audio-visual presentations, instant multiple translations, and elaborate social functions with entertainment to incentive travel facilities. Most of these organisers are members of the Association of Conference Executives (ACE).

2.4.3   Tourist boards
Tourist boards or organisations whether national, regional or area ones, of whatever title, are usually quasi-governmental bodies. Their work and aims are discussed in Chapter 9.

2.4.4   Automobile Association and Royal Automobile Club
These organisations provide essential support services to those

taking a motoring holiday. They provide advice and assistance on the best routes, maps and related matters. They also provide a breakdown and recovery service. The user must however be a member of the organisation or of an affiliated body in their own home country.

In Britain a few years ago they set up their own travel agencies. Besides selling the package tours of some tour operators, they also organised their own. These are not necessarily only motor tours. They have played a part in expanding domestic tourism, an activity that for the most part has been ignored by the major tour operators. The latter are mainly interested in overseas tours.

2.4.5 Tourist and trade associations

The tourism industry is characterised by having a number of associations, voluntary and compulsory, between enterprises in the same business (e.g. hotels) or which offer complimentary products or services. Their activities vary considerably in nature, scale and scope. While the promotion of their businesses and localities are their main objectives, they do also sometimes take interest in conservation, controlling standards, improving facilities and encouraging civic pride. Most are also concerned with providing information and liaising with other public and especially tourism interests.

These associations split into two distinct groups. First there are the professional bodies where the bulk of the membership is individuals involved, and enterprises active, in a particular profession. The individual members are mainly concerned with obtaining status or prestige through their membership but they also have a common interest in other objectives. These include establishing educational standards for membership, setting standards of behaviour, codes of conduct and limiting membership to those in the appropriate sector of the industry. An example is the Tourism Society while in the broader business context, the Institute of Marketing is another.

Trade associations on the other hand are groups of companies active in a particular trade. Their general objectives are very similar to those of the professional bodies. They are also keen to promote the standing and interests of their trade while furthering the exchange of views and achieving cooperation

with other associations in their industry. They may also be
involved in achieving representation on these other bodies and
any negotiations that may be necessary for mutual benefit.
They can be classified into three groups, covering tourism in
general, destinations and specific sectors of the industry. Some
of them are listed in Table 2.4. Destinational associations
contain members (private and public organisations) interested

Table 2.4   Tourist/trade associations

TOURISM ASSOCIATIONS

British Tourist Authority (BTA)
International Union of Official Travel Organisations (IUOTO)
World Tourism Organisation (WTO)
Tourism Committee: Organisation for Economic Cooperation and
    Development (OECD)
Tourism Society

SECTORIAL ASSOCIATIONS

British Hotels, Restaurants and Caterers Association (BHRCA)
Confederation of British Road Passenger Transport
Historic Houses Association
National Association of Holiday Centres etc.

Professional associations:
Association of British Travel Agents (ABTA)
Hotel, Catering and Institutional Management Assn (HCIMA)
Institute of Travel and Tourism (ITT)
International Air Transport Association (IATA)
Chartered Institute of Transport (CIT) etc.

DESTINATIONAL ASSOCIATIONS

National, Regional and Area Tourist Organisations or Boards
Pacific Area Travel Association (PATA)
Travel Industry Association of America (TIAA)
East Asian Travel Association (EATA)
European Travel Commission

---

in the development and marketing of specific destinations. Tourism organisations are interested in doing the same things for tourism generally and cut across sectorial boundaries. They may also be involved in research into tourism matters and the provision of international and national tourism statistics. Of the three, the sectorial ones are usually the most numerous. (See also Chapter 9 for a fuller discussion on National Tourist Organisations.)

2.5 Some cases

The following cases are of interest. One indicates a possible future, major development and the other the problem of customer dissatisfaction.

2.5.1 China – destination of the future

Considerable excitement and interest arose when it became known a few years ago that the Chinese government intended to open its country to tourists. They had realised the importance of tourism in earning much needed foreign currency and hoped, also, that better understanding of China would result. Initially there was talk of building one thousand Western-style hotels in areas of scenic and cultural interest to foreigners. These areas were to be designated Tourist Zones. It was also clear that tourists wishing to range over other areas would be discouraged. However the effects of the world recession in the early 1980s forced the Chinese government to cut back on their original plans. None the less more and more Westerners have been visiting China in organised package tour groups.

Prior to 1982 there was a cumbersome procedure whereby individual travellers had to obtain written permission to travel anywhere. The same applied to tour groups but the tour operators arranged this and usually encountered less delay. In 1982 this procedure was ended for about thirty cities and foreigners could enter them without permits.

Despite the current (1985) price of £1500 or more per person for a three-week tour, China will undoubtedly prove a considerable attraction to growing numbers of the higher income groups. Even middle income people might be tempted by 'economy' packages with the excitement of seeing the Great Wall at dawn, visiting one or two other places and being back in the Forbidden City by sunset. Other attractions include floating down the Lijiang River in Guilin on a raft, passing the humpbacked green mountains that most Westerners think are the creation of the over-indulgent mind of a Chinese artist or flying to Xian and Nanjing then taking a train to Suzhou and Shanghai.

For the individual traveller there are some drawbacks. The first is trying to get a train ticket while competing against the crowd of locals trying to do the same. Getting to the ticket office sometimes seems a near impossibility. Then there is the question of currency. There are the normal notes for the Chinese and special ones for the visitor. Getting change can often be a complicated business since foreigners are not supposed to hold or use the regular units of currency. Hotels are still limited. Turning up on the offchance of getting a room may prove futile. Then there is the problem of currency crooks on top of having to haggle over every purchase and the usual tourist traps.

Some of these difficulties also face members of groups. However the official guide accompanying them will smooth these out for the visitors. Despite all these difficulties, China offers the prospects of some new and exciting destinations for future long-distance vacationists.

2.5.2 A case of complaint

A retired couple living in Yorkshire decided to take a three-week winter holiday on an Atlantic island, a popular summer and winter destination. The wife, aged 75, was disabled. As a young girl she had had polio and now had severe arthritis and a heart condition. Though able to travel, care had to be taken over the choice of hotel. It had to have working lifts and be reasonably on the flat with few steps in the public areas. They selected one of the smaller but well-known tour operators based in the north of England, booking through their usual travel agent.

After careful consultation with the agent, when the wife's needs were fully explained, they and the agent selected two hotels. They would stay for two weeks at the first and be transferred by taxi to the second for the final week. The first hotel was reasonably acceptable except for damp beds and sheets! This gave the wife a severe chest cough. Several others also developed coughs and the people in rooms on both sides of the couple were heard to cough badly during the nights. On the day of the transfer although the couple had been assured they would have a taxi on their own, they were crammed with two others into a small taxi. It was extremely difficult to get the luggage of four people into the luggage boot and the passenger compartment. The ride was extremely uncomfortable, especially for the wife.

On arrival at the second hotel the couple found there was no room booked in their name. The other couple however had one although they had booked only three weeks before departure with the same tour operator. The couple making the complaint (the 'plaintiffs') had booked three months in advance of the departure date. The local courier of the tour operator had no record of the plaintiffs' reservation and there was no free room they could have. What made matters worse was that the courier did not come on duty until the afternoon. The plaintiffs spent a very uncomfortable seven hours sitting in the hotel lobby waiting for a solution.

The courier then went around the resort looking for a room and in the early evening the couple were told to take another taxi to another hotel where a room was free because of a late cancellation. This hotel had apparently deteriorated into a shabby gentility and the husband noticed that its tariff was considerably less than for the original hotel they had selected. The alternative hotel was very unsatisfactory in every way. The food was of poor standard, the couple had to wait some time to get into the ill-lit dining room and they had to wait a long time before they were served.

In addition the lifts were inefficient. There were long waits and at times they had to walk up the stairs to the upper floor where their room was. It was a slow and painful process for the wife. On the ground floor there were several open steps, including the access to the open area where there was a small swimming pool. There were no handrails. The only safe way the wife could negotiate these steps was to sit down and lower or raise herself step by step on her bottom. They told the courier that the hotel was unsatisfactory for these reasons and received the reply that the courier could not see them until after 12.30 p.m. the next day. So that day they sat for hours in what they described as the railway station atmosphere of the hotel. Some time after 1.00 p.m. the courier arrived.

She took the couple to view some apartments. These too were unsatisfactory. The view from the lounge was the roofs of other apartments and from the dining room, an ill-lit dirty place, was on to a wall very close to the window. The lounge was reached from the dining area by a steep flight of steps without a handrail and proved difficult for the wife to negotiate. They judged the apartment to be unsuitable. On return to the hotel they had stayed at the previous night they found that their room had been given to others. There were no free seats on any return flight until the one they were originally booked on a week later.

So they had to take the apartment. Apart from four rolls delivered in the morning for breakfast, they had to go out to restaurants for their meals. These were few and all at some distance from the apartment. Steep steps and paths had to be negotiated and they were made more difficult by the debris from building and other construction work still going on. Instead of being a good rest for the wife, this 'holiday' reduced her to a nervous and exhausted wreck and she took many weeks to recover.

On their return the husband wrote immediately to the tour operator and travel agent, recounting all the above in detail. The subsequent correspondence with the tour operator covered several months with the operator trying to fob off the couple with vague replies. They claimed they had attended to the needs of the couple to the best of their ability! Eventually an 'ex-gratia' payment of £130 was made and the operator claimed this was the difference between the cost of what had been booked and what was provided. The husband, however, had access to facts that showed the correct difference to be about £220. He pressed for the difference, leaving aside the discomfort and pain suffered by the wife. The travel agent tried half-heartedly to help but without effect. The husband raised the matter with ABTA but the response he described as tardy. He formed the view that ABTA was really only inter-

ested in protecting its members, not their customers, in a case
like this.

A travelling representative of the tour operator felt sorry for
the couple and tried to help. She gave them the name of the
director in charge and has apparently since been sacked by the
firm. Finally after much more correspondence with the director, a further sum was paid over to the couple. The money was
donated to a charity. Perhaps the irony of this affair is that the
couple in their working days owned a travel agency! They
thought they knew their way around this type of problem. Yet
it took many months before a reasonable settlement was
achieved. The result, as far as the couple are concerned, is that
they will not use that tour operator again and their many
friends knowing of their experience, have probably been put
off that operator also.

Assignments

1   Study the second case above and write a report on
    (a) what you would have done had you been the resi-
         dent courier?
    (b) how you think the tour operator should have han-
         dled the problem?

2   Discuss the role and importance of ABTA in the travel
industry. In the light of the second case quoted above, do you
think the husband's view of them is correct? If so how do you
think ABTA's role should be altered to benefit both its members and their customers?

3   If you were an executive with a major travel agent how
would you see China as a great, future tourist area? What do
you think you should do to ensure that your company will be in
the forefront of tours to China when the time is ripe? (Study of
relevant sections of Chapters 3 to 6 should help you to answer
this comprehensively.)

4   How did modern tourism begin? Discuss how the nature
and type of tourism has been changed by recent developments.
Forecast what you think will be the nature of package tourism
by the end of this century, giving particular reference to the

possible economic condition of the world and the major tourist generating areas (countries).

5   Discuss the role of the travel agent, especially those based in city centres, suburban areas and county towns.

6   Discuss the suitability of the different types of accommodation available for the different categories of consumer going on holiday and the prices they can afford.

3

Products and Markets

The tourism industry is like any other in that its products and markets are closely interrelated. In the jargon of marketing, the product-market concept applies here also (see Chapter 7). The products (tours and travel facilities) required by different types of customers or markets vary according to the latter's reason for travelling. These are listed in Table 3.1, a restatement of Figure 1.1. Thus the tourism products that should be offered will depend on the choice of markets or types of customers the tour operator and travel agent wish to serve. However, as stated before, the tourism product is an amalgam of resort, accommodation and other support services. It is not a homogeneous item: it is heterogeneous. The components used will themselves depend on the needs of the tourists. When these needs change it may be necessary to alter one or more of the components of any package.

3.1 Types of tourists and their needs

The basic motivations and determinants were summarised in Section 1.4. In this section more detailed consideration will be given to this matter.

3.1.1   Rest and relaxation
Tourists seeking rest and relaxation generally will require

accommodation of as good a quality and efficiency that can be expected for the price they can afford. The mode and standard of transport will also be dictated by these considerations. The resort or destination chosen will depend on the form of relaxation required. For those who want to spend most of the time lying on a warm, sunny beach (the 'sun-sea-sand set') an appropriate coastal resort will be chosen. Those wishing to make several day trips to other towns, cities or events, the choice and quality of the excursions will help to determine the choice of resort.

Tourists who wish to see as much of the countryside as possible may elect to take a coach tour staying at different places each night. The size and quality of the hotels used may be of secondary importance to the route and itinerary of the trip. Then there are others who wish to avoid the strains of one night stands, who will pick two or more resorts for their holiday. They may experiment with the hotel used at one (or all) of the destinations. Further, if the resort they wish to visit has limited accommodation facilities, the short-stay tourist might accept this, although for a longer one-resort holiday they might demand better quality and so choose a different resort. The support services in the packages will also be affected by the above considerations.

3.1.2 Cultural visits

In the case of tourists interested in other cultures, the location and availability of the cultural event will determine the destination selected. In this case also the standard of accommodation will not be of prime importance. Its closeness to the event is more important. If there are no hotels within the price range the tourists can afford, then the better guest house, or even a holiday village or camp, would be acceptable. Take for example the Passion Play at Oberammergau. This is held in a small town with only a few small hotels and pensions with inadequate capacity for the crowds that visit this event. The majority of visitors accept staying in small guest houses or living with local families in their homes. In many cases they are prepared to take lunches and dinners at outside restaurants and cafés.

In other circumstances many of these tourists would not

accept such accommodation and conditions. If the cultural event is in a major town with a reasonable range of hotels (e.g. the Bayreuth Festival) or in a major city with full facilities, the accommodation chosen will be the best that can be afforded. If the event is some distance from their accommodation, tourists expect either good, frequent and inexpensive local transport or well organised coach services organised especially for the purpose.

3.1.3 Educational visits

Tourists taking holidays for educational purposes, whether to learn something or to attain new knowledge, will choose destinations appropriate for this purpose. Again the type and standard of accommodation are of secondary importance. For example, people wishing to study art, music or another skill are now accepting accommodation in universities and colleges that run such courses during the vacations. There may be a certain cachet attached to this and frequently the customers are those with limited means. They find the low costs linked with the learning aspect as representing very good value. These holidays provide a rest of a different sort, a change of interest from people's daily lives. The support services can also be rudimentary. However those who take these holidays are prepared to make their own spare time activities such as walks in the surrounding countryside, community singing at night, concerts and so on.

3.1.4 Exotic and unusual holidays

There is now a wide range of these on offer. If visits to faraway but sophisticated destinations are involved (e.g. Southeast Asia, Australia, South America) the tourists normally expect everything to be of a high standard, provided this is possible and they can afford it. If adventure holidays are concerned they will take what is available but expect it to be in character with the vacation, for example, living under canvas if foot or pony trekking around the Himalayas, America or even the Lake District, is involved.

While some trekking holidays provide basic facilities (a tent, sleeping bag and cooking over a camp fire), others are not quite so basic. Their tented camp precedes them from camp site to camp site and has refrigeration facilities for drinks and proper facilities for baths. Dinner, perhaps cooked over a camp fire, awaits them. Any discomfort, including the high cost, is balanced by the chance to walk in unspoilt terrain not normally possible for all and sundry. They enjoy the spectacular scenery and rare flora and fauna. On the other hand rafting along the Amazon River involves very basic facilities on the raft even if nights may be spent ashore at whatever 'hotel' is available. These primitive and slightly dangerous facilities are accepted happily. They see it all as a great adventure with lots of 'local colour', local colour they would not accept with other holidays.

3.1.5　*Travel as a norm of behaviour*
During the last three decades, travel for pleasure has become a norm of behaviour for many millions. In some cases a certain prestige value is ascribed to 'going abroad' or on a cruise. In some societies, not going abroad for a holiday is seen as a sign of failure or has some sort of mysterious stigma. Those who travel for travel's sake or because it is the done thing, will usually go for accommodation, mode of travel and activities they think appropriate to their social or job status. In instances when they cannot really afford what they see as appropriate to their status, they will save, scrimp, borrow and go into debt to be able to take that holiday.

3.1.6　*Other travellers for pleasure*
The other categories of tourists (or markets) have needs and attitudes very similar to one of the foregoing. For example, the *common interest* tourist will follow a similar reasoning and response as that of the *cultural tourist*. So also will those who travel for a *religious purpose*, or to *shop* in some new (exotic) place or to *gamble* at some resort such as Monte Carlo or Las Vegas. While most will want the best accommodation they can afford, the compulsive gambler may show little interest. Any bed will do! The location, status and other aspects of the casino will rank more highly. For a sophisticated person not too addicted to gambling and with sufficient means, the standard and quality of the accommodation, mode of transport, support

services and other attractions will be rated equally with, or higher than, the destination and its casino.

3.1.7 *Business traveller*

In the case of the business traveller, the five points mentioned under this heading in Table 3.1 are paramount. These influence decisions made on time and mode of travel, routes, duration of trip and destinations. The priority ascribed to each can vary. The executive whose company has encountered an unexpected development abroad will catch the first available plane and will not worry if the hotel normally used is fully booked. The next best will do. The duration of the visit will

Table 3.1 Reasons for travel

Pleasure

Educational/need for learning about other peoples, cultures, etc.
Experience – beauty and wonder: from natural or manmade things
 – power and freedom to travel
Following hobbies and special interests (cultural, etc.)
Need for change
Need for rest and relaxation
Search for the exotic and unusual
Sporting events of interest to traveller
To shop in new places
Travel as a challenge
Travel to gamble!
Travel seen as a cultural norm – 'everyone takes a holiday'
Travel for travel's sake
Travel for religious reasons

Business travel

Type of customer to be visited
Type of industry to be visited
Locations of customers/industry
Timing and duration of visits
Reason or need for visit

---

depend on what has to be done and how long it will take to persuade the visited to respond. The route may be influenced by necessity but if it is a routine trip, the executive may stick to a favoured route, also carrier. Usually one executive travels alone but groups of up to six executives may go together. It depends on what has to be done at the destination (e.g. attend a conference, negotiate a major sales agreement or sort out a major technical problem and so on). The executives who travel range from company chairmen and executive directors to technical and sales personnel. For very important purposes much larger groups may have to undertake a trip together.

Business trips are seldom one night stands though this may be the case with sales and marketing personnel. Others stay for longer periods depending on the purpose of the journey. Various surveys in industrialised countries indicate that about a quarter of all trips are of seven to ten days duration. Also, nearly a third of all those who travel for business make more than five trips a year. In the USA about 10 per cent of all trips involve up to thirty nights in an hotel. This is because executives are sent for training or on familiarisation trips to factories and offices outside the executives' home bases.

Britain, with an international or export-orientated business activity was in the upper end of these figures. Executives with overseas responsibilities can make twelve or more trips a year and stay away for an average of five nights per visit. Nearly 50 per cent of them in fact undertook more than twelve trips in a year and about a quarter spent seven nights or more away from home on each journey. About 20 per cent of them made up to six trips a year but covered considerable distances involving twenty-eight days or more away from home. These were mainly visits to several important overseas markets. On the other hand the Japanese tend to exceed even these high figures, not only when travelling abroad but also in circuits of their own country. Note also that 'business travel' includes not only overseas and home journeys by nationals of a country but also visits by foreign nationals.

Regarding accommodation, most firms have an hierarchical approach to the subject. Company chairmen (and women) and chief executives may stay only at five-star, or equivalent, hotels. Other directors and general managers may be restricted to four-star establishments and so on. This is one reason why travel agents involved in business travel arrangements must have detailed knowledge of client firms, their needs and usual code of conduct in this matter.

Business travel requires individual arrangements and thus involves high costs. Within reason costs are not important. However in times of recession, or when companies are not doing too well, limits may be set by clients. With the growing internationalisation of business, this form of travel is covering an ever widening sector of the world. Executives also travel more frequently (especially during times of recession when they have to fight harder for their business). They try to avoid peak holiday periods (except company chairmen who may wish to be in the Caribbean or Far East in the winter!) but their stay at any destination will be shorter than that for a holiday. They may or may not hire self-drive or chauffeur driven cars at important destinations but they have tended in recent years to add a short-break holiday somewhere *en route*. This eases the strain involved and can take advantage of any special offers hotels might be making.

So business travel tends to be price inelastic and non-seasonal. It is often big-city orientated. It is also influenced by business related attractions such as exhibitions and conferences. It has to be tailored to each executive's needs. While it involves a lot of work for the travel agent, for an agent with the right knowledge and awareness of clients' needs it can be profitable. This is even when clients drive a hard bargain on costs when several executives use the same travel agent or if the latter has some sort of agreement with the firm.

3.2 Tourism products

It will be appreciated from the foregoing that tour operators and travel agents wishing to have a viable, successful business must offer a comprehensive range of packages and travel facilities. In addition the tourism product is a non-material, intangible thing. Unlike a manufactured product, the potential customer cannot feel, taste, touch or sample a package tour in advance of any decision to buy it. (The aircraft seat and hotel room are just components of a package that are made available for the duration of the flight and stay. Ownership of them does not pass to the tourist!) Because of the intangibility of the product, potential customers have trouble in identifying whether the package on offer will really meet their needs. Therefore consumers need considerable amounts of information and constructive advice from the sellers before a travel decision can be made correctly.

To the various members of the tourism industry the tourism 'product' is different things. To the hotel it is 'guest-nights' (the number of guests times the number of nights they stay at the hotel). To the airline it is the 'seats flown' and the 'passenger miles' (number of passengers and the distance they fly) that result. To the museum, art gallery or archaeological site, the product is measured in terms of the number of visitors. However for the tourist the product is the complete experience resulting from the package tour or travel facility purchased, from the time they leave home until their return. The 'experience' covers the entire amalgam of all the components of the package including their attitudes and expectations. The last two are important. No matter how well the package has been assembled, if 'experience' does not match customers' expectations nor satisfies their needs which are governed by their attitudes to holidays, they will judge it to be unsatisfactory.

3.2.1 Major considerations

Thus in formulating tourist products many other things must be considered, not just accommodation and transport. These include the attractions, support facilities and services at the resort, the ease of access to it *and* the attitudes and behaviour patterns of target markets or customers. The attractions cover both natural elements (landscape, seascape, climate and ecological factors) and manmade ones (reservoirs, chair lifts, cable railways to scenic viewing points, cultural activities, historical sites and buildings). The facilities include the infra- and superstructure of the area (accommodation, local transport, roads, railways, airports and other public services). Accessibility is measured not only in the time taken to travel to the resort but also by the modes of transport available (air, sea, rail, road) and the degree of comfort involved (for example the use of smaller aircraft or widebodied jets).

A few examples might help to illustrate the points made about customer attitudes, behaviour patterns and possible satisfactions. First, the tourist taking a sea cruise is looking for perhaps a new or unique experience. In addition they want a clean, comfortable, safe and efficiently run ship, providing good accommodation and food. The route must cover ports of call that interest the traveller. While on board they may assume attitudes and behaviour patterns superior to those they follow in their normal lives. They may be more critical of shortcomings, especially if these spoil what is for them a very special holiday.

Then there are the special interest and cultural tourists. Besides expecting acceptable standards of accommodation, food and comfort, they will expect the special interest or cultural event to be what is claimed for it. If the event is also their hobby, their knowledge of it will be more extensive than if it is not and they will be critical of any shortcomings. The golf addict does not want a holiday with golfing facilities but one that offers excellent golfing experiences throughout the length of the holiday.

Finally, for those attending conferences, the location and standards of the hotel must be appropriate to the conference. If any customers or influential people have to be entertained, there must be good facilities in the hotel or close to it. For those who want to stay at an hotel of high or special repute (e.g. Reids Hotel, Madeira; Hotel im Palais Schwarzenberg, Austria; Lake Palace Hotel, Udaipur, India) lesser substitutes will not do. It is the hotel that counts not, within reason, the efficiency of the courier. The latter is of secondary importance.

3.2.2 Other considerations

Other items which go to make up a complete package and which influence the success of it, include the need for visas, whether they can be obtained easily, foreign exchange controls and regulations and health controls and risks. No matter how attractive a country or destination might be, if it is a long, difficult and tedious task to obtain a visa and the tourist is left to struggle through it on his or her own, the tour package will lose some or all of its attractiveness. Similarly if the health risks are high and need various inoculations before departure or a complex regimen of regular pill-taking while at the resort, an alternative holiday may be preferred. The same goes for countries with difficult or very restrictive regulations and controls on currency matters.

3.2.3 Product development

The various components that form the 'raw material' from which holiday packages can be created are set out in Table 3.2. Which of the alternatives should be selected will depend on the type of holiday the operator wishes to create, the target markets for which it is intended and thus the needs, requirements and expectations of the people comprising those markets. Not shown in the table is price. Obviously this must be taken into account. The cost of the components, competition, the profit margin required and the ability of consumers to pay, all help to determine the tour price that can be set.

The costs set the bottom limit to the price that is possible if the operator does not wish to incur a loss on sales. Competition sets the upper limit to the price that could be charged. Unless the package offers some special or unique advantage (marketing jargon: 'unique selling proposition' or USP) over competitive packages, sales will fall below expected limits. The ability of potential customers to pay the asking price will indicate whether the intended price will be acceptable and if the desired profit will be obtained. Thus the construction of tour packages and their prices require careful and detailed study of all these relevant factors (see also Chapter 7).

Once a series of packages have been formulated and marketed, the operator cannot sit back for too long and forget further product development. Market conditions (economic, costs and competition) change. Customers' needs and expectations also change. The product range will have to be altered to match these changes. For example, people who have spent their younger years on sun, sea and sand holidays, in their maturer years will seek something different. They may wish to pursue hobbies, other cultures or special interests. If their incomes have improved and with it their net discretionary incomes, they may expect better standards and quality of everything or more exciting holidays.

So even the most successful package, especially one that has been sold profitably for years, will need re-study in the light of perceived or forecasted changes. If competition has become fierce should the operator change the resort or hotel? Should some of the existing programme be phased out ('rationalised') and replaced by new packages? Should diversification into quite new activities, such as sea cruises, be advisable for the operator's continued, profitable survival? All this takes time. Even just adding a new hotel to some resorts could take two or more years. Accommodation has to be booked in advance and nothing suitable may be available for a while.

If new resorts are to be added it may take even longer. If the new destination or country is unknown to the operator, suitably experienced new staff will have to be found. Time has to be spent by executives in visiting these new resorts to learn as much as possible about relevant aspects. Is the infrastructure adequate? If new facilities are being constructed, when will they be completed and will they be adequate? Table 3.3 outlines two simple cases of what may be involved if product modification, new product development and diversification are needed.

Developments are taking place most of the time. A few years ago only one small company organised foot-trekking holidays in the foothills of the Himalayas. Now several do, including treks to the base of Mount Everest. Trekking holidays are now not only available for Nepal and India but also in Kenya, Peru, Chile and China, to mention a few. Unfortunately the most popular ones have the usual drawbacks of overcrowding and pollution which destroy the original appeal of walking in remote areas. Finally, packages must be suitable for the period of the year when they will operate and new ones should not compete so strongly with existing products that they take business away from the latter.

3.2.4 *Touring*

Most holidaymakers fly to the international airport convenient for their resort, or fly to a main or capital city and stay a night or two before moving on to their resort. They may then stay

Table 3.2 Tourism products – range of components

Country*	Destination*	Location	Accommodation type	Facilities	Meal service
Spain	Costa Brava Costa del Sol Madrid Grenada etc.	Seaside	Hotel: 5 star 4 star	Shopping arcade	Full-board
France	Riviera Paris etc.	Country Mountains/hills City/town centre	3 star etc. Guest house Motel/motor hotel Youth hostels	Hairdresser Pension Valet/dry cleaning service	Half-board Bed & breakfast Buffet service
Austria	Kitzbuhel Seefeld etc.	Business location	Camping sites Hired caravans/ motorhomes	Nurseries and night watch service	
USA	Disneyworld Tampa, Fa.	Near place of interest etc.	CRUISE SHIPS	Sports facilities etc.	Choice of restaurants etc.

Table 3.2 Tourism products – range of components

No. in group	Duration	Mode of transport	Type of tourist	Special interests	Excursions
Mass mkt, i.e. large gps (60 +)	1 week	Air – scheduled charter	TOURISTS: A; B; C1; C2; D; E.**	Sporting (golf etc.)	Half-day visits Full-day visits Extension tours
Popular mkt, say 40–60	2 weeks	Road – coach car (own) car (hired)	Retired people	Historical Art/museums Archaeological Antiques	Short stopover Long stopover Special events Shopping visits
Small groups, say up to 24	3 weeks			Wine and food Bird-watching	
Families/clubs	4 or more weeks Short break	Rail	BUSINESS TRAVELLERS		Visits to factories
Individuals	Weekends Other	Sea – ferries ships (cruises)	Co chairmen etc. Co directors Other executives Salespersons Others	Industry (type of) Training Conferences Meetings Other	Visits to special organisations/ centres Visits to conferences etc.

* A few examples. ** See Chapters 7 and 8.

Table 3.3 Tourism products – product development: Some examples

A Medium-sized tour operator whose range of products include the following:

I SPAIN 1. Costa Brava	(i) Lloret del Mar	2 and 3 star hotels all-inclusive; table d'hôte, no choice	Mass market: Cl, C2, D. Excursions extra
2. Costa del Sol	(i) Torremolinos	As above but full- and half-board	As above
3. Costa Blanca	(i) Benidorm	As 2 above but buffet service	Club groups and popular market: C1, C2. One excursion included in price.
II USA 1. Florida	(i) Tampa area	4 star hotels; B&B, buffet	Groups of 24 mainly B and C1, excursions extra

(a) *Product modification: options include:*

I
    (i) Add one or two 4 star hotels with better locations and facilities
    (ii) Costa Brava: offer choice of menu for small extra charge
    (iii) Costa del Sol: offer another resort, greater choice of hotels, etc.
    (iv) Costa Blanca: offer other resorts and hotels; also B&B; choice of à la carte menu; more excursions included in tour price; more facilities including nurseries, etc.
    (v) All may necessitate price changes (increases) but some might not. If modifications not possible consider price reductions

II
    (i) Add other destinations, e.g. Disneyland, Miami Beach
    (ii) Offer alternative of half-board
    (iii) Include some excursions in tour price
    (iv) Offer some better hotels to attract more B group consumers

(b) *New product development: options include:*
    (i) Open up new resorts in Greece, Tunisia and Egypt at same or better standards than offered for SPAIN – higher prices. Target markets: B and C1 with possibility of some As

(c) *Diversification: options include:*
    (i) Go into sea cruise business and/or Nile cruises

(ii) Offer new and if possible, unique safaris in East Africa or India etc.

B   A specialist tour operator offering 3-week air tours of SE Asia in 'economy' and 'luxury' packages.

Both tours involve 4 nights at Penang, Kuala Lumpur and Bangkok/ Pattaya Beach, 3 nights at Singapore and 5 nights at Bali. The route used is London–Kuala Lumpur–Penang–Singapore–Bali–Bangkok or Pattaya–London.

The 'economy' tour uses 3-star hotels or equivalent while the 'luxury' tour uses 4 star or equivalent. All on half-board terms.

Extension of 1 week is offered as an optional extra and this is for 5 nights at Cheng Mai.

Various local half-day and day excursions possible; costs not included in tour price.

Travel by 2nd class rail from provincial cities to London charged extra at cost.

(a) *Product modifications: options include:*
>(i) If competition strong, keep same packages but look for cost savings to pass on in lower prices, 'special offers' or to include one local excursion in tour price, etc.
>(ii) To improve sales of 'economy' package change some or all hotels to 4 star at either small surcharges or at same price if savings elsewhere are possible (e.g. negotiate fare reductions, or if demand sufficient by using charter flights)
>(iii) For 'luxury' package use 5 star hotels, especially if economy tours start using 4 star ones; meet increased cost in similar ways suggested in (ii)
>(iv) Include one half- or full-day excursion in prices
>(v) Include choice of à la carte for main meal for small surcharge or at no extra cost. Consider possibility of better rooms at no extra cost (e.g. rooms with better views, locations in hotels, etc.)

(b) *New products: options include:*
>(i) Offer alternative tours e.g. London–Penang–Singapore–Bali–Manila–London or any combination thereof; option of adding Bangkok/Pattaya at small extra cost and also extension for stay at Cheng Mai
>(ii) Offer package of London–Kuala Lumpur–Penang and sea cruise from Penang around Indonesian Islands incl. Bali, ending at Singapore for return to London

(c) *Diversification: options include:*
>(i) Air tour to Rio–Peru (including overland tour to Inca sites) etc.

there for the entire holiday. If a two-centre holiday is taken they will move to the second resort in due course. Touring as such, travelling around to different parts of a country with stops of only two or three nights at any place, is still not as widely in demand as it could be. Even those who do, tend to concentrate on major centres. Touring remains the preserve of those with wanderlust who are not content to remain on a beach all the time but wish to see as much of a country as possible. Even many who hire cars at their resorts use them only for localised trips.

Many people who do undertake touring are motivated by a desire to visit as many countries as possible. They seem less interested in the places actually visited! Often they remember little about the trip or even the places visited after they return home. People coming from far afield (for example Americans and Australians visiting Europe) may cram too much into their visit if they think it will be their only one. Their touring is very high speed stuff (21 countries in 14 days!) and not surprisingly, memories of it may be very blurred. Such rushed journeys are not touring at its best. A more leisurely schedule with 'time to stand and stare' at whatever interests the tourist is necessary for full enjoyment of the trip.

The ability to undertake touring in the past has been restricted by lack of facilities such as suitable roads, coaches and hotels at overnight stops. Touring requires a reasonably developed infrastructure if it is to be enjoyable and free from problems for the customers. The exception is safari trips where the tourists' interest in seeing animals in the wild takes precedence. Travelling along bumpy tracks and staying overnight in basic accommodation is all part of the fun. However many countries known for their safaris (e.g. Kenya and Tanzania) have built very sophisticated hotels ('lodges') with facilities equal to the best in the world. So people can relax in relatively pampered luxury after a hard day on the trail!

The availability of modern, airconditioned coaches with reclining seats has stimulated interest in touring. Many of them have toilets on board and can serve hot and cold drinks *en route*. They have taken much of the discomfort formerly associated with long-distance coach tours out of this type of holiday. For those who hire or take their own cars the availability of good, safe, scenic roads adequately served by petrol and service stations and good accommodation located at well selected sites have also stimulated demand. However the drawback for some people is that these routes can become overcrowded at peak holiday periods.

3.2.5 Ancillary services

Ancillary services are important contributors to the success of any tourism product. Those of particular importance include *good guide or courier facilities* and appropriate financial services. The latter cover *insurance, foreign exchange* and *credit facilities*.

Most travellers like to be insured against personal accident, holiday cancellation, hospital and other medical care, delayed departure, loss of money or luggage and fast repatriation by air in case of serious accident or illness. What many do not realise is that most of this cover could be null and void in the event of wars, riots and civil commotions. Whether insurers will change these exclusion clauses in the future is doubtful. They claim it is difficult to assess these eventualities. The premiums would be heavy. Insurers claim that most travellers want reasonable premiums for policies that cover the risks that are more likely to arise. However the growing political instability in many parts of the world in the 1980s and the high cost of medical attention in the USA and some other countries, show up the inadequacy of most current insurance cover.

Regarding foreign currency, there is now a good choice open to tourists. Subject to the laws and regulations of the home and host countries, currency notes in sterling, any other hard currency (such as US dollars, German marks or Swiss francs) and sometimes currency of the host (destination) country can be taken. However taking notes increases the risk of losses due to theft. A safer method is to take travellers' cheques in any major currency, or that of the host nation if available. For example in the last instance, while Austria is a major holiday centre for British residents it is not possible to obtain travellers' cheques in Austrian schillings. Usually major organisations such as Thomas Cook, American Express and the clearing banks offer instant replacement of lost cheques on notification of the loss to the issuing organisation. Which currency to use will depend on the international economic and financial conditions at the time.

There are also several credit cards which can be used on holiday, subject to conditions ruling at the time. First, there are VISA and ACCESS cards which have set credit limits depending on the financial standing of the holder. Repayment can be extended over any period provided the minimum monthly payments are made. Interest on unpaid balances is at a rate considerably higher than bank base rates. Then there are cards like those issued by American Express and Diners Club which have no limits but repayment in full is expected at the time of billing. Finally, several other organisations have their own cards. These include hotel groups, some airlines, one or two tour operators (e.g. Portland Holidays) and the Universal Air Travel Plan (UATP). The last can be used to purchase IATA tickets.

Most tour successes also stand or fall according to the standard and efficiency of the courier and guide services provided. Couriers, often employed on a part-time basis, shepherd and supervise groups of tourists from the airport of arrival throughout their stay at a resort to their eventual departure for home. Some operators also have couriers at the airport of departure in the home countries to see their groups safely on the right plane. With coach tours the courier travels on the coach and also acts as guide, giving the necessary commentary as the coach travels through places of interest. These couriers are sometimes called tour escorts or leaders. Some coach tour firms have dispensed with separate couriers. They use driver-couriers who combine driving with commentaries on the sights *en route*.

Guides on the other hand are involved in giving information on the places and sites seen on foot such as art galleries, museums, archaeological and other historical places. Sometimes with coach tours the tour escort or leader may have to do this. How the work is allocated depends on the availability of suitable staff, the need to reduce costs and the complexity of the tour. On the other hand some developing countries insist that guides and couriers must be local nationals. This is especially so with nations having high, permanent unemployment. Language problems can sometimes arise in these cases. Some countries (e.g. Russia and China) insist on local nationals being the guides and couriers for political reasons rather than any other.

3.3 Characteristics of tourism markets

Section 3.1 discussed the different types of tourists possible and their basic needs. These influence the characteristics of the resultant, different tourism markets to which these individuals belong. This section studies these aspects further. Markets from a marketing point of view are discussed in Chapter 7.

3.3.1 Definitions of 'market'

The word 'market' has several meanings depending on who uses it. First, it can refer to the people who buy and sell any product or service and all the transactions involved. To the economist it usually means 'all those buyers and sellers of goods and services who affect the price'. Or it can refer to (sales) demand for an item and can be stated in units (volume) or its value $(£)$. Thus the market for tourism products in a country (a tourist-generating area) can be stated as say, ten million people, or fifteen million journeys, or £300 million, or any combination of these. The third possibility above usually refers to the total expenditure on tourism by residents of, and visitors to, the country. 'Market' can also refer to the place where the transactions are done. To the stockbroker it is the stock market or stock exchange.

For management and marketing purposes it is *all those actual and potential customers who do or could buy a product or service*. For this book this last definition is the most appropriate. In this case it means 'the actual and potential demand for a tourism product based on a specified tourism motivation or purpose'. 'Market' can also refer to a tourist-generating area. Here it is using a geographical basis for the definition.

3.3.2 Holiday market

This normally refers to all who go on a general vacation. The holiday is usually of two or three weeks' duration but there are now some long-distance and other tours where four, five and even six weeks are the usual duration. Buying decisions can also be influenced by interest in, or liking for, a particular resort or country. Prices vary from the 'economy tour' with low prices to 'luxury tours' involving much higher ones.

Within the price range, tourists have freedom to choose any resort or hotel but not necessarily the timing of the holiday. Some tours may only be available at certain times. Also if the tourists have children at school, the timing will depend on when the school holidays are. Or if they work for an employer who specifies the time when annual holidays may be taken, then their choice will be constrained by this factor.

Vacationists can be categorised into two groups. First there are the more *conservative* people who are less likely to take risks and minimise these by sticking to the same resort or country each year. Then there are those less sophisticated people who do not wish to venture out of their usual social environment or who are introverts. Their decisions are usually influenced by emotional considerations though some rational ones may also apply. Finally, young couples with small children and heavy financial commitments may feel constrained by these circumstances.

The second group could be called *experimentalists*. They are more adventurous and are prepared to try something new, if they can afford it and it is put over well to them, especially if it satisfies some new interest. Many just do not like going to the same place or country every year. They believe a change is as good as a rest. They are willing to accept reasonable challenges if they offer new and exciting experiences in scenery, local culture, climate, people and so on. They are usually better informed, especially about less sophisticated destinations and are not put off by the inherent drawbacks. Usually they have travelled extensively and have the net discretionary income to try new things. Instant colour TV transmissions stimulate their interest. Their decisions are based on rational considerations though some emotional ones may also be present.

Both these groups can be further subdivided by socio-economic factors. The more usual ones are age, income, social and job status. These are discussed further in Chapter 7.

The holiday market may also be sub-classified in terms of

demand. First there is the *mass market*. This involves the largest number of vacationists who travel in large groups (say forty or more) usually taking the less expensive all-inclusive tours. The customers are usually drawn from the conservative group mentioned above but a few experimentalists may be included in the groups. The latter are those who may be temporarily constrained by financial limitations or who wish to try different resorts and countries without risking too much money in the first instance. The bulk of the customers are usually from social group C2 (skilled and semi-skilled factory workers and artisans) and D (unskilled workers) with some E (retired people on limited pensions in particular and some unemployed who can still find the money for inexpensive holidays). There may also be a few C1 people (white collar/office workers and junior executives) with financial limitations.

Another sub-classification is the *popular market*. These involve smaller groups going on inclusive or semi-inclusive tours, more usually the latter. With these the hotel arrangement is for half-board (dinner, bed and breakfast) allowing tourists a free choice for lunch and the excursions they can take at the resort. This contrasts with the all-inclusive holiday where the price covers three meals a day and one or two excursions. The popular market customers are mainly from the C1 and C2 groups and pensioners and retired people (E group) with more substantial incomes. Middle executive and middle income people (B group) also use these semi-inclusive packages though they tend to patronise the more expensive ones, sometimes with bed-and-breakfast arrangements only at the hotel. All are more sophisticated than is the case with the mass market, expect better accommodation and like to have some freedom of choice regarding meals and menu, especially lunch.

Finally there is the *individual holiday tourist*. Independently minded, they do not wish to be confined to a group and prefer to do their own thing. One of their motivations is being able to get away from their own nationals and live amongst the society of the host country. Usually they have the income to afford this more expensive holiday which is usually tailor-made to their individual requirements. They travel independently and stay at hotels of their own choice. They are drawn from social group A (company chairmen, senior executives and professionals) and B. A few C1s in the upper income groups of their class and self-employed artisans are also customers of this type of holiday. In several instances they may stay at their own time-shared or fully owned villas or apartments. In recent years some are prepared to travel with small groups to benefit from the cheaper fares, becoming independent on arrival at their chosen resort. They use the courier as and when it is convenient to them.

Retired people with good occupational pensions may also take independent holidays. Most people in this classification either use their own contacts to make their reservations or major, leading travel agents. If they have friends at the destination they may stay with them. The duration of these holidays varies according to the time the executives have available. Usually these holidays are for three or more weeks.

3.3.3 Business travel market

This has been discussed fully in Section 3.1.7. All that needs to be added here is that most executives on this type of journey prefer bed-and-breakfast, or at most half-board, arrangements at hotels. It depends on how much entertaining is involved, the quality and reputation of the hotel's restaurant and whether they intend to eat in, or out of, the hotel.

3.3.4 Cultural tourism market

People who take these holidays have a state of mind and pattern of behaviour that are influenced by their love of, and search for, new cultural events, ones new to them that is. They are not motivated by geographical considerations and distance is no problem provided they can afford to pay for these holidays.

The activities that attract them depends on their interest and background. For example, a citizen of the USA with European ethnic roots will want to visit the region of their ancestors. British people whose ancestors served the old Raj would want to visit the Indian subcontinent. Europeans may be interested in Egypt and the Pharaohs and so on.

There is a substantial element of learning involved in cultural tourism but there must also be the will to learn. Although normally undertaken by the better educated, others

interested in self-betterment or overcoming the lack of opportunities when they were young will also go for cultural tours.
They are generally well read on the subjects that interest them.
Customers can be from any social group. Many will save for
some time to be able to afford these tours.

Again the duration can vary from two to six weeks with
three or four appearing to be the norm. The choice is limited
by the cultural event, when it is held and the number of tour
operators active in each case. The tourist's freedom of choice
about when holidays can be taken is another influencing
factor.

3.3.5 Common interest tourism market

Common interest subjects can cover cultural activities as well
as sports and sporting events. The characteristics of this market
are similar to those described in the previous section and both
may involve the use of a suitably knowledgeable courier. The
difference is that the groups may be drawn from those belonging to the same club, association or church but this is no longer
mandatory to gain the benefit of former 'affinity group' terms.
One example is members of the congregation of a church going
to the Holy Land for Easter or Christmas. Another is members
of a sporting club going to America for their open golf or tennis
championships. A third may involve visits to the historical sites
in the Indian subcontinent by members of a camera or
archaeological club. In this last case they go to see and
photograph the places and are not so intent to learn about
them as is the case with cultural tourists. The duration is
normally two to four weeks.

3.3.6 Conference/congress tourism market

This is a variation of business travel since mainly business
people undertake such visits. However where the conference
has wider appeal private individuals may undertake them.
Examples include conferences on ecological matters, wild life
and new developments of all kinds. Organised on a group basis
they offer cost savings but since a wide range of people may
attend them, the accommodation facilities must offer a wide
choice to potential customers. They are not cheap since the
speakers usually expect to receive reasonable fees for their

trouble, local transport will have to be included and there is the cost of hiring the hall. The duration can vary from a few days to two or three weeks.

The important factors that influence the decision of executives to accept the offer include:

(a) the accessibility of the venue and the availability of sufficient transport, international and local;
(b) sufficient and efficient conference facilities and arrangements;
(c) sufficient accommodation over all grades required;
(d) venue in relation to the home base of the participants;
(e) importance of the function and venue;
(f) the tourist attractions available and time allowed for relaxation by participants, especially on free evenings;
(g) cost, relative to the importance and standing of the event.

3.3.7 *Classification by age of tourists*

Classifying markets by the age of the customers is obviously important for the tour operators involved in product development. People of different ages have different interests and thus travel and holiday needs. Younger people are restricted by their low incomes. Of necessity, they will go for the cheaper packages (mass or popular market) and they are also more adventurous and will accept quite basic facilities (travelling by converted truck on trips to India, sleeping under canvas whether on camp sites or not and generally 'roughing it' are common examples). The young marrieds with young children have financial constraints but also give priority to the needs and safety of their children. If they know that long air journeys upset the younger children they will seek destinations involving short (two to three hours) flying times.

The older people perhaps having 'slummed' when young now wish to experience better quality hotels, holidays and so on, especially if they have the necessary income. If they are adventurous and seek new horizons, long-distance holidays are attractive. Thus this age classification also gives indications of the price range that should be used for facilities aimed at the different age groups.

3.3.8 *Classification by demand trends*
This method takes into account what is happening in the general field of tourism. It divides markets into primary, secondary and opportunity ones.

Primary markets are those tourist-generating areas which are actually providing the main portion of the tourist traffic to a destination or resort. The people from these areas are generally knowledgeable of the destination. While the untapped potential may be less than half total demand these are the markets where sellers of tourism products should concentrate their efforts. It should be relatively easy to achieve optimal sales from them. (For example the USA is a primary market for tourism to the UK. Ethnic, historical, language and health safety are all factors that work in Britain's favour.) However it is important to keep track of changes in customer needs so that the packages and facilities offered keep pace with their changing requirements.

Secondary markets are those providing some tourist traffic but their potential is much greater. Either the majority of potential tourists are not aware of the attractions of a particular country or have been better sold to go to others. These markets can be turned into primary ones if the right research and then marketing approach is used. Germany because of the Germans greater interest in Spain, some other European countries and North Africa are secondary markets for tourism to Britain. Efforts in recent years have done much to start turning Germany into a primary market for Britain.

Some countries are secondary markets to Britain by reason of distance. For example, despite the ethnic and historical links, Australia and New Zealand are too far away. Travel to Europe costs too much to allow easy development to primary markets. Others, such as developing countries with low *per capita* income have few nationals who can raise sufficient funds to make the trip. Yet others may be restricted by government controls on foreign currency used for personal, as apart from business, travel. While much has happened to reduce the cost of travel in recent years (e.g. Australia and New Zealand Family Reunion Clubs; the widening range of discounted air fares, etc.) it is still difficult for many, even in more affluent but far distant countries, to raise the funds for a visit to Britain.

Opportunity markets are areas distant from the destination country and normally providing few tourists. On the occurrence of some special event, there can be a sudden but short-lived increase in tourist traffic. For example in 1977, the Silver Jubilee in Britain turned Australia and New Zealand into opportunity markets. In general however it is seldom that opportunity markets can be turned into long-term secondary or primary ones.

3.3.9 *Some other classifications*
There are some other classifications which may be helpful in the planning and management of travel and tourism. These include mode of transport used, educational travel and the scope of the envisaged travel or journey. However these are used more effectively as sub-classifications of those discussed in the rest of this section (3.3).

3.4 Special characteristics of tourism

In product-market planning for any industry it is necessary to take into account, and allow for, any characteristics which are special or unique to the business. Tourism has several.

3.4.1 *Rigidity of supply components*
Rigidity and inelasticity of the supply components in tourism (accommodation units, airports, railways, roads, etc.) arise for several reasons. First, these are all capital-intensive items and take some time (years) to complete and open after they have been approved and the time-consuming planning stages have been completed. Since several organisations may have to reach agreement on the development of any part of the infrastructure, allowing for the independence shown by the organisations, the planning stage can be protracted. Further, once the facilities have been created they cannot be converted for other uses. An under-utilised international standard airport remains an under-utilised airport. An hotel which does not meet viable levels of occupancy cannot be used as an apartment house very successfully (as some hotels in Singapore and elsewhere have discovered). So if demand has been over-estimated or has

fallen drastically since development started, a resort will find itself with substantial under-utilised assets which will be a drain on its receipts or income from tourism.

If demand has been under-estimated then many potential customers will have to be turned away and this could damage the goodwill and image of the resort. Since it will take years to create additional facilities, by the time they are available for use it may be very difficult to regain the business that has been lost. New target markets may have to be developed and this too takes time and is expensive. Given that these facilities cannot be 'manufactured' in periods of slack demand for use during times of peak demand, as is the case with manufacturing industry, it means that the tourist infrastructure, even with the best plans, will be under-utilised at times and unable to meet demand at others. (See Chapter 7 on how marketing tries to overcome these problems.)

On top of all this, skilled and semi-skilled staff will be needed to operate the facilities. These may not be readily available and considerable training in advance may be needed. Even then there may be insufficient people to meet peak demand. Where staff available is limited, it may be advisable to keep a maximum number on full employment and this is a heavy drain on overhead costs. The ideal situation is to keep the number of staff to that required for the median (middle level) of demand and recruit part-timers for peak demand periods but as stated, this is not always possible.

3.4.2 *Instability of demand*

Tourism is subject to instability of demand, posing problems in planning and increasing the business risks. There are several reasons for this. First, there are still pronounced seasonal variations in, and high elasticity of, demand. Next, there are the sudden, often unpredictable impacts of external and environmental factors. For example, economic recession or boom depress or increase demand. Certain destinations go out of favour for political reasons or because some new attitude to health hazards has arisen. Sudden political changes in host countries can close or open frontiers and so on.

Then there is the quantitative and qualitative changes in the demand structure, sometimes for no apparent reason. Consumer tastes and preferences can change for predictable or unpredictable reasons. Often it may be just a fashionable thing to move away from one holiday country to another. In other words there is little customer loyalty to destinations or to modes of transport, type of accommodation and travel trade intermediaries.

3.4.3 *Elasticity of demand*

This elasticity of demand in tourism is due to income and price elasticity. Their effects are not uniform but they are major contributors to the instability of demand for tourism products. *Income elasticity* describes the changes that take place in the (incremental) volume of demand because of (incremental) changes in income of the potential customers. *Price elasticity* describes the effect of any (incremental) change in price on (the incremental change in) demand. Generally demand for tourism products is very responsive to changes in price and incomes. Tourism being considered by most consumers as a non-essential (if desirable) discretionary consumption, it does not rate as highly as other more essential expenditures (for example a new car). The wide choice of destinations, prices and modes of travel accentuates this problem for any one destination or tourism product.

3.4.4 *Seasonality of demand*

Tourism is still a business subject to seasonality of demand. This may be due to habit, climate or tradition. Also seasonal variations may be caused by institutional factors not under the control of the customer (e.g., school holidays; factory or office annual vacation periods). It may also be geared to specific events such as Christmas, the Salzburg or Bayreuth Music Festivals and carnival time in Rio. In 1973 IUOTO attempted to quantify the 'seasonal factor'. They found that the factor was greatest for Europe (an average factor of 9). In Europe, Greece had a factor of 9, Bulgaria 11.8, Roumania 13.7 and Yugoslavia 21.8. Other European countries had factors of 5. A factor of 9 meant that arrivals at peak periods were nine times greater than at the lowest demand periods.

3.4.5 Competition

In tourism, direct competition exists between destinations and resorts and modes of transport. With destinations, competition between resorts in the same country or region is strong. Examples include the wide choice of resorts on the Costa Brava and the other 'costas' of Spain. Then there is the competition between countries, for example the French Riviera, the Italian Riviera, Greek Islands and North African Coast to mention a few. If tourists cannot find what they want in one resort or country they can switch to another. If their new choice proves to be very good, tourists may switch their loyalty to it, at least for a while, especially if the cost is within the right price range.

With transport a considerable degree of substitution is available. For short and medium haul journeys, tourists can choose between air, sea, road or rail. In the case of road travel this can be by car (own or hired) or coach. Competition is also strong between airlines serving the same destinations with similar aircraft and timetables. When too many airlines operate over a route a fares price war may result or as summarised in Section 2.1.3, a bewildering plethora of cheap fares can arise.

Because of this wide choice and the strong competition between tour operators and also resorts, customer brand loyalty, to operator and resort, is low. The fact that customer motivations, preferences and attitudes to their lifestyles change and can do so quite quickly, reduces brand loyalty even further. However if a tour operator has taken the trouble to discover in detail what its target markets (customers) want and has gone out of its way to meet these needs at acceptable prices, then higher levels of brand loyalty can be achieved year after year. It will find that a good percentage of its annual business comes from repeat business, customers who come back to them every year, even if they choose different resorts or countries. In Britain, Thomson Holidays is an example.

Then there is what can be described as indirect competition or substitution. Expenditure on holidays can be curtailed by the need to buy a new car or house. High maintenance costs on the home or car or the payment of school fees can have the same effect. Or a new type of holiday (sea cruises) can become very fashionable and replace package tours taken previously. Thus the scale and nature of competition can be substantial and intensive.

3.4.6 Distribution

Distribution in tourism is discussed in Chapter 7. Here only the fundamental differences need to be mentioned. In manufacturing, distribution involves the packing and packaging of the finished product and its shipment to the customer via different channels of distribution. In tourism the product is made up of different supply components, most of which have to be *in situ* at the resort. So distribution is concerned with taking the tourist to the product (resort).

Prior to that there is the need to distribute all the information needed (via brochures, leaflets and letters of advice) by potential customers to allow them to make a decision in favour of the seller (tour operator or travel agent) making the offering. Finally customers have to receive confirmation of the reservations and eventually their tickets have to be sent to them. So distribution in tourism involves the despatch of a lot of paperwork. The introduction of the computer has simplified and speeded up this work.

3.4.7 Other special characteristics

Another special characteristic is inherent in the fact that quality and service standards depend on the availability of good staff. Trained and experienced people are needed. It is essential that they should be good at handling customers efficiently and courteously, even under trying circumstances. This applies to office staff as well as couriers and guides. Failure here can damage the goodwill and image of tour operator, travel agent, airline or hotel. Deficiencies in equipment and facilities can sometimes be compensated by the use of efficient staff. There is no compensation for the lack of competent and courteous employees.

Next there must be 'complementarity' between the different enterprises providing the tourism product and support facilities. Primary resources (accommodation and transport for example) can only attract business if the essential support facilities (access, airports, entertainment and so on) are there to back them up. If the primary resources are inadequate, overcrowding, overbooking and damage to the environment occur and even the most attractive support facilities will be of little avail. If the quality and other standards of the different components are not comparable, customer dissatisfaction results. Thus there must be a good balance between primary and support resources.

Finally, it must be remembered that tourism demand and the attractiveness of a resort, are considerably influenced by external factors beyond the control of tourism enterprises. Political instability, financial and currency uncertainties and labour unrest often cannot be predicted precisely. It is also difficult to forecast their effect on demand. Consumer response can be contrary to what logical considerations may suggest. It depends on what other motivations are predominant. Therefore the industry must always be prepared to take any remedial action that may be necessary if the industry is not to be unfairly blamed by customers for failures due to events beyond its control.

3.5 Demand forecasting for tourism

Demand forecasting and its many techniques are subjects that are too big to cover in detail in this book. Those who wish, or have to, go into this subject in depth should turn to the many good, specialist books on it. Only the general principles relevant to tourism will be mentioned here.

Any company embarking on demand forecasting for the first time cannot expect to achieve a high degree of accuracy with its first forecast. Successive predictions should improve in accuracy as executives learn and understand more and more about their markets, the factors affecting demand and the techniques used. It may also be advisable to call on the services of experts, suitably qualified and experienced consultants. This may be expensive but not as costly as the errors that could arise from faulty forecasting, when eager amateurs are allowed to bumble through the work.

Other general guidelines include the necessity to stick to the same forecasting periods, whether twelve, eighteen or twenty-four months for example. Otherwise the predictions will not be comparing like with like. Errors in subsequent decisions and planning will result. Next, the accuracy obtained and the causes of erroneous forecasts should be known and discovered. These lessons can then be applied to future efforts, so improving the forecasts. Further, predictions should not be made for forward time periods that are longer than the business requires. For example, it takes at least three years to develop and launch a new tourism product so five-year forecasts may be sufficient. Predictions for periods of more than ten years, especially in very uncertain economic conditions, are of little value. They may prove to be no better than gazing into a crystall ball! Finally, techniques that are faster and more sophisticated than are needed, or which an unsophisticated executive team cannot handle, should be avoided. Use of simpler methods may prove more effective. The availability of computers overcomes this particular problem provided executives can interpret the printouts correctly.

3.5.1 Meaning of forecasting

Forecasting is a prerequisite for successful planning and is the art of predicting events before they happen. It allows decisions to be made in advance of events that would otherwise affect the business. It is difficult to formulate sound plans otherwise. It helps managers to look ahead to assess if demand and resources can be brought into reasonable balance to obtain optimal levels of profits, over the longest possible period.

For example, the construction of airports, hotels, transport and other utilities take time and are costly. If they are designed for a level of demand that will not be realised, the result will be a waste of resources. It should also be remembered that forecasts based on inadequate or inaccurate data is a waste of effort. Further, executives should not try to push predictions beyond the (limited) objective of the analysis.

3.5.2 Elements of tourism demand

Demand forecasting for tourism should cover not only the total demand for tourism products but also all the supply elements involved. Sometimes this is not always practical. For example, estimating the souvenir, photographic materials and other consumables needed by tourists may only be possible by observation. So in most cases demand forecasting will concentrate on:

(a) accommodation requirements at the resorts;
(b) need for all forms of transportation (local and international); and
(c) the other support facilities, including excursions and entertainment, expected by tourists at each destination.

3.5.3 *Quantitative and qualitative forecasts*

Most demand forecasts are quantitative. They indicate the volume of demand and how that is changing. It is also important to have qualitative forecasts. These indicate the trends in the mix of customers, or customer groups comprising the demand for particular packages, resorts and type of travel. For example, it is useful to know how the relative importance of holiday tourism and business travel is changing, or the change of interest taking place regarding the different types of holidays. Then changes in attitudes and preferences of potential tourists towards all forms and modes of travel must be known if future plans are to be successful. Both types of forecasts are needed to predict tourist movements of all kinds between countries.

3.5.4 *Factors affecting tourism demand*

These factors can be divided into a number of groups. First is the *purchasing power* of consumers. This measures their ability to buy holidays, in addition to other important products and services having higher purchasing priorities in their lifestyle (such as clothes, fuel, school fees and so on). Purchasing power depends on income levels, taxation and thus the discretionary incomes that remain. About 80 per cent of tourism emanates from developed countries with high *per capita* incomes. This indicates the correlation that exists between the standard of living and travel intensity.

The next factor is the *demographic structure* of a country. While population growth and size as such appear to have little effect on tourism, what is important is changes in the age structure. As the age median rises so more people should move into income levels that permit participation in tourism. If the average income is very low, countries with large populations, even if the age median is rising, will still have limited demand for tourism.

Travel motivations, social and cultural factors also influence tourism demand. As Table 1.1 and Section 1.4.1 have shown, many travel motivations exist. Any tourism product could appeal to customers with heterogeneous or even diametrically opposed, motivations and needs. This is probably because of the abstract or subjective nature of the satisfactions and benefits stemming from tourism activities, the intangible results of an intangible service. Nevertheless the strength of the motivation and its importance to customers does influence demand response. Which motivations are paramount depends on the social and job status of the consumer.

The higher the status, lifestyle, attitudes and expectations, the more people are likely to indulge in tourism for at least part of their vacations. A further social impact on tourism demand arises because of the stresses and strains of daily life. The greater these are the more people are likely to seek recuperation through some form of tourism, domestic or international. Finally, peoples' cultural interests influence where their demand for tourism will lie.

The *availability* of suitable tours and the *successful marketing* of them also influence demand. It is not only the desire and ability to buy tourism products but also awareness of their availability that helps to create demand. Other factors influencing demand for a particular product include *price, accessibility, the image and attractions* of the resort. Its *uniqueness* is another. For example by 1984, in Britain, at least two operators were offering three-week package tours to Tibet. Despite the high cost of them, demand exceeded availability.

Economic factors affect costs, prices, resource availability, productive capacity and demand. To limit the uncertainty here analyses of the relevant trends are essential before accurate demand forecasting is possible. Even then, forecasts can be undermined by unforeseeable events such as the sudden leap in oil prices at the end of the 1970s. This put up the cost of fuel and all transport fares. The 'knock-on' effect on manufactured goods and other services increased the costs for hotels, airlines and providers of ancillary services. Only by finding cheaper alternatives did the tourism industry manage to keep price increases to a minimum.

Political developments affect tourism. So forecasts should try to allow for major political changes. The latter could involve a change to a totalitarian government, or new legislation on visas, movements of foreign nationals or foreign exchange and currency controls. Legislation designed to restrict or control tourism also affects demand.

Changes in the *demographic structure, social attitudes* and conditions also affect demand. So do *technological changes*. Growing concern about *pollution* and growing active interest in *conservation* could restrict demand. Tourism enterprises insensitive to these factors could experience a fall in demand for their products.

Many of the above have a complex, inter-locking effect on each other. This make analysis of tourism demand a difficult task. As a result, forecasts can be subject to various errors, injecting unsuspected bias into the predictions. Misunderstanding can result over the inter-relationships between all the factors discussed earlier. Only people with the relevant knowledge and experience should undertake demand forecasting. Amateurs should beware!

3.6 More cases

Here are two more cases that highlight the challenges that face the tourism industry. The economic recession at the end of the 1970s heightened the difficulties.

3.6.1 A Phoenix arises

This is the story of a tour operator that arose from the ashes of the original parent company, one of the pioneers of modern package tours. It is an independent company now. Its original parent no longer exists. It has overcome many problems though its recently formed airline has added both to its problems and profits.

The economic recession put pressure on tour operators to achieve growth and stability for their businesses if they were to survive. By 1983 this company was high in the growth league. The gross return to shareholders was over 2000 per cent for the period 1972–81. By 1981, turnover was in excess of £95 million and the company had an 80 per cent rise in profits to about £13 million. Although it had set up its airline in that year, the company had an end-of-year balance sheet showing more than £18 million in short-term deposits and cash. The management like to see the company as the 'Sainsbury' of the tour business with Thomson Holidays as 'Tesco'! In fact with about a 9 per cent market share it is closer to Intasun (12 per cent) and Cosmos (6 per cent) than Thomson's 22 per cent.

It has relied partly on geographical expansion. Originally operating out of Birmingham, complementing its original parent's use of London airports, by 1984 it was also operating from Bristol, Glasgow and Newcastle as well as the East Midlands, Gatwick, Luton, Manchester and Birmingham. The collapse of the original parent initially brought various problems, including those associated with going into and coming out of receivership. Eventually the company was free to sell its holidays anywhere in Britain. Financial support from the Greater Manchester Passenger Transport Executive and Nottinghamshire County Council (keen to protect its interests in the East Midlands Airport near Derby) provided considerable assistance.

The company saw its growth potential as lying in its ability to take into new marketing areas the same products that had earned them their initial success. In practice this meant flying more planes into existing destinations and finding more hotel beds in the hotels they were using. They insisted also that quality control and consistency of product should not be undermined. They applied sound, prudent management to the decisions that had to be made.

The company has worked hard to win the friendship and support of travel agents who are the 'shop windows' of the tourism business. They have no plans to sell direct to the consumer as Thomsons have done through their direct-selling subsidiary, Portland Holidays. The company has achieved its success despite having to face many problems during the recession.

When increasing competition, static demand and shrinking profit margins forced Thomsons and Intasun to introduce 'no surcharge' guarantees to improve their market shares, the company followed suit. The companies hoped also that this inflation-proofing of prices would reverse the trend to late bookings by customers hoping to benefit from last minute 'special price' offers by operators desperate for business. In January 1982 only about 40 per cent of those taking holidays abroad had booked. This played havoc with operators' plans and advance reservations. Even then, by June 1982 some 20 per cent had still not booked their holidays.

Another problem was the need to achieve high overall load factors on aircraft, especially when they are owned by the tour operator. In 1981 the company achieved a load factor of nearly 95 per cent, though by 1982, because of the deepening recession, this was down to 87 per cent. According to accountants in the business, every one per cent lost represents £0.5 million less profit. The reason is that the marginal cost of carrying more passengers when flights have load factors exceeding 90 per cent is very low. Thus passengers forming the top slice (above 90 per cent) give an equivalent gross profit margin of about 40 per cent. When faced with a last minute shortfall of passengers, the average company prefers to cancel flights (called 'consolidation'!) rather than rush out offers of discounted prices. This is because it is believed the latter will spoil any 'up-market' image and encourage late bookings.

There is room for greater efficiency in the tourism industry and this case company is trying to achieve it. They are trying to do so by use of staff incentives with profit sharing and share purchase schemes. Provided the company survives the 1984 price war, it appears to have an interesting future.

3.6.2 *A refurbished hotel group*
This hotel group, formed in 1959 by a conglomerate around the purchase of a well-known Brighton hotel built in Victorian times and opened to the public in 1890, became a major hotel group in the 1960s. Then sister hotels were opened in Birmingham and London. In 1977 the conglomerate sold the hotels to an even larger, international group, another conglomerate,

with over 800 subsidiary companies and a turnover exceeding £3 billion a year. The new owners invested heavily in the hotels.

The Brighton hotel had deteriorated somewhat by then. The new owners spent £2.5 million in refurbishing it and it has regained its reputation with the business community it aims to serve primarily. The group opened a new hotel in Blackpool, a conference and banqueting centre in Solihull, a new pub in London and a contract-managed hotel in Cairo. Future expansion is not planned to come from acquiring new hotels but through contract management of existing properties in suitable locations.

The group has always based its activities on offering a full range of facilities to business users. These may stay for one or several nights, especially when attending a conference, exhibition or meeting in the vicinity of the hotel. They are also suitable venues for dinner parties and banquets. They provide a level of service that is difficult to better. This depends on having an adequate number of well-trained, courteous and efficient staff, including managers. Senior executives see the importance of efficient management as one that cannot be overstressed. The fact that staff move to other jobs and establishments more frequently in the hotel business does not worry them. If the atmosphere and efficiency have been right and staff enjoyed working for the group, they return quite often in more senior positions. They then bring a much wider experience to bear on their new jobs.

The aim of the management is to maximise the expenditure of their guests by making the hotels attractive places to visit. The Brighton hotel for example averages about 7000 guests a year. Even if they spend only £1 or £2 extra each, this is a substantial addition to the cash flow. This group is clearly a growing force in the hotel industry, where investment has been scarce.

The hotel business can be lucrative. However a high average, annual occupancy rate is needed to achieve this. In competitive times it means that an hotel must provide guests with a consistently good service and use innovative marketing.

Assignments

1 You are an executive with a major tour operator and have been asked to recommend ways in which the turnover and profitability could be improved. Of all the different types of tourists in existence, which ones would you recommend as offering the best chance of achieving these goals?

2 Having accepted your suggestions (above) in principle, you are asked to consider the tourism products the company should offer. What factors should you consider carefully and which target markets would you select for each product group? Explain fully the reasons for your choices.

3 Why is demand forecasting for tourism a complex subject? What important, general considerations have to be taken into account?

4 Tourism is said to have certain unique characteristics. What are they? Discuss fully the effects they can have on demand and in the planning of the products a tour operator can offer. How should the operator select its target markets?

4

Accommodation and Catering

This subject was discussed briefly in earlier chapters where it was relevant to do so. Here a wider discussion will be made.

The *lodging industry* or market is comprised of all the accommodation listed in Table 4.1, though some purists maintain that only the first four types do. This industry is also part of the much wider *travel industry* or market which of course includes tour operators, travel agents, air and shipping lines, railway, coach and bus companies, car and plane rental enterprises and other organisations providing the attractions such as sightseeing excursions and so on. Tourist boards are also part of this total travel scene. Accommodation is an important component of the tourism product. The category and grade available at a resort sets the parameters of the type of tourism that can take place there and the numbers that can be handled efficiently. If there is any discrepancy between demand and the quantitative and qualitative supply of beds, things can become chaotic. Customer dissatisfaction will result. Resources will be wasted. The profit potential will not be fully realised.

In the United Kingdom before the Second World War, the hotel industry was dominated by large independent units. It was only after the war that the big hotel groups (e.g. Grand Metropolitan; Trust Houses now Trust House Forte) emerged.

Table 4.1   Types of accommodation

Serviced sector
Hotels: licensed and unlicensed
Motels/motor hotels/motor inns
Private hotels
Guest/boarding houses
Cruise ships
Youth hostels
YMCA/YWCA
Farmhouses

Self-catering sector
Caravans
Camping sites
Apartments/villas/chalets
Other time-sharing accommodation
Hired motorhomes
Private (owned) caravans/motorhomes/yachts
Second homes/visiting foreign relatives (VFR)
Home exchanges

Serviced or self-catering sector
Holiday villages/centres/camps
Hired yachts
'Up-market' hired villas (e.g. in the Caribbean, etc.)

© D.W.F.

Now in Britain, hotels belonging to even larger international groups (Intercontinental, Hilton, Sheraton, Holiday Inns, etc.) are established. They have intensified the competition with their high standard of service and the range of services provided. In France and Italy where the hotel industry was well established a long time ago, the hotels found themselves unable to respond rapidly to the new mass tourism boom but they have long since caught up with the rest of the developed countries. Spain's hotel industry on the other hand had not developed so early and was not so deeply entrenched in the former business of individual, private guests. They have responded more quickly to the needs of the package tourist from the lower income groups (e.g. C2 and D).

The move to larger groupings after the war was prompted by the realisation that the economics of operation favoured large hotel groups over the individual units. By the 1960s this realisation and intensifying competition from the large groups led to voluntary groups being formed by independent units (e.g. Golden Tulip Group; Best Western Hotels). In the case of units with outstanding reputations and/or some historical connections (e.g. the Lygon Arms Hotel at Broadway in the Cotswolds), they formed themselves into the Prestige Group of Hotels.

The large chains have the advantage of being able to operate central reservation and marketing systems (now computerised). Guests at one hotel can book a room at another group hotel at their next destination. There are also centralised reservation systems which are used by a number of (smaller) hotel groups and individual hotels who do not wish to set up their own, exclusive system. Many groups also have their own sales offices in a nation's capital city and/or other major centres. All this is to make things easier for potential guests to make reservations. They avoid all the hassle of having to telephone, telex or write to the selected hotel and waste time waiting for the confirmation. Instant reservation, like instant coffee, is now very much part of the hotel scene.

The hotel groups can also centralise their purchasing. Through being able to order larger quantities they can obtain cost savings. Large chains also have easier access to sources of funds (see Chapter 9). This is important since considerable amounts of capital are needed to build, operate and refurbish hotels. The voluntary chains, while maintaining their independence of operation, can obtain similar advantages. If members of voluntary groups maintain similar standards and quality, customers are assured of what they will get.

Since the Second World War there has been horizontal integration by independent hotels joining existing groups. There has also been vertical integration with airlines, shipping lines and industrial conglomerates buying or building hotels (the economic difficulties of the late 1970s saw some of these withdraw from the hotel business). Hotels integrating with airlines ensured that reductions in air fares were not negated by increased hotel tariffs at destinations, eroding the benefit in cost savings that could otherwise be passed on to the traveller. Another motive was the increase in sales outlets for all the partners in a carefully planned integration. Where hotels and carriers are linked through a centralised or computerised booking system, customers can book rooms and buy their travel tickets at the same time and this has proved very convenient for buyers and sellers. Another outcome is that new hotels tend to be bigger, matching the increased capacity of aircraft and the greater tourist flows. However, the concept that big is beautiful (good) has been queried in recent years.

The advantages experienced by airlines' association with hotels has led some brewery companies, after the rationalisation of their traditional business, to expand their investment in hotels. One or two major oil companies also followed this trend. They were motivated by the fact that business and holiday motorists were inconvenienced by the lack of suitable hotels on their routes. Further, by placing accommodation units at scenic points not hitherto having hotels, they hoped motorists would extend their routes and so consume more petrol.

One result of all this is that many resort hotels are owned by parent companies from other countries. Generally the parent expects a substantial part, if not all, of the profit of the hotel to be remitted to it. Thus a smaller portion of the earnings from tourism may remain in the resort country. This has led to the argument discussed earlier, that the financial benefits of tourism to the host countries is not as great as had been first imagined.

The accommodation or lodging industry is now made up of a variety of serviced and self-catering units. These are listed in Table 4.1.

4.1 Demand for accommodation

The demand for accommodation stems not only from the vacationist (package tourist or other) but also from business travellers and nationals of the country where the accommodation unit is situated. The last may be visitors from other regions or local residents using the hotel for a night or two, for many reasons. Or local residents may just use the restaurant facilities for occasional meals. Having to satisfy such varied demand poses problems for hotel managers. These problems are outside the scope of this book (there are many good books on them) but tourism executives should be aware of them. The main one of common interest to both parties is the difficulty in forecasting demand for accommodation and thus in obtaining a profitable occupancy rate throughout a trading year. If forecasts are persistently over-optimistic, hotel tariffs may be cast at higher levels than might otherwise be necessary to ensure that the required profits are made. With accurate forecasts, keener tariffs are possible. Given that the clientele is drawn from more than one country, these problems are increased.

The demand for any one type of accommodation depends on how much guests will be prepared to trade-off one requirement against another. It will also depend on the relative importance of their different needs. For example, how important is the location of the hotel compared with its size, type or prices? Do guests wish to be near the sea, on a good beach or close to particular activities or cultural events? The business traveller may wish to be near the office being visited, or a factory, or the venue of a conference or exhibition, or an airport. However, if the tariff of the ideal unit is too high, the traveller may compromise and choose a cheaper, next best, hotel. Business travellers with limits placed on their expenditure by employers will be more price conscious than those without such restrictions. Then if the hotel does not provide the right image, especially for those who have to entertain customers, business people will seek a more impressive unit. Thus the nature of demand cannot be estimated only from the type of person invoved and the reason for their visit.

Further, demand is not uniform. For tourism it has a seasonal nature while with business travel it can be cyclical. There are periods of peak and low demand. For the business trade, demand is greatest for the nights of Mondays to Thursdays but practically nil for weekends. Hence the development of 'weekend breaks' of all kinds. These are attempts to improve the occupancy rates at that period. Lower tariffs apply for such 'breaks' and can include other attractions. These range from special functions (for example, classical music performances included in the tariff to half-board terms which include morning tea, newspapers, all taxes and service charges) to a half-day excursion to some historical site and half rates for the spouse accompanying an executive on a business stay of four nights or more.

Other special offers include very low tariffs for winter guests staying for one, two or three months, or attractive rates over Christmas, the New Year and Easter. In the first two instances the tariff usually includes the cost of special Christmas and New Year dinner parties and other jollifications. If hotels can even out demand by these methods, the staffing problem can be eased. Instead of depending on a small core of full-timers and topping up with part-timers for peak demand periods a larger core of full-timers can be justified. Part-time staff are not always easy to find and there is strong competition for the good ones. Closing the hotel at low demand periods may solve some problems but creates staffing difficulties. People laid off at these times may find permanent employment elsewhere and not return when the hotel reopens.

Other points that influence the demand pattern are worth noting. While over 60 per cent of British nationals stay in hotels when holidaying abroad, only 30 per cent do so when vacationing at home. In the latter case, many people may be visiting relatives or friends, or prefer caravanning, camping or self-catering facilities. Or it may be a question of cost. The individual guest does not enjoy the discounted tariffs offered to tour operators. The need to save money motivates people to break away from the sophistication of hotels. Further, some people feel restricted in hotels. They prefer the freedom of choice, action and dress possible when camping, caravanning or using self-catering units. The last has experienced considerable expansion from time-sharing apartments or bungalows to equally well appointed log cabins in remote places of great scenic beauty.

Thus more people are ceasing to see their requirement as finding an hotel room wherein to sleep. They are seeking a total leisure experience with considerable informality as well. Even with holidays abroad, the all-inclusive package providing three meals a day at set times and with fixed menus is losing its appeal. It is too restrictive and after the first week may be a bit of a bore. Despite language difficulties, self-catering offers adventure without too much risk, an exciting new experience, a chance to mix with local society as well as offering greater flexibility, with some cost saving. The chance to eat out and choose from a wide range of restaurants also appeals. However, the cost of meals out and of hiring a car may make a self-catering holiday only marginally cheaper than an hotel-based one. If tourists use their own cars, the actual cost saving is reduced when the depreciation and maintenance costs on the vehicle are taken into account. The growing interest in farm-based holidays at home and abroad is motivated by similar considerations as for self-catering.

4.1.1 British demand at home and abroad

Some basic statistics on British tourism are listed in Table 4.2. As shown, some 40 million holidays of four nights or more and 32 million of three nights or less were taken in Britain by Britons in 1981 and 1982. In 1983 the figures were 43 and 35 million respectively. For the main holidays in the UK about 19 per cent used licensed hotels or motels and 10 per cent used unlicensed hotels or various types of guest houses. Fifteen per cent used rented accommodation and 18 per cent used caravans. The last was a drop from the peak of 23 per cent achieved in 1977. Visiting friends and relatives and staying with them accounted for 20 per cent of all major holidays. Holiday camps took about 8 per cent and camping about 6 per cent.

For minor holidays, staying with relatives and friends was the main form of accommodation used (about 37 per cent) and is perhaps to be expected. The demand for other accommodation was licensed hotels and motels 17 per cent, unlicensed hotels and guest houses about 10 per cent, rented accommodation 11 per cent, caravans 15 per cent, holiday camps 3 per cent and camping 4 per cent. All these figures were for 1983, the latest available at the time this manuscript was being prepared.

In the same year, Britons going abroad for their main holiday stayed mainly in hotels (58 per cent) or with friends or relatives (23 per cent). Holiday camps, camping, caravans and rented accommodation accounted for about 17 per cent. The figure for hotels includes pensions but the use of the latter

Table 4.2 Some statistics on British tourism

Item	1981 £m.	1982 £m.	1983 £m.
Foreign currency earnings from tourism:	£3758	£4017	£4555
Comprising:			
Accommodation	£ 815	£ 870	1005
Eating and drinking out	440	470	540
Entertainment services and others	310	328	380
Shopping and other expenditure	1065	1135	1310
Internal transport	340	365	420
Fares paid to British air and shipping lines for travel to and from Britain	788	849	900
Overseas visitors spent in Britain	£2970	£3168	£3655
Britons spent on travelling in Britain for all purposes	£4600	£4500	£5350
Of which spent on holidays	£3075	£3100	£3625
Exchequer earnings in VAT and other indirect taxes from visitors	£ 500	£ 500	£ 500
Visits abroad by Britons; all reasons	19m	20.6m	21.0m
Expenditure abroad by them	£3272	£3640	£5104
Excluding fares to foreign carriers	£ 866	£ 963	£1050
For every £ earned overseas tourism contributed an estimated	5p	5p	5p
For every £ of invisible earnings tourism contributed an estimated	16p	13p	14p

Holidays of 4 nights or more taken by Britons in Britain remained at 40 million for 1981 and 1982 – 4 million less than in 1980 – but were 43 million in 1983.

Holidays of 1 to 3 nights by Britons in Britain remained at 32 million for 1981 and 1982 but were 35 million in 1983.

Nearly 1½ million people in hotels, catering, transport, retailing and entertainment depend directly or indirectly on tourism.

Source: BTA estimates based on International Passenger Survey and British Home Tourism Survey.
Note: 1983 figures are provisional at time of preparation of table.

declined from the 1950s peak of 25 per cent. The causes for this reduction were believed to be the greater affluence of many socio-economic consumer groups since then and the growth in the range of package tours on offer in the last three decades. Increased interest in rented accommodation and in time-sharing may have been other contributing factors.

4.1.2   Visitors to Britain

On the other hand, according to the International Passenger Survey (published annually) visitors to Britain used the hotel sector (described as paid accommodation of all kinds) for about 30 per cent of the total bed-nights spent in the country. Non-commercial private homes were used for about 50 per cent of the total bed-nights. However, it must be remembered that non-business visitors account for about 90 per cent of total demand for accommodation, divided almost equally between commercial and non-commercial units. It should also be noted that business visitors prefer hotels. However in recent years, major corporations renting apartments for their visiting executives and customers has reduced this dependence on hotels.

4.1.3   Changing patterns of demand

In most countries, accommodation facilities have been designed to cater both for domestic and foreign guests. In some countries the former predominate while in others it is the latter. However as attitudes to holidays of vacationists change so may the pattern of demand for accommodation. Despite the problems (high capital cost and time to make alterations) the industry has to be alert to the need for altering the accommodation mix to match demand. Countries with a highly developed domestic holiday market (e.g. Belgium, France, Italy) are less dependent on hotels. The pattern of demand is also distorted in countries with well developed camping facilities. However where large hotels or leisure complexes provide considerable in-house entertainment and other attractions (as in the USA), the pattern of demand will be altered in favour of these.

Then where transport facilities are good, tourists will be tempted to be more mobile. Even if they are prepared to be based in one country, they may stay in more than one resort.

Their accommodation needs may be varied deliberately for wider experience or to break the monotony of staying at the same type of unit, hotels or even camps of any sort. Some tourists may wish to enjoy the open-air life of camping for part of their holiday but use an hotel or rented accommodation for the remainder to add sophistication to their total holiday.

The car has also influenced the length of stay at any one resort. Often the motoring tourist may make few reservations in advance since this can be restrictive on the route taken or lead to hurried journeys to reach the predetermined resort. They may like to linger on the way if they discover unexpected scenic beauty spots which hitherto had not been visited. Thus the geographical area of a motor tour can be considerably extended. The car has also played a major role in the development of demand for short holidays and weekend breaks. The increased interest in self-sufficiency and informality when on holiday has led to greater demand for self-catering facilities.

4.1.4 *Expenditure*

Table 4.2 gives the BTA figures for expenditure by foreign visitors to Britain. This was £875 million in 1982. It is not possible to quote comparable figures for Britons using accommodation in Britain. However, local nationals and residents spent £4500 million on travelling in the UK for all purposes. Of this total, £3100 million were spent on holidays. If about 30 per cent of this is the cost of accommodation, expenditure on this item would be about £1300 million for all purposes and £900 million or more for holidays. On the same estimate, Britons abroad could have spent £1000 millions or more on accommodation.

Even if these figures understate the real position, substantial earnings are involved for all types of accommodation. However the growth in demand by tourists for other types of (non-hotel) units is eroding this substantial business. The situation for other developed countries is similar, subject to the relative size of their tourism trade.

4.1.5 *Supply and demand*

The continuing prosperity of the tourism and lodging industries depends on the demand and supply of accommodation being kept in reasonable balance. Balance here means, however, more than just matching the number of beds available with the number of tourist arrivals. The quality and standards must match and meet the needs and expectations of the visitors. For example, an abundance of deluxe hotels would be of little avail if the demand is for standard or economy units. Or the supply of beds may be in balance but if the restaurant capacity cannot deal with the volume of tourist traffic reasonably efficiently, customer dissatisfaction will result. Tourists have limited time for meals, especially when about to set out on an excursion or some evening adventure. They will not be pleased with any delays at meal times.

If supply exceeds demand, occupancy rates will be lower than desired and decreased profit (even losses) may result. Competition will be intensive and could lead to substantial discounting of tariffs. A recent example was Singapore with some 85 major hotels and relatively limited tourist inflows. Many hotels were offering substantial discounts, some as much as 60 per cent on their published rates. The exceptions, for various reasons like uniqueness and outstanding architecture and decor, were the Shangri-la, Mandarin, Hilton and Hyatt hotels. New hotels are still being added and it is hard to foresee what the tariff position will be by the time this book is published!

If demand exceeds supply many would-be guests will have to be turned away. This will damage goodwill for the hotel and the resort. Long-term demand will decline as disappointed consumers find other hotels that prove, subsequently, to be very satisfactory. This could inhibit plans for future expansion. It is difficult to win back lost cusomers and goodwill. It takes time and the necessary promotional work is expensive.

Thus the accommodation available limits the capacity of a resort for tourism. The number of visitors permitted should be geared to this. While lack of accommodation will automatically limit the flow of tourists to any place, less goodwill will be lost if suitable, nearby alternatives are available. Or alternative destinations and hotels could be actively promoted. For example, to ease the congestion in London during July and August, the attractions of provincial centres, for example Stratford-on-

Avon, the Cotswolds, Lake District and so on, can be offered and promoted as excellent alternative centres for holidays.

When tourists are dissatisfied because some element of supply they need is not available, they may make adverse comments on return to their home countries. This could further damage the reputation of the host country and reduce demand. The hotel element in tourism is the one most vulnerable to criticism either because of unsatisfactory facilities or service. This is a point for hoteliers to remember. Also, once an hotel has been built, it is difficult and expensive to make alterations, however essential. Careful forecasting of current and future demand and changes in tourism flows, is vital.

Other things to be kept in mind include improvements in transport which allow consumers to travel further, to more distant or exotic resorts and improved net discretionary incomes which permit longer holidays in better grade accommodation. Changes in tastes and attitudes including movements 'back to nature' or on to greater sophistication and thus changed needs, are other influencing factors. Thus the accommodation industry must remain alert to these if they wish to match demand with suitable supply elements. Above all, it must be remembered that changes in demand may arise from both rational and irrational thoughts or perceptions by the different types of traveller that have to be served.

Thus demand can ebb and flow. Increases sustained for a few years may diminish or demand may start to decline rapidly. This may be due to economic, financial or political developments. Or, more difficult to foresee, change may be due to the whim of potential travellers or the evolution of a new fad or fashion. Again, constant vigilance is necessary.

4.1.6 *Planning accommodation*
Thus the planning of accommodation for any purpose is not easy. It requires careful study of the points mentioned above, as well as estimated costs and expected returns. First, an estimate must be made of the number of visitors there are likely to be, the purpose of their visit and so the possible length of each stay and whether demand is likely to be affected by the

points discussed in the preceding sections. These estimates should be adjusted for any seasonal or cyclical fluctuations that are known, or anticipated, to affect demand. Answers to other questions are needed. Do vacationists favour only a few months of the year or is greater flexibility in the timing of holidays becoming evident? Do business travellers have specific times (months) for their visits? How are the latter influenced by regular, or occasional, conferences and meetings taking place at or near the destination? Will the guests be travelling singly, in pairs or in groups and what size of group will be involved? What locations will be favoured and how will total demand be split between available locations?

Other questions include the following. How many will be first-time visitors? What proportion is likely to make repeat visits (this depends on how satisfied they were with their first visit)? Are there any regular visitors and when do they come? What specific needs and attractions or entertainments are expected by different classes of visitors? What sightseeing tours or excursions are needed? Which type of travel (holiday or business) will have increasing or declining demand? What is the ratio of holidays to business travel? Are conferences and other meetings in the area increasing and how will this affect visitor flows? What are/may be the income, age, educational and social structures of visitors? Would it be better to influence one or two age or other consumer groups to visit the resort because of their greater expenditure, or their needs more closely match the facilities of the resort? Can this be achieved?

When these and the other questions have been answered and quantified, the planners of accommodation will have a more precise idea of what is needed. However they must not forget the attitudes of the local nationals and residents. Will they be antagonistic to the development or accept it? In countries with well developed tourist activities, the basic data will be easier to deduce than in countries new to tourism. Unfortunately few hotels keep and collate information and statistics on their guests. Yet the registration documents can provide hotel executives and developers with valuable basic facts on current business, apparent trends or changes taking place and thus possible future business patterns. With the increasing use of computers it would be a pity if this available information is not used for planning and development work.

4.2 Location and classification

Hotel facilities have to be provided where demand exists. If transportation is excellent (e.g. fast motorways, good rail or coach services, handy airports) then the accommodation can be a reasonably short distance from the area it serves. The positioning of an hotel depends on the location of its markets (guest-generating areas) and the purpose of the visits that give rise to the demand for accommodation. The location will also establish whether the hotel will prove viable and profitable. If the hotel is too far from the centre it is supposed to serve and/or is difficult to reach or find, then occupancy rates may be lower than intended.

In the case of hotels intended primarily for tourists, they should be located at or near major tourist centres. They will be dependent solely on this type of trade if there is little business in the area and so few business executives needing accommodation. The same problem will arise if there are few local nationals who could use the hotel or if they are not favourably inclined to tourists. On the other hand, hotels catering for business needs will be located near centres of economic and industrial activities. They may have to work hard to gain the necessary occupancy rates if few tourists visit these locations. Other establishments catering for a mix of business executives and tourists will seek the best, often compromise, locations for their intended customer mix. If the tourist interest is in cultural activities normally located in or near major towns, location decisions pose few problems. It is when tourist interests are some way out of town and business people wish to be close to or in towns that difficulty in finding the best location can arise. Select the wrong one and the profitability and viability of the hotel could be in jeopardy.

The formal classification of hotels has been mentioned in Chapter 2, Section 2.2. In addition the public and travel trade have unofficial ways of describing hotels by their location or purpose. Thus there are 'city hotels', 'seaside hotels' and so on. Or they may be described as 'holiday hotels', 'conference hotels', 'business hotels' and the like. Hotels are also described according to the facilities they provide such as 'bed-and-breakfast hotel', 'apartment hotel' and occasionally, 'sport hotel' if it caters specifically for one or more sporting events. Finally the description might be based on ownership (independent, group or voluntary group). For tourism planning and management purposes the safer basis is to use the official classifications mentioned in Chapter 2. However, if it helps potential clients to understand what sort of hotel is on offer, these official descriptions can be embellished by the appropriate unofficial description.

4.2.1 Franchising

In the USA and in Europe in more recent years, franchising has been applied more widely in the hotel industry. In this, the franchisor (vendor) supplies the franchisee (buyer) with a developed product having an established image, being known to a large proportion of potential users, having been well advertised. Holiday Inns is perhaps the best example. With hotels the franchisee has to use the established logo of the franchisor, adhere to various critical dimensional standards (size of bedrooms, size and number of public rooms), the facilities provided (car parking, room and other services), standard of furnishings and decor and so on. All this helps to identify the franchised hotel with its 'parent' organisation. Usually an initial capital sum has to be provided by the franchisee. Sometimes a sale-and-lease-back arrangement may be used. There is also an operating royalty payment to be made annually based on the occupancy rate achieved, with a certain base occupancy specified (that is the franchisee has a minimum royalty payment to make). The last is meant to ensure that the franchisee has an incentive to optimise the marketing effort to sell the accommodation. There are other variations to the franchising agreement.

The benefits to the franchise holder include limiting the capital outlay needed since both parties contribute to this cost. Then there is the advantage of having a known name and the cooperative or linked advertising that is usual. In some cases there can be some central purchasing arrangement for consumables. In most cases there is also the common use of a computerised, centralised reservation system.

In the day-to-day operations the franchisee has reasonable independence provided nothing is done that may be detrimental to the name. Occasional checks are made by the franchisor to ensure that the range of services, standards and quality are up to those of the franchised name.

4.2.2 Training
This subject of training for tourism was discussed in Chapter 1 (Section 1.5.6). All that is required here is a statement of the training needs of hotels. The benefits that can accrue can be experienced in Kenya and some other places.

First of all, regular, phased training helps to improve the standard and efficiency of the service, improving customer satisfaction and helping to increase customer loyalty, important in competitive times. Second, through increasing staff motivation, training can improve staff loyalty and recruitment. With the latter it also ensures that the right calibre of people are recruited. Absenteeism, a bane of the industry, and staff turnover may also be reduced. Thus management stress is also reduced. Finally, accidents, breakages and waste of raw materials of all kinds can be kept to minimal levels.

However, if the ongoing training programme is to achieve all this it must be properly planned and structured. The services of someone experienced not only in the hotel business but also in organising and running training programmes is needed. The eager amateur would be a disaster here also. Thus careful thought is needed. In addition an appropriate training policy should be agreed between all concerned and an adequate budget allocated to this task. The policy will identify the qualitative and quantitative goals for all training needed by all grades of staff and must be kept under regular review. The person responsible for training must maintain close liaison with colleges and others offering suitable programmes, while being able to plan and mount programmes to suit the hotel's special needs. These should cover induction and orientation courses as well as refresher ones which bring to the attention of staff, new developments and concepts in hotel management. Liaison with the Hotel, Catering and Institutional Management Association (HCIMA) is also an essential part of the work.

4.3   Some economic aspects

Accommodation units pose one great problem in that they lack flexibility of supply. The capacity of a unit cannot be adjusted to match periods of high and low demand. Because of this fixed capacity, when any room remains unoccupied this represents a waste of that portion of the hotel's resources and a drain on its profits. So in low demand periods there can be a considerable amount of idle capacity. Also, during peak demand periods the hotel is limited by its maximum capacity and will have to decline all business in excess of this, representing a loss of part of the potential profit that could be possible if capacity had been greater. Thus the product is perishable since unoccupied rooms represent an irretrievable loss as when a consumable item has to be thrown away because it has perished in some way.

Hotels also have fixed locations and cannot be moved around to follow demand. The hotel product has to be consumed at the place (location) where it is produced (available). Thus the hotel business is unique in that these three conditions (fixed capacity, fixed point of consumption and perishability) apply together at one and the same time, a fact which no other business, other than transport, has to face. Yet the transport operators can vary their capacity to suit demand changes by altering schedules and the number of units (trains, planes or buses) operating at any given time. Hotels do not enjoy this luxury! The economic aspects of building and operating an hotel are made more difficult by these three special characteristics of the industry.

4.3.1   Investing
Capital investment in hotels and other accommodation units can be classified into two: first, investment in land and buildings which takes the bulk of the money and second, in the interior assets (furnishings and decor) of the completed build-

ing. These are fixed costs which have to be incurred before an hotel can be operated. Variable, operating assets (labour costs, purchase of consumables, etc.) form a relatively small part of the total capital required, although labour costs represent a substantial amount of the outlay needed when the hotel is operating. Although technically a variable cost, given the standard and quality of service required, the ability to alter the number of staff employed is limited. So labour costs are not all that variable (see also Chapter 9, Section 9.1).

There are various methods of financing a project. The first and original, traditional method was for the owner (individual or group) to put up all the capital. For major developments in current economic conditions it is no longer advisable and is sometimes impossible. A favoured alternative is the sale-and-lease-back approach. The owner sells the land and projected buildings to a finance house, bank or insurance company and other financiers and leases back the property at an agreed fee or rent. Sometimes the latter varies with the occupancy rate achieved by an hotel when it is the property involved in this arrangement. Or the land may be owned by a developer and if it is part of a bigger development (a leisure centre, theme park and so on), the land is leased to an operator. The latter finances the building of the hotel. Finally the interior assets (furniture, fittings, kitchen and laundry equipment) may be leased and not sold to the hotel by the suppliers. All these reduce the amount of venture capital needed by the hotel development and the resulting leasing costs can be paid from gross profits, reducing perhaps, the tax bill on the trading profits.

For hotels the ratio of capital to revenue is high. There is a long pay-back period for new hotels, perhaps ten, fifteen or more years. The capital needed will be of different natures. That for land and buildings is long-term finance while that for the interior assets is medium-term, say up to seven years. Finally there is short-term finance to cover operating costs and minor capital costs for refurbishment and minor alterations.

4.3.2 *Operating costs and occupancy rates*
The operating costs fall into three groups: labour, materials and overheads. Labour costs are not just the wages and salaries but should include any other emoluments whether in cash or

kind. An example of the latter is the cost of meals provided free of charge to the staff, also national insurance payments and free transport. Materials costs include the food, beverage and other costs such as bed linen, towels and cleaning materials, provided to serve the customer. Overhead costs cover all the other items, usually ones that cannot be properly proportioned to a guest or specific activity. These include rates, heating, lighting, insurance, maintenance, repairs, depreciation and the salaries of senior, group management.

Total fixed costs do not vary with the occupancy rate but variable costs rise and fall to some degree as occupancy rates rise and fall. However, using unit cost as the measure, the variable unit cost is not altered by the occupancy rate but the fixed unit cost falls as occupancy rates rise. When occupancy decreases the income earned by each occupied room must make a higher contribution to fixed costs since the unoccupied ones make no contribution at all. Thus the unit operating costs have an inverse ratio with occupancy. Obtaining high occupancy rates is important since they improve the overall profitability of the hotel.

In bad economic times the problems of covering costs and making a profit are increased. This is especially so for all serviced units with their substantial operating costs, including fixed overheads and depreciation (often referred to as *unavoidable costs* since they are incurred whether the hotel is full or empty!). High, average occupancy rates are needed. Hence the various special terms, discussed earlier, which are offered in off-peak periods of demand. There is also the need to keep costs down consistent with the quality, standards and services that must be provided.

Generally city and town-centre hotels have higher occupancy rates than out-of-town establishments. Hotels at seaside resorts have the highest degree of seasonality and the lowest average, annual occupancy rates. Units in scenic mountainous terrain can have good occupancy rates if demand is high throughout the summer and winter for sporting or other reasons. Hotels catering mainly for the tourism trade have low average annual occupancy rates if they do not have an all-the-year-round demand. The seasonality of the demand can also be unstable, especially when consumers are going through a phase of changing attitudes and needs. Yet to show a profit the occupancy obtained in most cases should exceed 75 per cent.

So the operating costs and occupancy rates required and being achieved influence executive decisions on the basic and differential tariffs to be charged. When occupancy rates are low, advantageous prices may be offered for group reservations. When the rate is high only the standard tariffs may be applied. Different tariffs may also be applied for 'normal' weekday periods and off-peak, low occupancy weekends. The tour operators, when they are assembling their holiday packages and travel agents making arrangements for business travellers must take all this into consideration when they make their own decisions on these matters.

4.3.3 Size

Much discussion continues on what is the best size of hotel to have. The decision must depend on the general economic and demand conditions as well as the type of business to be obtained. For a tourist hotel at a major resort, 300 or more bedrooms may be right and prove most profitable. However, when such an hotel is full it may appear overcrowded to many guests and uncomfortable for most. If the public rooms and other services cannot cope efficiently then everyone may be dissatisfied. If the hotel is taking a mixture of tourists and other types of guests the latter may find the former too noisy and monopolising the facilities. If there are major conference and other business groups using the place, the holidaymakers might find themselves elbowed out of the bars, restaurants and public rooms. The staff may give priority service to the business guests to the detriment of others.

A small hotel will not have much in the way of public rooms and may not be able to afford many other services. This may be acceptable to tourists seeking basic, unsophisticated and inexpensive accommodation. It would not please those expecting higher standards. All the problems mentioned above could also apply to the smaller hotels who tend to be the least profitable. If they have 25 to 50 bedrooms, or are in a poor location (even if they have say up to 80 rooms) they experience the greater problems.

The major development of recent years has been the formation of hotel groups. In the UK by 1984, there were some twenty groups with a total of more than 1000 bedrooms each. Trust House Forte has over 200 hotels and Post Houses in Britain with a total number of bedrooms exceeding 20,000. They have interests also in a number of overseas establishments. Besides owning hotels outright, groups may operate establishments on lease from other owners or manage them as agents for the owner under a management contract. Current examples include the Hyatt Carlton Tower Hotel in London and some Hyatt, Intercontinental and Oberoi hotels around the world. The excellence of the service provided will depend even more on the efficiency of the management team, and the terms of the contract.

Large groups enjoy economies of scale (of their operations). Because of their greater profit potential and ability to spread their risk, groups usually have easier access to capital. Financiers feel safer in providing funds for groups rather than individual units. All these help them to provide more comprehensive and efficient services for their guests and should be kept in mind by tour operators when they have to select the hotels they will use for their package holidays. Tariffs, or prices, are not the only important consideration.

4.3.4   Some other aspects

Some of the other points tour operators should consider when selecting hotels are as follows. First, the larger the hotel group and the greater the degree of centralised control, the longer will be the lines of communication and control. Comments and instructions on all operational matters will take longer to filter through to and from all units. Opportunities for misinterpretations are greater. Thus operational efficiency can vary from hotel to hotel. If there is friction between hotel executives and group top management, long lines of communications and control can make matters worse. If a tour operator makes its block reservations through group headquarters, the interpretation of the terms and conditions of the contract at some hotels may not be what was intended when the bargain was struck. It may take time to resolve and meanwhile many customers of the tourist organisation may have been inconvenienced or made dissatisfied.

Finally, the aspirations, expectations and habits of the tourists and the hotel staff, together with the ways by which the latter make decisions and carry out their duties should not be ignored. The tourist organisation can only advise hotel staff on what the expectations and needs of the guests are likely to be. It involves a subtle educational task which may have to span a long period. Regarding the tourists, hotels should be carefully selected so that the latter will most nearly match the requirements of the former.

Being aware of the basic motivations for travel will help here. For example, nearly 60 per cent of Americans who travel are pleasure motivated. Less than 40 per cent of British travellers are so motivated. In the case of Japan the percentage is thought to exceed that for the USA. It will also be recalled that educational standards, hobbies, interest, accidents of history and degree of sophistication also influence travel demand. All these influence the choice of accommodation for tourists.

4.4 Catering

This section discusses briefly those aspects of catering relevant to tourism management.

The efficiency of a catering operation is often judged by its ability to satisfy the special needs of a minority of any group, without fuss or delay. The majority are relatively easy to cater for, if their needs and tastes have been correctly assessed or the range of food on offer is comprehensive. The minority tend to be more vocal if their special requirements are not met, especially when sufficient notice has been given. Tourist groups these days can number in their ranks, vegans (vegetables, fruit and nuts only), vegetarians of varying degrees, those who eat only Kosher foods, Hindus and Muslims. The ability of hotels to cope with these properly (and also airlines incidentally) must be considered when the accommodation element of packages are being selected.

The holidaymaker, besides, is looking forward to a pleasurable time. Nothing creates greater dissatisfaction than a mess-up over food and meals. Tourists realise they are a semi-captive market for the hotel restaurant and this makes them even more sensitive to what is provided. So they may exaggerate the dissatisfactions. If there are several unfortunate incidents they may start to imagine other, non-existent failings. The exaggerations can increase when they return home. Their remarks to friends and neighbours can damage the image of the hotel *and* the tour operator.

The catering sensitivities of tourists can arise from three basic holiday expectations. First there is the value aspect. They wish to eat, drink, be sheltered, relax and be served in ways *they*, not the hotelier or restauranteur, judge to represent good value for money. Second, they require menus that can be easily understood. So multi-lingual menus, or ones in different languages are needed. Also, any prices shown should not involve them in currency conversion problems given that as a whole they are not very good at converting currencies. Thus prices should be in the local currency, not US dollars unless the majority of the guests are American. Finally, except for unsophisticated or ultra-conservative people who wish to stick to familiar foods, most tourists are seeking some novel experience. They wish thereby to be entertained and interested by the range of dishes on offer. Typical, local dishes should be included in the menu. Thus some effort is needed to judge when different types of tourists may lose their addictive needs, or desire to play safe is overruled by their desire for (limited?) adventure. Local foods should be produced in a style that is not too alien to the tourists' palates.

4.4.1 *Catering products*
It follows that the range of dishes provided by hotel restaurants may have to be greater and more diverse than accommodation products, if maximising customer satisfaction is the aim of the management. However cost and other practical considerations may limit the degree of diversity possible. The diversity is a reflection of the different types of guests using the facilities. They can range from the actual residents of the hotel (whether tourists or business executives) to local and foreign nationals visiting friends or relatives, or attending some function (wedding, conference, meeting of some kind).

In addition there may be organised groups (sport, business,

professional and other clubs) who may require separate facilities, services and menu. Among the casual customers will be local residents who wish to entertain family, friends or business associates without getting involved with all the work if this was done at home. Their kitchen and dining-room facilities may be limited and they may not have any hired help. They too can have special needs or expect a cosmopolitan menu.

Hotels with one restaurant and a limited kitchen would have difficulty in catering for such diverse needs. Careful design of the menu is necessary. The availability of pre-cooked, deep frozen dishes quickly prepared in a microwave oven has eased the problem and reduced wastage but careless use of the microwave can produce culinary disasters. At best it is not real *cordon bleu* cooking. Many hotels now have more than one restaurant and some may specialise in Chinese, Japanese, Italian, French, English and other foods. Many also have coffee shops open for most of the day and offering a limited range of basic dishes. They are of course particularly popular for breakfasts.

Tour operators should consider all these aspects also when selecting the hotels they will use in their packages.

4.4.2 Individual restaurants

The individual, independent restaurant faces all the problems of those in hotels plus the fact that they do not have a semi-captive market. They are competitors of hotel restaurants and rely on offering excellent service and food, with perhaps one or two unique dishes, if not menus, to attract custom. The number and variety of these establishments can enhance the attractiveness of a region to tourists. When selecting destinations and resorts, tour operators should consider the availability of these restaurants and whether they will help to attract tourists to their regions. This is particularly important for self-catering holidays where tourists will wish to eat out for some, if not all, of their main meals. Then the variety of food on offer will be important.

4.5   Some cases

Here are just two cases which illustrate some of the challenges faced by hotel management and how their success with them can influence tourism demand.

4.5.1   *Smaller is beautiful*

At the time of the boom in demand for hotel rooms, especially in Britain, many hotels were built or new extensions added to existing units. The main aim was to add bigger and bigger hotels. However, to keep costs down the tendency was to build very similar structures with almost identical furniture (fitted-in bedrooms) and fittings. The result was that except for the decor in the public rooms, the new hotels were similar in aspect.

One medium-sized hotel group, with a few medium-sized hotels, each of which had some unique aspect (shape, layout, history, gardens) had to decide whether to follow the trend. After much heart-searching and study of the growing demand for hotels and the types of customers needing them, they decided not to follow. They decided that their unique appeal lay in the fact that their establishments did not conform to the monolithic structures being built.

Despite warning noises from experts and some financial backers, they decided the group would grow by adding hotels which fitted their image and offered some unique aspect. They stuck to the same general size of unit but a few larger and smaller hotels would be considered if they fitted the requirements of guests in their catchment area. They would also have to show a reasonable profit record. Over the years they proceeded along their chosen path.

They prospered! At times when the hotel business was not doing so well, the group maintained a high level of profit and a stable business. They found that their guests showed considerable brand loyalty to their hotels. Also the problems of management were minimal. Sometimes they had to talk loud and long to raise capital for new acquisitions but even here, their cash flow allowed them to generate some of the new capital they needed. When demand increased again their profits rose even higher. The occupancy rate also rose substantially. Their reputation meant that they did not need to embark on extensive and expensive selling to fill their rooms. They continue to prosper and maintain what is an amazing stability in their business in an industry sometimes noted for its instability.

4.5.2 'Go West (and East) young man'

On the other hand, there was a large hotel group with many big hotels in the UK. The management realised they must still seek to grow to maintain their market leadership and profitability. Economic conditions indicated that this was also necessary for long-term survival given increasing international competition. The problem was how should the group tackle this problem?

First, they identified a few areas in Britain where demand was not being properly satisfied. They acquired some carefully selected hotels, refurbished them and in some instances carried out some rebuilding within the existing fabric of the buildings. A few new wings were added. However they were careful to keep the room capacity of each hotel to a size that would allow profitable occupancy rates and reasonable market shares. So they avoided problems of staffing while offering efficient service.

They also identified the growth in motoring holidays and the places where new hotels were needed. These were designed to meet the special needs of motorists, combining the best of modern hotel-keeping with the concept of motels. However they realised there was a finite limit to growth by these two methods, especially as major American groups were also expanding in Europe.

They studied the continuing boom in tourism and decide there were interesting opportunities in certain places abroad where demand of specific types of accommodation was exceeding supply. So they bought and built a few hotels overseas in carefully selected locations. These ranged from city centres to major holiday resorts catering for popular tourism markets and upmarket destinations. The last were at more distant and expensive areas. The overseas development was planned to add about 10 per cent to their total room capacity in these regions. As a result, their business became more stable and profitable and they were helped by their ability to raise the capital needed for these developments. Also, their reputation has been enhanced by this expansion, so carefully planned.

Assignments

1 What were the major developments in the accommodation industry after the Second World War? Discuss the factors that influenced these developments.

2 What changes have taken place in the demand for different types of tourism and how did these affect the location and size of accommodation units?

3 As a member of the executive team for a major hotel group you have been given the task of investigating the points mentioned in assignments 1 and 2 above. You must then present a preliminary report on the course the group's expansion plan should take. Submit such a report and justify your recommendations.

4 Subsequently, you are asked to set out guidelines on the ways in which available new capital could be used. What guidelines would you set and how could forecasts in changes in tourism demand help you to decide these?

5 Why may the catering products of an hotel be more diverse than the variety of rooms on offer? Illustrate your answer with examples drawn from different types and sizes of hotels catering for different customer groups.

5

Transport

Some aspects of transport for tourism purposes have already
been discussed in Chapter 2. This one will consider other
important points.

Tourism is all about moving people from one place to
another for holidays and business reasons. The development of
public and private transport made mass-market tourism possible. As the discretionary incomes of more and more people in
developed countries increased, their propensity and ability to
buy more tourism products grew. However transport systems
are not created to serve tourism needs only. As stated in Section
2.3 they serve other markets which owe nothing to tourism.
Indeed most systems do not depend heavily on the demand for
transport for tourism purposes. The latter is an important
element but is not necessarily the predominant one, except in
undeveloped or poor countries whose economies are heavily
dependent on tourism. Even airlines operating charter flights
for tour operators have their own scheduled services for
passengers and freight. Road transport services (bus and coach
companies) as a rule depend on non-tourist traffic for more
than 50 per cent of their business. With the seasonality of
tourism demand they would face problems of staffing, idle
resources and negative cash flows if it were otherwise. Some
small coach firms do close down at off-peak periods but face the
difficulties of holding on to essential staff and maintaining idle
rolling stock.

Some transport experts believe that providing facilities for tourists can complicate the task of supplying the other services which form the bedrock of the business. Some of these other services may play a bigger part in developing transport systems. An example is the carriage of mail. The granting of a licence to carry mail helped considerably the development of facilities whose viability would otherwise have been in doubt. Similarly the withdrawal of the licence could lead to the eventual demise of the system, especially in sparsely populated areas.

Carefully planned and controlled transport systems designed to serve all types of traveller can be profitable. However they are capital intensive. Railways have to lay tracks and purchase substantial amounts of rolling stock. With road transport, there is the cost of purchasing vehicles of different capacities and maintaining and replacing them. Central and local government have to meet the high cost of building the road systems. With air transport, airlines have to purchase and maintain increasingly costly aircraft of different sizes. Bigger and better airports have to be built for the larger, sophisticated planes. As new holiday resorts are developed, so it may be necessary to build airports nearer to them. In every case, high utilisation of all resources is vital.

However while capital investment and fixed costs are high, there are economies of scale in using larger aircraft. Carrying more passengers in large planes that are economic to operate helps to keep air fares down. This is possible only if each aircraft can achieve high load factors. The latter is possible if total demand is large enough for the number of competing airlines flying each route. Limiting the number of flights can help to overcome this problem. However, if flights are withdrawn at the last minute, tour operators will be forced to 'consolidate' their bookings, that is put passengers on other flights which the tourists may not want and which creates all kinds of inconvenience for them. Customer dissatisfaction results. So close liaison and planning between carriers and tour operators is essential.

The design of transport systems requires careful consideration of a number of factors. These include the rolling stock, track and termini needed, the estimated total demand and the competitive position. The last includes competition within individual modes of transport and between modes. The instability of demand and increasing international competition aggravate the problems. The emergence of many new nations in the last thirty years has made the competition in air transport very intense. Each new country sees it as a symbol of its maturity and status to have its own national airline. Thus an increasing number of seats are chasing total demand which has not increased sufficiently to absorb this extra capacity. Hence the jungle that has grown up around air fares with a confusing number of different rates available but not always publicised by the airlines.

Thus there is a very wide choice open to tour operators for the transport element of their packages. However the mode of travel, timing and duration of journeys that are acceptable, will depend on the attitudes and preferences of the target markets (consumers) for which the packages are intended. Also it is not just a question of cost. With airlines, the standard and quality of the flight schedules and in-flight services and customers' views of their safety record play an important part in establishing ready acceptance of the holiday packages on offer. With coaches and trains, the punctuality and quality of the service and to a lesser extent, safety records, should be taken into account. For sea trips, the reputation and image of the shipping line and the inherent luxury of the ships, as well as the on-board entertainments, are important considerations. Therefore tour operators have to consider many things before sound decisions can be made on the transport services that will be used.

5.1 Role of transport

The role of transport systems then is to carry passengers and freight from place to place. However, devising an economical system is not dependent only on the points mentioned earlier. There are political considerations.

In many countries the major modes of transport are state-owned, state-controlled or subject to public regulation (by a government department or its agency). In these situations major decisions may be based on political considerations (for example, how many votes may be won or lost, or how voters' attitudes will be affected) rather than sound economic facts. Much capital has been wasted on developments which on economic grounds would be unjustified but they have been pushed through to meet some public or political fad. Often the objectives of a project, especially its purpose and the markets it should serve, have not been thought through clearly, if thought about at all. If the investment aspects are evaluated, they may be done project by project, without thought of a national transport policy or whether the project would support the national economy and help it to grow. All this can create problems for the tourism industry who may find that the resultant services are a jumble and do not meet its needs efficiently.

Only in developing countries conscious of their limited resources, are attempts made to plan their transport services on a national basis. Unfortunately for many reasons which cannot be discussed here, national planning is subject to long delays. Serious mistakes result. The last may be due to lack of experience or sophistication of the planners. Of course political factors can lead to greater distortion of the work!

5.2   Modes of transport

The modes of transport are air, rail, road and sea. Dividing transport up in this way has the advantage that in analysis and planning work, each mode is easily identified. However in Britain the statistics for Channel and other ferries are found in shipping records. Also while the hovercraft is considered an aircraft for the purpose of safety regulations, their significance is as competitors to conventional ferries.

5.2.1   Air transport

This mode can be subdivided into scheduled air services, non-scheduled or charter services and air taxis. The first operate on defined domestic and international routes under licences granted by the governments of the countries they serve or overfly. They are required to operate in accordance with published and agreed schedules regardless of the passenger load factor. On some routes which are not commercially viable the year round, they can operate during peak demand periods only. The airlines can be state-owned or private enterprises depending on the policies of the government of their home countries. Usually the publicly owned airline will be the country's *flag carrier*. Other carriers, according to their relative importance to the total system are known as *second* or *third force* airlines. Leading competitors of national flag carriers are usually considered second force airlines. Those providing a network of local or regional services are referred to as *feeder* airlines.

On a cost per kilometre basis, short-haul flights are more expensive. This is because they involve more frequent landings and take-offs and on take-off they consume more fuel than when they have achieved their operational ceiling. Further, aircraft on these routes spend more time on the ground and incur more airport charges. When launching a new route, there is the greater risk because of the lower load factors. This may lead to higher fares than those that would be charged when more seats were sold, that is when the load factor is higher. Higher fares may inhibit growth in demand.

When fixing fares, airlines have to consider the size and type of aircraft to be used, route traffic density, potential total demand and competition. In addition, the regularity of demand, whether it is balanced in both directions, the mix of passengers between first, economy and tourist classes, any discounted ticket sales and the estimated break-even load factor are other influencing factors. Further, demand can change at short notice and this instability can effect the viability of a route.

Non-scheduled or charter services appeal because of their more attractive price or fare per passenger. These lower fares are achieved by working to high load factors, around 85 to 90 per cent and keeping overhead costs low. The marketing costs are non-existent since these services are sold to tour operators and do not need to be advertised to the public. They are not obliged to work to a set timetable and so avoid the costs and losses of scheduled operators whose planes may, on many occasions, be flying with only a few seats occupied (very low load factor). The in-flight and other services provided will depend on what the hirers (customers), usually tour operators, require. In recent years some tour operators have taken over or formed their own charter airlines. These take mainly their owner's tourist groups but do take other groups and sell empty seats on the discounted fare market.

Air taxis are private charter planes, usually able to carry from four to about eighteen passengers, used mainly by business executives and teams on various trips for their companies. They offer convenience and flexibility to the users and the routes are tailored to their needs. In many instances they allow the executives to fly out to their meeting and return home on the same day, not always possible on scheduled flights if the timetable does not match executives' needs.

Air transport is the dominant carrier for the tourism trade in most countries. However while it provides fast and convenient transport to more distant destinations, in total fare terms, it is not cheap. Nor can it match the unique advantages of the other modes discussed in the following sections. Depending on the terrain, other modes may be better for shorter distances. The development of cheaper domestic air services, especially shuttle flights, has however intensified competition against these other modes. If shuttle services are extended to other European countries, assuming the governments concerned can reach agreement, then airlines might extend their competitiveness against other modes of transport on medium-haul journeys.

5.2.2 Railways

In Britain the railways have taken some time to adapt their services to the needs of modern mass tourism. While they played a major role in the first half of this century in providing tourist transport, by the middle of the century they were losing out to aircraft and the greater private ownership of cars. By the 1980s British Rail had become more marketing orientated and made determined attempts to win back some of the tourist traffic. Various special offers were made and they devised 'Golden Rail' tours in conjunction with their own hotels and those of other hotel companies. Short-break packages were introduced and more recently, substantial discounts were offered on some day- and period-return journeys. One of these was their 'Away-day' fares.

Although the standard of service has declined and route mileages cut drastically all over the world, railways still carry a substantial proportion of vacationists, especially domestic tourists. Once a cheap and convenient way of travelling for the mass market, mainly lower and middle income groups, railways have lost some of these advantages because of rising costs and hence fares. The closure of many branch lines, often serving traditional holiday destinations and scenic areas, has reduced its utility. Growing competition from travel by air and the privately owned car has further eroded the position of railways as a passenger carrier.

The development of private railway lines and companies by the growing number of steam train enthusiasts has served to balance a little the loss of amenities of the major, often state-owned, network. Since most of these private ventures are in scenic areas, they have added a further attraction to the tourism market of their regions. In Britain over forty such ventures are in operation and while some depend heavily on the patronage of tourists, others also serve local residents with commuting and other services. They depend in the main on voluntary labour drawn from the membership of the organisation running the line, or enthusiasts, to operate and maintain the system.

5.2.3 Coach operators
The coach appeals to many as an ideal way of touring a region and seeing all there is to see. Coach tours account for some 10 per cent of the UK domestic holiday business and the operators see an improving future for their business, especially if rising costs further disadvantage other modes of transport. Four factors are thought to work in favour of these tours.

First, there appear to be moves by some sectors of the market to more fuel-efficient forms of transport. Second, the building of hotels, particularly in scenic zones, has overcome some of the shortage of suitable accommodation which inhibited the expansion of coach tours in earlier years. Third was the more liberal licensing laws in favour of coaches and the raising of the speed limits on them. With the latter, using motorways for journeys between scenic areas, coaches could cover greater distances in a day. Finally, the development of larger, modern coaches, with improved in-board facilities has helped to increase demand. So the coach is a good mode of transport for those seeking inexpensive holidays. These factors have also helped in the growth in demand for international coach tours.

5.2.4 *Cars and car hire companies*

As stated earlier, the growth in ownership of the private car has seen this mode of transport grow as a major competitor of airlines, railways and coaches for tourism purposes. Its apparent cost is lowest but its real total cost is not quite so cheap. This postwar boom in car ownership has also seen the growth in demand for car hire facilities. Car owners have come to appreciate the flexibility and convenience of travel by car especially in selection of routes and stopovers. So many people's lives are geared to the car that often they cannot appreciate other modes of transport. Even tourists who fly to their holiday destinations may wish to hire cars on arrival, either for local excursions or to continue on the rest of their holiday. The fly-drive tour is now good business.

In the last three decades several car hire companies have come into existence and operate profitably. The better-known international names are Hertz, Avis, Budget and Europcar. They offer a wide selection of cars and rates with many offices (or 'stations'). Many offer the facility of being able to collect a vehicle at one airport of arrival and leave it at another when return flights are taken from a different airport. In addition there are several small companies operating from limited locations. They are useful to tourists who need a car for local mobility or who will return to the original location before flying home.

Hire companies are useful to tour operators, hotels and airlines who wish to offer car hire facilities. They may do so at very competitive prices or to add as a further attraction to their services or packages. In the latter case the price of the package may include the hire of a small car for three or five days. British Rail established links with Godfrey Davis (now Europcar) while Sovereign and Enterprise Holidays (owned by British

Airways) and other tour operators have arrangements with Avis, Hertz and other car hire firms, for European, American and some other destinations.

5.2.5 Cruise ships and other water transport
Ocean-going cruise ships, ferries, hovercraft, river and canal boats form the water transport sector. For British holiday-makers going abroad other than by air, they cannot avoid using ferries (traditional) or hovercraft (new and possible if a car is not being taken abroad). Numerous car ferries operated between the UK and Europe, Scandinavia and Eire but the economic squeeze of the 1980s has seen some contraction in these services. The demand for canal and river boats, including cruisers on the Norfolk Broads, are other popular forms of waterborne transport for those seeking a leisurely and quiet holiday. Ocean cruising has grown in popularity in the last decade or so.

In 1932, in the depth of the Great Depression, Cunard Steamship Company (now part of the Trafalgar House Group) and P & O began using some of their ships for cruising. Other lines (e.g. Furness, French Line and Matson) soon followed. After the Second World War, ships as means of transport for long-distance ocean voyages went into decline with the arrival of large, fast intercontinental aircraft. By the 1960s, shipping lines were forced to abandon many traditional routes and operations because of rising operational costs and falling demand. Some ships were put to cruising but they were not ideally suited for this. They were not economical to run and because of their draught could not tie up alongside the docks of traditional holiday destinations. In some cases shallow water prevented them from visiting some destinations at all.

It was necessary to build ships specifically for cruising. These have smaller cabins and more extensive public rooms. Their daily operating costs must be less than traditional liners. Those companies that did not embark on a rebuilding programme soon had to withdraw. Happily the sea cruise has caught on and demand is buoyant. There is a certain cachet, or status symbol, about taking a cruise. Also the customers see the fares – which are not particularly cheap – as acceptable because of the unique experience and high quality of service provided.

Some see cruising as less tiring than other forms of travel. They get on the ship and let the destinations come to them. After an exhausting day ashore they can return to the comfort and luxury of the ship. The cruise market has changed from older persons who did not wish to fly to younger and middle-aged people. Also people who might otherwise never have dreamt of going on a ship accept cruises as a good holiday prospect.

A further development has been the fly-cruise. Developed in Britain towards the end of the 1960s, passengers are flown to or from the port of departure or return. This saves time that would otherwise be spent on a long sea voyage at the beginning or end of the holiday. This also permits the ships to make quicker turn-rounds, saving on harbour dues. Use of charter air services kept the cost of air fares to reasonable limits. It appealed to the younger age groups who had no liking for long sea voyages and saw the ship as a luxury floating hotel taking them to various destinations by short trips of a day or less.

A recent variation on this idea started by Cunard and British Airways using Concorde is to travel one way by sea and the other by Concorde. This provides an interesting method of travel for those taking independent holidays to North America. P & O had started a similar idea, before Cunard, where passengers would fly one way to or from Australia and make the other journey by ship. For their world cruises, customers may pick up and leave the cruise at any destination, using a designated airline to complete their journeys. For the upper income groups who do not wish to spend 70 days or more cruising, this was an attractive alternative.

5.3 Patterns of demand for tourism transport

Further remarks concerning patterns of demand and consumer choice of holiday transport are necessary. The choice is influenced by consumer preference, opinions and prejudices for each mode and the degree of comfort, convenience and flexibility they require. The demand for transport for tourism purposes is heterogeneous in nature. It varies according to the type of tourist to be served and the purpose of their vacations.

However for international tourism, air and road transport predominate while for domestic tourism, road (car and coach) and rail transport are still the main competitors, though under competitive pressure from domestic air networks. The demand for transport is of course seasonal like tourism itself. Until people can be more flexible on the time they can go on holiday, for most school holidays and the set holiday periods of their employers currently make this impossible, this seasonal demand will continue.

Consumers using the holiday packages designed for the mass and popular markets, although not very knowledgeable on transport matters, assume that the operators will select the most economical routes and modes available. That is the transport element of the total cost will be the most economical possible. Only for special instances, for example flying by Concorde, will they accept higher costs. They also expect departure and arrival times and the duration of journeys to be as convenient as other considerations permit. Some may be prepared to pay a little extra for the use of airports nearer their home base or more convenient departures and arrivals but many may not be able to afford this.

Consumers taking package holidays, in the main, travel to Europe, Scandinavia and the Mediterranean coast of North Africa. In more recent years demand has grown for holidays in North America, the Far East and Australia, both packages and individual trips. The Caribbean has always been popular with the better off, especially during the winter. Thus the spread of demand for transport (air, road, rail) is considerable in geographical terms. Packages to the first three destination countries involve relatively short flight durations of four hours or less. Package tourists in general are not too keen about long flights. If the flight to a resort takes five or more hours, some tourists may seek alternative destinations with shorter flight times. However provided the air journey is not too long, many people will put up with quite long coach journeys to and from their resorts. This allows tour operators to use smaller, less expensive and less congested airports. When people are travelling to distant and exotic resorts, these time considerations are of less significance. The exciting prospects of the destinations exert more influence on buying decisions.

While most travellers accept that meals are not often served on domestic flights, they have not accepted so meekly the attempts to replace hot meals with packed sandwiches, often handed to passengers as they board the aircraft, for holiday flights. If other airlines provide full in-flight services for tourists, including free wine with meals, customers tend to pick the packages using these carriers. People from all sectors of society, from socio-economic group A to D, use air transport for their holidays.

On the other hand, motor and rail transport are patronised by groups C1, C2 and D in the main though some Bs also prefer these modes. Members of the A group use motor transport on individual holidays but if long distances are involved, air will be used. Some of them use rail and sea transport if they do not like flying. For organised groups comprised mainly of the first three categories of people mentioned above, coaches and minibuses are preferred, even when quite considerable mileages are involved. However they prefer to avoid long stages between stops even in modern air-conditioned vehicles with comfortable aircraft-type seats and other on-board facilities. Demand for coach travel is stable but seasonal and coach operators expect demand to grow in future years if cost of other packages increase and more sophisticated vehicles become available.

The alternative to the coach is the car, whether owned or hired and this mode is used by all the socio-economic groups. The Cs and Ds perfer using their cars if they have large families. The *per capita* cost is less than by any other mode. As mentioned earlier, the flexibility and convenience of this mode also attract demand.

Rail travel, despite recent fare increases, is also attractive to families with limited incomes, especially for domestic holidays. The special offers mentioned in the preceeding section are aimed primarily at groups C, D, and E. These special offers, made at peak holiday periods tend to maintain the seasonality of demand. Rail travel is a good alternative to use instead of the car and is claimed to reduce fatigue especially over long journeys.

As already mentioned, sea cruises have buoyant demand even though passenger fares are close to, or in four figures.

They are patronised mainly by social groups A and B with a good number of C1s who are in the higher income bracket of their group. Some C2s and Ds will save up to go on one. Other users are drawn from the E group, those retired people with good occupational pensions or retirement jobs. Those Es with only the state pension cannot normally afford this type of holiday. Demand is less seasonal since most A and B people can take their holidays at off-peak periods and often prefer to do so.

5.3.1 Leisure

The introduction of the shorter working week is the main factor why there has been an increase in leisure time for many people. This increase in leisure time, without loss in earnings, has contributed to the growth in demand for tourism products of all kinds. More leisure has also seen a growth in demand for sporting activities and this has increased the demand for sporting holidays. Here also the increase in car ownership has been a factor since more people can travel with ease to major sports centres, golf courses, marinas and so on. Many will travel long distances to get to a favourite sports resort, increasing the opportunities for further development of the tourism industry.

Another contributory factor is the change in the occupational structure of the country. While the total workforce may be permanently reduced by the recent recession and its effect on traditional labour-intensive industries, there has been an increase in the number of 'white collar' workers. These are salaried, clerical and administrative people in industry, the professions and service industries. Traditionally they have longer holidays than the average 'blue collar' (shopfloor, skilled, semi-skilled and unskilled) workers and greater net discretionary incomes. Many can afford the more expensive, up-market tourism product.

5.3.2 Cost of travel

The costs of the different transport modes are listed in Table 5.1. With air travel a distinction is possible between flying or cruising costs and those associated with landing, take-off, parking and storage dues. So with short-haul flights, the ratio of flying time to time on the ground is less than for long-haul flights. A fast turnround of aircraft on short-haul flights is very advisable if operating costs are to be held down.

Table 5.12   Transport costs

AIRLINES

Fixed costs   aircrew administration
                     depreciation on aircraft and other plant
                     interest charges on capital, etc.
                     insurance
                     engineering overheads (at base)
                     all other ground costs

Variable costs   aircrew salaries and expenses
                     direct engineering costs (overhauls)
                     fuel and oils
                     passenger meals and in-flight services

SHIPPING

Fixed costs   annual surveys and overhauls
                     depreciation
                     interest
                     insurance, protection and indemnity costs
                     all other shorebased costs

Variable costs   deck and engine costs (non-hotel crew, maintenance
                         during voyage, fire prevention)
                     hotel and catering costs (hotel staff, cleaning, main-
                         tenance, furnishing, entertainments, victualling)
                     Master's costs (fuel and oil, master's salaries, marine
                         insurance)
                     port costs and fees
                     loading and discharging costs

PUBLIC SERVICE MODES

Fixed costs   depreciation, interest
                     workshop overheads and all head office costs

Variable costs   fuel, oil and for road vehicles, tyres
                     salaries, uniforms, licences, insurance, cleaning
                     ticketing

In the case of ships, cruising costs per mile are less than for liner (scheduled) services, because of the former's more leisurely speed and the new vessels are designed for more economical running. Fuel consumption is reduced. Cruise ships are charged yacht rates at many ports, reducing the port dues that have to be paid. The ratio of the number of crew to the number of passengers is usually lower, reducing labour costs. With the demise of the large passenger liner on scheduled routes, most of the 'shipping conferences' that regulated fares have ceased effective existence.

Only the harmonising conference to which most ferry companies belong continues in operation. Even this was referred to the Monopolies Commission in 1972 which reported that the conference's activities were not in the public interest. It recommended that the government should supervise the fare structure and the work was given to the Office of Fair Trading.

Short ferry services, although in demand for tourism, face the problem of high operating costs and the price war of the early 1980s cannot have done much to improve the situation. Ferry companies try to overcome this difficulty by having round-the-clock sailings to achieve a stable demand all the year round, and quick turnround at both ends to minimise harbour dues and maximise resource utilisation. On-board sale of duty free goods also helps to achieve acceptable profit levels. Because holiday demand peaks in July to September and to a lesser extent in December to March, ferry companies try to stimulate demand at other times by offering lower fares then.

Railways in Britain are free of the type of regulation applied to air transport except for some obligations imposed by various Acts of Parliament. To counter the effects of rising costs with this mode, entrepreneurs have taken advantage of the continued fascination people have for railways, especially old or unique steam systems. They have organised special programmes. These include the resurrection of the Orient Express but operating only between London and Venice, travel to China and Hong Kong via the Trans-Siberian Railway and the Palace Express in India which recreates the splendour of princely times during the British Raj.

The demand for transport services is price sensitive and subject to price elasticity. The vacationist will seek other holidays using cheaper modes of transport if this reduces the cost of the package, provided the alternatives are acceptable. Special and common interest tourists will do the same but are more likely to find the extra money for more expensive forms of travel if there is no alternative way of getting to their destinations. If fares are kept artificially high and appear unreasonable, they will do without the special holiday for a year or two.

Thus transport firms, through their fares, can influence the choice of destination and tourist product by vacationists of all kinds. If tourists' work situations permit flexibility in the timing of their holidays, they may switch their travel to off-peak periods when fares and the total cost of their holiday package will be lower. Pensioners and retired people with limited incomes will certainly do so. On the other hand, the business traveller, within reason, is not so price sensitive. They have to travel at specified times for specific reasons and will not change their schedules for a limited price reduction. The mode of transport chosen will depend on the distance to be travelled, the workload involved and whether the overall costs fall within any limits set by the employer. Other important considerations include the punctuality of the carrier, the standard and quality of the in-flight or on-board services and meals. If the business traveller is dissatisfied with any of these he or she will switch to another carrier.

Charter airlines have lower total costs than their schedule competitors. They do not need the large and elaborate reservation and station services of the schedule flight operators. They are presented with details of the number of passengers that will be on each flight, destination and departure points, timing and duration of flights required and so on, by the tour operator making the charter. That is the tour operator chartering the plane does all the administrative work.

5.4 Transport economics and regulation

Consumers of transport services expect a wide choice of options regarding departure times, duration of journeys, routes and carriers. This ignores the hard realities of modern economic conditions. Maintaining such a wide choice results in the under-utilisation of all modes, especially as demand for transport services has seasonal *and daily* peaks. The peculiarities of human attitudes and behaviour to transport services should be kept in mind by tour operators as they can influence consumer decisions on the choice of holiday and the mode of transport they will use.

Then the economies of scale set minimum limits to the levels of usage of airport, aircraft, roads, railways and so on, if unit costs are to be kept within reasonable bounds. Yet the minimal economic activity for any item of plant is usually greater than the immediate demand for it, when room for future expansion has been allowed for, or when demand is very seasonal. This prevents the full exploitation of the potential economies of scale. For example, a single-runway airport with sophisticated landing control systems can handle more arrivals and departures than would be the case without these control systems. If demand for these sophisticated airports does not match their capacity they will be operating at uneconomic levels.

A large airport in theory, is more economical to operate. However congested terminal buildings, access roads and parking facilities, with insufficient staff to handle the passenger traffic flow efficiently, put a practical top limit on size. For example, there was considerable argument on whether London Heathrow needed a fourth terminal or if other London airports (Gatwick, Luton, Stanstead) should be used with better effect. One had only to be at the Heathrow International Terminal (no. 3) between 9.00 and 10.30 a.m. during the peak summer period when it is congested to see the problem. Yet at off-peak periods the terminal can be relatively deserted.

These are some of the points that need consideration when airports are being planned, especially if they are intended primarily for tourist traffic. Should the plans be based on peak demand when assets would be under-utilised at other periods? Or should they be designed for some estimated mean minimising the congestion at peak times and under-utilisation at off-peak ones? For airports designed for mixed demand (ordinary travellers and tourists) the peak demand periods of other types of user will not coincide with the off-peak ones of tourist traffic. If peak periods coincide, the congestion problem is worsened. Similar problems can arise with road and rail systems. These problems are not easily resolved and get worse when tourist and non-tourist traffic have to be handled. Here are further points tour operators should keep in mind when selecting the airports to be used.

For tourism, the choice of several airports and destinations increases the potential range of tours possible. However, closeness to resorts, ability to handle substantial nunbers at peak times and the safety record, are factors which should also influence the choice of airports used. Within reason, the closeness of the airport to the resort should be subordinated to safety aspects. Forecasting airport needs is difficult and it is easy to exaggerate what studies in depth can achieve in tackling the problem. A national study to establish a national plan is preferable to the occasional, *ad hoc* study of one airport or location. What can happen if there is no coherent study and policy is illustrated by the situation on the Atlantic seaboard of the USA.

In addition there is the problem of too many airlines chasing insufficient demand to satisfy all their capacity. This has injected further instability into the air transport business and much fare-cutting. In the end no one, not even the tourists, will benefit. Further, modern aircraft use complicated and expensive electronic control mechanisms thus increasing operational (maintenance) costs. This has put more pressure on profit margins, increasing the need for even higher load factors.

5.4.1 *Regulation of air transport*
Air transport is subject to regulation at national and international levels. The main concern is safety. For this reason aircraft have to be licensed, controlled and supervised. Next, because air transport has an important impact on the economy, governments support and encourage the development of profitable routes. They oppose or prohibit those which only intensify competition further or where there is already over-capacity. Third, as a result of noisier engines and aircraft, controls on permitted noise levels at landing and take-off are applied by many authorities. Concern about pollution has also spawned controls on engine emissions and the discharge of excess fuel on

landing. In countries with state-owned airlines, regulations may exist which control the development and operations of private ones. The balance achieved between public and private services depends on the political views and attitudes of the governments.

International routes are assigned by mutual agreement between interested governments, those of the countries of departure and arrival and those overflown or where stopovers are made. For the last, agreements will also specify if new passengers can be taken on and the terms and conditions when this may be done. Political attitudes can cloud these decisions.

Domestic routes and their allocation to competing airlines are determined by the government. In democratic countries these decisions can sometimes be challenged in the courts. Thus in Britain, domestic and international route allocation can involve tussles between British Airways and such independents as British Caledonian, Dan-Air and British Midland Airways for example. These aspects may also influence decisions by tour operators on the choice of carriers they will use for their packages.

International, scheduled flight fares are established through mutual agreement of the airlines, through the mediation of traffic conferences of IATA, the trade body of the airlines. These agreements are subject to ratification by the appropriate governments. However it is not all plain sailing. Disputes and disagreements do arise between airlines and governments, especially if a major country refuses ratification. Then the proposed fares cannot be introduced. The dissenters either have to be talked out of their dissension or some compromise has to be found.

In Britain the Civil Aviation Authority (CAA) acts as the government's agency in the regulation and approval of fares. It is also responsible for the licensing of charter airlines and tour operators who organise package tours abroad by air. The International Civil Aviation Organisation (ICAO), a United Nations agency, established what are called the *five freedoms of air travel*:

(1) the freedom to overfly another country without landing

(but some Middle Eastern countries insist on overflying planes landing in their countries, presumably to earn airport dues);

(2) the freedom to land for technical reasons (e.g. refuelling);

(3) the freedom to set down passengers, mail and freight;

(4) the freedom to pick up passengers, mail and freight (but some totalitarian regimes may severely limit or prohibit this right);

(5) the freedom to set down and pick up passengers in the territory of a third party (e.g. British Airways flying London to Delhi may do so at Rome, Athens, Cairo or any other stop *en route*).

Items 3 and 4 are known as the commercial freedoms and cover most point-to-point traffic. As noted, not all countries adhere strictly to the above.

The Anglo-American agreement known as the *Bermuda Agreement* originally restricted carriage between these two countries to their national or major airlines and imposed restrictions on the permitted capacities. Other countries have similar bilateral agreements or predeterminist ones which specify a fixed percentage of the total traffic that must be carried by their own national airlines. Britain's aim was to use the Bermuda agreement to avoid overcapacity being offered by restricting the routes to two American and two British carriers.

Cabotage routes, those within the national territory of a country, are not subject to international agreement. They are controlled by the government, who normally restricts them to their national carriers. These routes are also not subject to fare ratification by IATA.

IATA (whose membership includes some 80 airlines) and its fare control policies have been subjected to increasing criticism. It is claimed that international fares are being kept artificially high and are often the result of political considerations, for example, inefficient national carriers can achieve higher fares than normal competitive considerations would permit. Without these higher fares, many airlines would be bankrupt if their governments were not prepared to subsidise their operations. IATA also establishes agreements on the meals and other services that can be supplied, the pitch of the seats and the leg room allowed each passenger.

The general criticism is that IATA has injected inertia into the management and running of airlines, through its desire to avoid damaging controversy between its members. Its cartel approach has not led, however, to sustained profitability for members since they face fierce competition from non-IATA airlines. The latters' more aggressive marketing, superior in-flight services, more efficient handling of passengers and generally more dynamic approach to the business have led many travellers to prefer the better established non-IATA carriers.

As a result, with increasing interest in freer competition in the USA and Britain, IATA reorganised itself. It now has two sections, one a tariff section dealing with fare agreements and the other is a trade section. All members belong to the latter but membership of the former is voluntary. Many American operators have withdrawn from the tariff section.

Regulation of domestic air transport in Britain is done for the government by the CAA. The equivalent body in the USA is the Civil Aeronautics Board (CAB) which approves fares and routes. There is also the Federal Aviation Agency (FAA) responsible for overseeing air traffic control and the safety and efficiency of air travel. The CAA assumes all these responsibilities in Britain and at the moment, also owns some Scottish airports.

5.4.2 *Road passenger transport*

In Britain between the two world wars, competition between coach and bus companies was so severe it became necessary to introduce a national licensing system via the Road Traffic Act of 1930. This created a number of Area Traffic Commissioners who hear applications for proposed services and grant road service licences to approved operators and routes. Drivers and vehicles have to be licensed but here the important criterion was safety for passengers and other road users. Provided the safety regulations are met, licences are granted on a non-discriminatory basis. Drivers must hold a valid Heavy Goods Vehicle driver's licence if handling buses and this or other appropriate ones for coaches and mini-buses. Licences granted by the Commissioners depend on their opinion of existing demand for such services by the public. The use of lower than normal fares with any proposed new service is not seen as in itself, providing a valid reason for the granting of a road service licence. However, in 1984, the then Conservative government in Britain published a White Paper proposing the deregulation of road passenger transport to increase competition by allowing more private companies to operate these services.

The Transport Act of 1968 brought about changes in the organisation of passenger road services but was largely concerned with commuter and other socially desirable services and safety. By the early 1980s in Britain, pressure was growing for more control of holiday coach traffic with the increasing number of serious accidents that had happened. The introduction of the tachograph, to conform with EEC regulations, does at least restrict the number of hours a driver may be at the wheel. Relief drivers must now be available on all long-distance coaches. Off-duty sleeping on the coach, while the other driver is at the wheel, is not seen as a true or correct interpretation of the use of rest periods!

Most European countries have regulations controlling the operation of long-distance coaches. France, for example, because of the terrible accidents that happened to coaches full of young children, in 1983 imposed a restriction on the maximum number of such children who could be on a coach, both French and foreign operated. For international traffic, many countries restrict the use of foreign vehicles. Those that are approved must meet various safety regulations. Some countries also place restrictions on the ages of coach drivers.

The private car, except for road taxes, has not been subjected to similar regulations. However pressure is growing in some countries that similar regulations are needed. In Britain the Ministry of Transport Test Certificate (MOT certificate) for cars over three years old has gone some way in removing dangerous cars from the road. However the requirements of this test are not considered to be as comprehensive or stringent as seems necessary, despite some recent additions to the requirements. The regulation on the minimum depth of thread for all tyres, making it an offence for people to use tyres having less than this minimum, or which are bald or otherwise defective, has increased road safety. The compulsory use of seat belts for driver and front seat passenger has minimised serious injury in an accident. The use of belts by back seat passengers may also be demanded in the near future.

5.4.3 Deregulation

IATA plays an important role in providing a clearing-house system which allows quick financial settlements between members and in establishing standardised air tickets and other documents that are interchangeable between carriers. It also provides compatability for the basis of calculation of air fares under fluctuating foreign exchange rates. It sets the standards for operating procedures and relationships with travel agents and tour operators. Its abolition would inconvenience travellers. For example, in the USA the lack of interlining facilities between non-IATA members (permitting through fares on a single ticket for multi-stop journeys) has proved a problem for travellers.

Nevertheless in the USA a drive for the deregulation of air transport was pressed home. In 1978 the Airline Deregulation Act was passed. This required the abolition of commonly agreed fares. In that year also, the CAB ordered IATA to justify its fare-fixing policy, derived by agreement between member international carriers. This was seen as a contravention of anti-trust laws. By the beginning of the 1980s the British government was supporting a drive for a more liberal approach to fares for the North Atlantic routes. It asserted pressure on its European partners for a similar approach for European routes. This was strongly opposed by many airlines. The price fixing of North Atlantic fares ended in 1980 after the American carriers withdrew from the tariff section of IATA.

Unfortunately deregulation coincided with the start of the severe recession of the last few years when high inflation, static demand and rising costs (of fuel, new aircraft and maintenance) all combined to produce difficult operating conditions for the airlines. This led to many empty seats and substantial operating losses. A mad scramble to fill seats at any price produced a plethora of fares that only confused the user even more. The user had to do quite a bit of shopping around to find the lowest fare for a route and to discover if in-flight and other services had been slashed as a result. The growing interest of business executives in discounted fare tickets posed a further threat. Travel agents' incomes were also reduced as their remuneration is based on a percentage of the actual net fare paid by users, their customers.

However one benefit has been that these results of deregulation forced airlines to seek greater efficiency of their operations. Costs were cut savagely and staff made redundant. For example, British Airways turned substantial losses into profit by 1983 through slimming down its organisation and making other changes. The British government's intention to sell the airline back to private ownership may have been a further spur.

5.5 Some cases

The following are just two cases that illustrate the attitudes of travellers to the modes of transport they choose and the problems airlines had to overcome.

5.5.1 The cost-conscious business traveller

The business community has been subjected to many economic pressures with the world recession of the early 1980s. Until about 1982 the cost of their business journeys was accepted as an unavoidable cost of their business but as profit margins were squeezed more and more, they began to look carefully at these expenditures. This pressure from business executives for greater economy in their travel costs became more significant for the travel trade.

In 1982, travel agencies, supported by the airlines, made more concerted efforts to develop alternative sources of income and business travel was the one that received most attention. Corporations with large travel accounts began to receive worthwhile offers of discounts if the company agreed to place most of its business travel requirements with a particular airline and travel agency. Airlines in particular were desperate for new business and came up with some extraordinary offers. They offered substantial inducements, over and above the standard 9 or 10 per cent commission, to travel agents who promoted the sale of their tickets. With these enhanced commissions the agencies could pass on attractive inducements to their business clients. Since these higher discounts from airlines were 18 per cent or more, the inducements were worth consideration.

Agencies also realised that they had to offer a better level of service and not neglect the personal touch. Without these, the initial inducements were often treated with suspicion. Sophisticated reservations systems using a computer or linked by terminals to the associated airline's computer, allowed major improvements in the speed and efficiency of the service to business organisations. Travel clerks who were traditionally order-takers, were trained to become travel counsellors able to handle the intricate problems of business travel requirements. They were expected to build up detailed knowledge of the business client's needs, how these could be met more economically and the best routes from all considerations. They were then in the position to give valuable money- and time-saving advice. Some major agencies created central departments to monitor the bewildering fare structure available so that up-to-date advice could be given on the latest bargains, official and unofficial.

Thus the recession has forced travel agencies to pay attention to the specific needs of their corporate customers. The complexion of the business travel market has been transformed in recent years. Hopefully this will prove of mutual benefit to the travel industry and the business world.

5.52 Struggle of the airlines

1982 was a bad year for airlines. Two, Braniff and Laker, had collapsed. Several others were clinging to survival. British Airways sustained a loss of about £500 million. If it had not been state-owned this would have led, almost certainly, to bankruptcy. It was the year when growth in air travel virtually ceased. Further, while revenue and profits declined, operating costs rose alarmingly. The US dollar strengthened against most other major currencies. This put up the cost of fuel, new American-built aircraft and their spare parts, all paid for in dollars. Interest rates and inflation rose, increasing the cost of capital and loans for the purchase of new aircraft and other plant.

The airlines were forced to get out and attract passengers (old and new) in an increasing number of ways by attractive offers. These ranged from fares, better ground services at airports, in-flight services, greater punctuality and better food. In other words, they had to give better all-round value to their passengers. The frequent business traveller was singled out for special treatment, with preferential check-in and boarding facilities and their own special seating sections (cabin class with British Airways and other similar arrangements by other airlines. These were meant to separate the full-fare paying passengers from economy class ones, usually tourists, who paid less for the flight). It became difficult for travellers to know which was the best deal on offer. They had to become well-informed and know where to get the latest, accurate information on all these points.

The airlines learnt to tailor their services to match the changing needs of customers. Besides the frequent travellers who got their own cabin area with special facilities for which they paid with higher (full-rate) fares, the first class passengers were assured of sleeper seats in which they could stretch out comfortably, with a better range of in-flight food and drink. Tourists were confined to the rear of aircrafts with basic services. The airlines realised that tourists were mainly interested in cheap fares and did not mind some loss in services. Some airlines offered very cheap fares which did not include hot meals. If tourists or economy passengers wanted meals they had to order them when checking-in and pay a supplement (not particularly cheap) for them.

In the USA severe competition led to many airlines offering different types of airpasses. These allowed the holders, on payment of the asking price, to travel freely for up to 60 days along the airlines' domestic network. Some airpasses were restricted to foreign visitors but some were for local residents only. They were good value for money, especially for tourists from overseas who wished to see a lot of America.

Finally, a number of round-the-world fares came on offer. While conditions varied, in general passengers were allowed to stop-off anywhere along the airline's route but travel had to be in one direction. Backtracking was not permitted. Booking restrictions, maximum and minimum stay requirements, period of validity and penalties for changes in itinerary were applied and varied from airline to airline. Some of these offers were operated by two airlines (e.g. Singapore Airlines and TWA) where one or both on their own did not fly right round the world. These offers stimulated demand for world tours.

Assignments

1   Why and how has the development of mass transport systems helped to increase demand for tourism?

2   Why should transport systems be subjected to regulation? You work for an independent airline and have been instructed to prepare a paper for your managing director who is to address a conference attended by government officials, on the subject of deregulation. Prepare a paper.

3   Discuss the merits and demerits for tourists, of the different modes of transport available. How do costs, or fares, affect the position?

4   As a member of a team planning a new transport system (choose either air, road or rail) you are asked to make a special study of relevant economic factors. Which would you study and why are they important?

6

Infrastructure and Superstructure

To attract tourists and provide them with a satisfying experience on which long-term, profitable business can be built, construction of suitable accommodation, restaurants and passenger transport terminals at the resorts is necessary. These form what is called the *superstructure* of the region. In addition there must be a sufficiency of roads, harbours, railway lines, airport runways, water, electricity, other power supplies, sewerage disposal systems and other utilities to serve not only the local residents but also the tourist influx. These are normally referred to as the *infrastructure*. It is argued that the infrastructure is not constructed primarily for the tourists but for the local inhabitants. The former are taken into consideration only if the region has tourist appeal or is destined for development in that direction. The implication is that superstructure items such as hotels and restaurants are constructed with tourists in mind but many experts disagree with this. They maintain that most of these establishments are designed with a mixed trade in mind, some tourists, some casual visitors and some local residents. While some are intended almost exclusively for tourism purposes, local inhabitants can and do use them. Other experts believe the above definitions to be false but the use of the words 'superstructure' and 'infrastructure' is useful 'shorthand' for reference to the components of these groups.

If the infrastructure is insufficient to support the total number of people at a destination, both local inhabitants and tourists, then the full potential of the superstructure elements, especially hotels, will not be realised. Customer dissatisfaction may be high as a result of the failings of the infrastructure. If local transport is inadequate and results in long, tiresome journeys, with delays and bottlenecks between say, the airport and the hotels, all travellers will be inconvenienced. Tourists may then avoid return visits. Worse still, the stories they tell their friends, embellished in the retelling and by time, may deter other potential visitors. This will inhibit the development of the tourist trade to that resort. Similarly, if the accommodation is of poor quality or there is severe overcrowding, tourists will be displeased. Again they will not return and may persuade others to go elsewhere.

In an ideal situation the infrastructure should be created in advance of wholesale development of hotels, restaurants and associated attractions. The timing has to be carefully planned. For existing resorts a careful balance has to be maintained between the infrastructure and superstructure. However the infrastructure usually covers a substantial area, takes considerable time to create and involves substantial capital investment. Because of this, it is usual for the central and/or local government to initiate work on the infrastructure. The capital required is found from public or official funds. They may also be motivated by other considerations such as improving the economy of the region, increasing the employment opportunities and increasing foreign currency earnings. Also, since the infrastructure serves the local population, who may be almost the sole users at off-peak periods of a seasonal tourist trade, this approach makes sense. None the less these facilities, bus and coach companies, airlines and others may be owned and operated by a number of private companies, not only state-owned organisations.

Superstructure elements like hotels and restaurants cover more limited areas and need less capital. They are usually developed, owned and run by private commercial companies. Only in countries where state ownership is predominant, such as India and some developing nations, will hotels be initiated and owned, perhaps in some partnership arrangement with private industry, by the state. Even then the running of the hotels will be done by a private company on a service or management agreement.

6.1 Planning and development

In practice the planning and development of tourist resorts can take many forms and involve different consortia of organisations, public and private. Thus there is not one archetypal form. Some resorts have developed spontaneously because of inherent attractions such as superb scenery, coastline or beaches, thermal springs, excellent climate and folklore. Others have grown as a result of imaginative planning by private or public interests. However it is only recently that attempts have been made to regulate and coordinate various tourism projects. This has become necessary especially where improved transport services have opened up new regions and taken increasing numbers of tourists to hitherto unexplored regions.

This put increasing strains on infrastructures created for a more static age and designed mainly to serve local residents. Industrial development also increased the flow of visitor traffic for industrial and commercial purposes. This growth was stimulated further by the interest in adding on short or long holidays at the end of business visits. It became necessary to rethink and replan infra- and superstructures. The shortage of suitable land and capital emphasised this need for more coordinated planning and development. Otherwise scarce resources would be wasted.

6.1.1 *Estimating future demand*
Estimating and forecasting the growth in demand for the elements of infra- and superstructure is just as difficult as forecasting the need for new tourism products in the future (see Section 3.5). Again, decisions will have to be made on imperfect intelligence and assumptions have to be made where necessary data is not available. These assumptions may often be inaccurate and lead to incorrect decisions. However estimat-

ing future demand may be easier for some destinations. For example, an island resort may be judged by its controlling authority to be sufficiently saturated with tourist traffic. If the authority wishes to preserve the special character or appeal of the place that originally created tourist interest, it can ban or restrict further development and entry. An example is Bali with its natural, spiritual atmosphere. Other destinations can restrict development to appeal only to the luxury trade by price or entry controls. Or they may be dependent on the vagaries of foreign exchange advantages or competitive air fares for their growth. Examples here are the USA and Far East. In addition, the nature of demand may vary. Glamorous or exotic coastal resorts and islands may get mainly excursionists off cruise ships with few accommodation needs. Industrial centres and those on the crossroads of international air traffic (e.g. Singapore) may get mainly short-stay visitors taking short-break holidays before moving on to other destinations.

While the volume of demand for the luxury trade may be small, it is reasonably constant. For resorts enjoying cheap fares or exchange benefits, provided these do not alter too frequently, demand can be substantial but somewhat unstable. In both cases they may be subject to normal seasonal fluctuations. Other types of tourism may fluctuate seasonally and according to changes in taste and fashion regarding holidays. All this makes it difficult to forecast demand and thus the support services needed (see also Chapter 4).

Given this difficulty in forecasting future trends, the substantial capital needed and its high cost, there is reluctance to launch out regardless, on what may prove to be a high-risk venture. The need to improve the profitability on all investments increases this reluctance. Experience in tourism also suggests that it can be unwise to assume that even the most attractive resort will enjoy indefinite growth or that the local inhabitants will accept this growth and its concomitant social costs. Economic factors alone can bring a sudden and drastic halt to growth. Another restricting factor is the shortage of skilled labour. Even if a substantial reservoir of unskilled labour is available, it takes time to train. By the time this has been done demand could have fallen substantially.

6.1.2   The planning process

In planning the infra- and superstructures, the inter-relationships between the supply components, accommodation, transport and the others, must be considered. How do or will
potential visitors view what is provided for them in relation to
their holiday objectives? Are they visiting the resort only to
spend most of their time on the beach in the sun? In this case
extensive shopping facilities may not be essential. Or are they
also interested in the area because of its reputation for producing certain items (leatherwork, shoes, clothes, wood carvings,
etc.) as well as the attractions of beach, climate or mountains?
Then the shopping facilities should be more extensive. Or are
they attracted by the local culture or food when the provision
of these should be accentuated? How extensively do they wish
to travel in the region and what forms of transport are
preferred?

Estimates of the capacity required can be made by standard
market assessments and experience. These should be adjusted
to allow for seasonality and competition from other destinations, nearby or distant. These estimates and those on the
viability of the project form the major elements of a total
feasibility study. Demand estimates are critical since they set
the scale of the whole development and the infra- and superstructures needed. The organisations providing all the services
must participate in this forecasting and planning work if a
successful development is to result (see also Chapters 3, 4 and
5).

Because of the uncertainties and the high risk involved, a
gradual stage-by-stage development is financially prudent.
However this poses other problems for the developers. For
example, they might begin by building an airport with one
runway and limited number of buildings sufficient for initial
traffic flows. Expansion could come when demand has
increased. However, extending an airport is a major undertaking and expensive and can cause considerable inconvenience to
the users for years. A recent example was the development of
Los Angeles airport for the 1984 Olympics, which took several
years. Similarly, a two-lane, twin carriageway road may be
sufficient initially. Adding a third lane in each direction will
cause traffic congestion (and accidents) for some time. Finally,
with all developments, delays can arise due to shortage of

labour, capital and equipment not to mention labour disputes.

Problems also arise with the expansion and development of existing urban areas when they become attractive to tourists. The number of people to be served by facilities designed for local residents only, can increase substantially. Expansion of the infra- and superstructure becomes necessary. When the resort is reachable by motor transport, greater car ownership and increased use of express coaches, swells the new influx.

First, accommodation facilities have to be expanded and the availability of suitable sites for this may be restricted. Then, increased road, air, rail and waterborne traffic will require development of terminals and other facilities. There is also the increased pressure on, or demand for, police services and other public utilities. Finally there is the change in the pattern of employment that would arise. Labour of all kinds may be diverted to the tourism industry from traditional work. As the competition for labour intensifies, shortages and rises in labour costs will result. Importing labour, usually foreign nationals, can lead to social and political problems.

With development of rural areas the same problems can arise. The creation of tourism infra- and superstructure will change the land usage of the area, taking substantial amounts of land away from forestry, agricultural and conservation uses. Damage to the environment and increased pollution could result if development is not carefully controlled. Improved road, rail and air networks, not just accommodation, require considerable land areas and pose problems of increased waste disposal facilities.

The need for integrated, coordinated planning and development is necessary and *ad hoc* methods must be avoided. The roles of the private and public sectors should be clearly defined to avoid duplication of work, neglect of some tasks and unnecessary competition, all of which waste resources. (Readers wishing to study more deeply the subject of tourism planning should turn to the many specialist books available, a few of which are given in the bibliography.)

6.1.3 *Decision levels*

In an ideal situation decisions on tourism planning should take place at several integrated levels.

First there should be a comprehensive *national plan* specifying the objectives to be met over about ten years and allocating resources on a 'global' basis. This will be the master plan for a nation's tourism development. Next, there should be a *regional plan* which spells out the development details for each region in which resorts are to be created or revitalised. They specify in detail the infra- and superstructure needs and the economic and social costs of them. They are usually for a shorter time scale, say about five years. Or there may be *sectorial plans* which are similar to regional plans but deal with one specific sector of tourism activity such as skiing resorts, marina and folklore development.

These last two will be supported by *programmes* covering the different components making up the regional or sectoral plans. For example, there will be one covering the building and expansion of hotels, another for other forms of accommodation, a further programme for transport development and so on. The programmes themselves will be composed of various *projects* covering the different elements of a programme (e.g. hotels – foundations and fabric; furnishings and decor; kitchens; restaurants; bars and car parks.

This approach permits effective implementation and control of tourism development intentions. It will also highlight possible problem areas. Finally, it should give a properly integrated development that should meet all the objectives stated originally for it.

6.2   Agents and types of development

Many organisations in the private and public sectors are agents or initiators of tourism projects and development. In the public sector, central or federal governments and their agencies, state and provincial authorities in the USA and France and local authorities in Britain (county councils, boroughs and others) may initiate schemes and will certainly be involved in those launched by the private sector. In many instances, these authorities will coordinate activities through a national or regional tourist organisation (see Chapter 9) or other government department. For developing countries some international organisation may be involved. This can range from some agency of the UN to the World Bank or one of its offshoots. In the private sector, large companies or consortia will take on major projects while smaller ones tackle regional and local projects.

6.2.1 Types of development

Tourism development falls into different categories. The factors influencing the type of development possible are listed in Table 6.1.

Spontaneous development may take place in a region if the scenery and climate are attractive, there are few large towns, only a collection of villages and little or no other commercial or industrial activity. An example was the Costa Brava of Spain which had a rugged coastline and a few fishing villages originally. Rapid development will result if the place appeals to the mass market, capital is available at reasonable rates and there is little or no control of development by central or local government. This assumes that total demand will be buoyant. If the existing population is small there will be ineffective

Table 6.1 Factors influencing tourism development

1 Size and extent of existing population
2 Diversity and vitality of existing activities prior to the introduction of tourism
3 Extensive or localised nature of the area
4 Whether the facilities were planned or grew spontaneously because of some natural or manmade attraction
5 Availability of land and finance
6 Impact on the local community; the resultant benefits and social costs
7 Relationship of local traditions and attitudes of local residents to the tourism project
8 Magnitude and speed of development
9 State of the local economy and possibilities of other forms of development or expansion
10 Size, dynamic nature of the local community and its facilities
11 The characteristics of the site and the financial and technical possibilities for development

protest against the anarchic development that could result. Indeed in some developing countries small local populations have been resettled elsewhere, to make way for the tourism project, when they could not be used to provide the required labour force.

With *planned, localised development* the decision follows careful analyses of all relevant points, including assessment of potential markets and the tourism capacity of the region. The economic and social costs should also be estimated. If properly planned there should be hardly any adverse effects. Examples of this form of development are to be found in Bulgaria, Roumania and parts of Malaysia. In the last case, tracts of undeveloped areas have been turned into very attractive tourist centres catering for the luxury and popular markets, without ecological damage.

In the case of *extensive developments*, whether of new complexes or expansion of existing resorts, all the points shown in Table 6.1 have to be considered. If the project is in undeveloped areas the major criteria are the net benefits that would accrue to the country (economy, foreign exchange earnings, additional revenue and others) and the damage, if any, to the ecology. In developed regions, the net social costs and the inconvenience imposed on the local population need careful assessment. All these are really different forms of the cost/benefit studies used when considering the advisability of any new business venture. This type of development may be initiated by the state, private industry or a joint venture.

Integrated development occurs when the project is undertaken by a single developer, usually a large company. If wise, the developer would check the proposal against all the points in Table 6.1, when checking the short- and long-term viabilities.

Catalytic development occurs when the activities of a major developer triggers off complementary projects by other independent organisations. It would be mutually beneficial to all parties if a high degree of cooperation could be achieved. The activities of the major developer inspires confidence and creates interest in those involved in supporting activities, whether they are creating new facilities or expanding existing ones. Provided the total development by all parties does not exceed the potential demand and capacity of the region, all is well. If the total facilities are excessive, under-utilisation of them would result. Hence the need for cooperation.

6.3 Amenities and attractions

There are several natural and manmade amenities which give appeal to a region and these are listed in Table 6.2. All of them are not found in a single location. Some may have just one or two and others have several. However if the locations or amenities are widely dispersed and some are difficult to reach, their appeal can be reduced. These attractions can be spoilt if uncoordinated or excessive development is permitted.

In addition similar attractions may exist in many locations. If some are closer to potential markets, they will have greater appeal because they are easier to reach. The region offering the right range and quality of amenities will have greater appeal than competitive locations that do not. Sometimes the political and economic structures of a country may make it difficult for coordinated development to occur. Other nations may be willing to promote development while at the same time protecting their natural assets from over-development, for the mutual benefit of the region, its local people and the tourists.

With historical and archaeological attractions their protection and preservation are important. They can be included in tour packages but the number of visitors each year may have to be controlled to prevent the destruction or deterioration of the site or building. Careful and skilful maintenance is also vital. Since the traditions, folklore and handicrafts of a country are usually linked to historical sites, their inclusion into the packages mentioned above would make sense. By highlighting them, local residents may be encouraged, with the government, to revitalise and maintain their folklore and handicrafts. Otherwise they may go into decline and eventually be lost forever. Nevertheless proper presentation of them is necessary.

On the other hand, festivals usually have religious origins. They occur at specific times of the year and are of short duration. They may not be well known, tourists may have difficulty in obtaining information about them and they may occur in regions difficult to reach. Tourism authorities should

Table 6.2 Tourist attractions

Scenic
   Natural beauty
   Spectacular panorama
   Wildlife, flora and other fauna
   Attractive beaches or mountain locations
   National, game or safari parks

Cultural
   Historical buildings and monuments
   Areas of historical significance
   Culture, religion
   Archaeological sites

Traditional activities
   Art
   Folklore and unique crafts
   Other handicrafts
   Music
   National festivals
   Native life and customs

Entertainments
   Cinemas and theatres
   Cuisine
   Nightlife
   Health resorts and spas
   Recreation parks and associated amusements
   Sporting activities (participation or viewing)
   Zoos and oceanariums

Climate
   Hours of sunshine and low rainfall
   Temperatures
   Weather generally

encourage selected operators to include these attractions in appropriate packages, while at the same time controlling the total influx of visitors. Otherwise the spirit and purpose of the festivals may be destroyed. Many countries now present many stylised shows (dance and other) for tourists which bear only a passing resemblance to the originals. In the process the essential spirit and purpose are lost and eventually the true folklore or religious basis may be lost. The synthetic replaces the authentic, which is a pity. Tourism authorities should ensure that their countries do not fall into this pit.

6.4 Resource evaluation and analysis

The 'resources' from which tourism projects are evolved include:

(a) locational and geographic factors (scenery, climate, land availability, accessibility and transport facilities);
(b) accommodation (existing and that can be created);
(c) historical aspects and festivals, as mentioned above;
(d) other manmade facilities (including art galleries, concert halls and the like);
(e) the supporting infra- and superstructure;
(f) labour availability.

Further, there is a correlation between the attractions on offer and the distance people are prepared to travel to enjoy them. Things that appeal to the local populace are usually within ten or fewer miles from their target markets. Sub-regional attractions are those which appeal to people who are within a 30-mile radius of them. Those with wider appeal, or with some unique aspect, will attract people from 45 miles or more and from abroad. Thus the Channel resorts appeal to people living in London, the Home Counties and Southeast England. Many may be day trippers. The Cotswolds appeal to the same people and those from the Midlands. However the attraction of historical sites and those connected with the culture of England attract people from all over the country and from abroad.

For most countries the climate is a critical 'resource'. The ideal for coastal resorts is long hours of sunshine and in peak seasons, limited rainfall (preferably at dead of night!) with a temperature range that avoids excessive heat and great differences between daily maximum and minimum temperatures.

For hill stations as in India and other tropical zones, summer temperatures should be moderate, humidity should be low and there should be maximum number of hours of sunshine with minimum rainfall. Island resorts are often considered best for winter holidays but it must be remembered that some (e.g. Mauritius) are very humid in December, or have their main rainy season then.

Other major constraints on development include restrictions on land tenure and use, and questions of access. There may be legal constraints, building codes and zoning regulations. Some regions (for example near national parks) may have restrictions on the amount of commercial accommodation that would be permitted. Similar constraints may apply to transport facilities. Other regions may limit the height and size of accommodation units or have regulations aimed at stopping land speculation resulting from proposed tourism developments. In some countries land in areas of great beauty may be state owned or controlled, involving several agencies. Cautious development by government agencies may then provide the main impetus but in other countries joint ventures may be encouraged.

6.4.1 *Economic, market and investment analyses*

As discussed elsewhere it is necessary to analyse the economic situation of the host country before embarking on new projects. Economic factors have considerable bearing on the success or failure of such ventures. With tourism, some of these economic factors may have different effects than in other industries. For example, a weak pound sterling is beneficial for incoming tourist traffic. If foreign nationals can buy sterling more cheaply than before, more of them may be encouraged to visit the country. However for British nationals going abroad, a weak pound may discourage some and demand falls. Despite the unpleasant effects of high inflation rates, especially rising unemployment, for long-term projects with high investment costs inflation may be beneficial. It will increase revenue in money terms. If the interest charge on capital is fixed, the project will become profitable sooner. This assumes that demand will not fall too much because some people cannot afford the higher prices resulting from high rates of inflation.

Besides considering these general points, the economic analyst must also be deducing the cost data for the project. The points that should be covered include the gross investment in the venture, the related depreciation and the discounted cash flows. These are normally done in conjunction with financial analysts or accountants. Then (quarterly) capital requirement and cash equity schedules can be prepared. The developer can then estimate the total investment needed, what proportion can be covered by interim financing and how much by cash/equity during the construction stage.

All this cannot be done effectively if market factors are ignored. The market analyst will have to study the potential total visitor market for the project, what other resorts will be major competitors and what unique propositions (or attractions) the new resort will have to attract business away from the competitors? In addition, the success rates of the latter, their operating costs, prices and quality ranges should also be known. The market specialists will then have to advise the development team on the capacity that is required at specific prices and quality standards, the usage/occupancy rates that can be expected and the time when the new project may be opened and launched.

The basic aim is to get a good balance between estimated construction costs and trends in market prices and demand. If a satisfactory balance is not possible the team will have to consider what reduction in quality is permissible or what items may be omitted or if a really unique factor could be added to justify the higher prices that would have to be asked. In some cases the entire proposal may have to be reconsidered (see also section 9.3).

6.5 Future policies

It is possible that any increased demand for tourism will be for areas already substantially developed, possibly at the limit of their capacity. Even when demand is for new destinations it is important that the mistakes made with earlier developments are not repeated. Further, protection and conservation of the environment must feature strongly in future policies.

With unrestricted growth of tourism, resorts and other towns or cities can be swamped with more and more hotels, apartment blocks, holiday homes, fast roads, restaurants, car parks, aerodromes, playgrounds, sports centres, caravan and camping sites. The importance of maintaining the environment can be overlooked. Yet the environment and its attractions are the prime resources of the tourism industry. In other businesses capital can be lost but new funds can be obtained to revitalise the firm. With tourism, once the environment or ecology have been destroyed they can never be regained. So future policies must take all these points into consideration.

These policies should indicate ways by which existing facilities may be better utilised thus limiting expansion needs. They should also set limits to the size and style of tourism projects and carefully designate which areas may be used for tourism development and which cannot. It is suggested also that these policies should shift the responsibility for pollution control to the developers and operators of resorts since they stand to gain from their operation. The need for better control of tourism development arises because of the irreversible nature of the development processes, the vulnerability of the environment and its vital role in the maintenance of all forms of life, fauna *and* flora.

All this means more than just passing laws to regulate tourism. Inventories of any unused land suitable for tourism and the designation of areas for tourism development, the acquisition and restoration of city centres and historic sites are also needed. Measures will also be required to combat purely profit-motivated and irresponsible development and their harmful effects on the ecology and other resources.

6.6   Skirmish in Paradise – an Australian case

Yeppon is a town on the coast of central Queensland, Australia's 'Sunshine State'. Its 6000 inhabitants consider it a paradise. The climate is said to be glorious, days of cloudless sunshine with cooling breezes in the summer. The views are superb, miles of white sandy beaches, undulating coves, tropical islands and deep blue water. There is no industry or pollution, traffic lights or parking meters! There is no petty crime, houses are left with their doors unlocked and valuables can be kept on the seats of unlocked cars. There are good schools, a good if small hospital and the necessary shops and other services. Naturally the local inhabitants wish to keep it that way.

In 1980, a Japanese businessman whose enterprises had expanded into the creation of leisure and tourist resorts, visited the area. His eyes fell on some 20,000 acres (8000 hectares) of beachfront land just north of the town. The beach here is ten times longer and wider than Waikiki and he saw it as the most beautiful, natural resort in the world. He saw the possibility of a large, international holiday 'village' with a variety of accommodation and golfing, fishing and other sporting facilities, wildlife parks, marina and botanical gardens, featuring Australian and imported flora. A wildlife reserve, bird sanctuary, nature and forest reserves were planned. The proposed five luxury hotels, ten motels, 85 holiday units and 1200 villas would provide accommodation for 18,000 tourists at a time. He estimated the development cost in 1983 as £63 million.

The state government took the views of the Australian Heritage Commission and the Queensland Ornithological Society, amongst others, and then announced that the scheme had been approved. From the start the local inhabitants, some more than others, objected. They saw that their way of life would be disrupted, feared what effect the influx of so many tourists would have on the area and disliked the prospect of having at least 4000 people on their beaches at any one time. Attempts to win over the locals, including a party when the guests were entertained by Japanese drummers, dancing girls and fireworks, appeared to have failed. In November 1981 a bomb exploded under the A$3 million Iwasaki motel then in the final stages of construction and did an estimated A$300,000 worth of damage. Legal (criminal) proceedings followed.

Although the development has progressed and by 1983 the motel had been completed and work on the first golf course had progressed well, considerable resentment is still felt by many of the inhabitants. This is despite the fact that the businessman and his wife have jointly pledged a total of A$5 million for the building of a retirement home near the resort. They also created a Scholarship Foundation for youths from Yeppon who wished to visit and study in Japan.

This case illustrates the problems that can face tourism developers especially when big projects are involved. The need to carry local inhabitants with a project and to convince them that their way of life would not be spoilt (at least too much!) is obvious.

Assignments

1   You are a member of a team formed to consider the creation of a tourist complex in a sparsely developed part of a foreign country, on an otherwise deserted coastline. Roads and other services are rudimentary. What are the major points that must be considered when planning the infra- and superstructure that would be needed? Specify the type of resort and holiday facilities contemplated.

2   The scheme is approved. Prepare an outline of the planning process and timing that would be needed. Which facilities should be constructed first? What tourist traffic flows are intended? How may initial facilities be expanded to meet growing demand?

3   How would you establish the maximum capacity for the resort? What steps would you recommend to protect the environment and minimise pollution?

4   How would you evaluate and analyse the resources, local and imported, which would be needed? How would you use or exploit natural resources and attractions?

7

The Marketing Mix

This and the next chapter will discuss briefly the major aspects of marketing relevant to tourism management. Readers wishing to learn more about marketing are advised to read one of the other books by this author, *Mastering Marketing* published in the *Mastering Series* by the Macmillan Press Ltd (2nd edn, 1984). Other titles listed in the Bibliography will also be helpful.

7.1 Activities and purpose

The management activities normally considered the responsibility of a marketing division or department are listed and summarised in Table 7.1. However, some of them may be carried out by separate departments of equal standing with marketing, if the volume of work is substantial or complex, or forms the main business of the company. For example, a major company making and selling an extensive range of consumer durables (cookers, refrigerators, freezers, washing machines, irons, toasters and other small appliances used in the home) had a sales department under a sales director. The marketing department, under a marketing director, handled all the other activities shown in the table. In reality the latter department was a 'marketing services department'. The physical distribu-

Table 7.1 Basic marketing techniques

A MARKETING RESEARCH

(i) *Economic research:* study of the economy of a country, region, industry or market to establish key economic and related facts. Should indicate what is happening in the economy under study.

(ii) *Market research:* more detailed study of a market, however defined, to identify total demand or volume of business available for products/services under study. Should also show how demand is growing or declining, competitors active in market, market shares, ruling market prices, trends, developments and market factors affecting all these.

(iii) *Demand studies:* even more detailed study of specific products/services to establish clearer picture of what is happening to demand for them, especially if results from (ii) above are not specific enough for marketing purposes, or when some special aspect requires detailed study.

(iv) *Consumer studies:* detailed study of specific types of consumer to establish their '*consumer profile*', i.e. their behaviour as buyers, propensity to buy a product/service, why, how, when and what they buy, likes, dislikes, prejudices, etc. Important when planning marketing strategy and policy, selecting markets and segmenting markets (see Sections 7.4 and 7.5).

(v) *Competitor research:* detailed study of competitors, their products/services and prices, how, when and where they compete, etc., i.e. to establish the 'competitor profile' for a specific market, product/service and customer group, why they are successful, etc. Needed if information from (ii), (iii) and (iv) above is insufficient for marketing purposes.

(vi) *Product research:* studies to discover what products or services are required or being bought, their specification and the performance needed, the price that customers would pay for the 'right' product, its expected lifespan, etc. Helps to determine what a company's product or service range should be.

(vii) *Sales research:* studies the pattern and nature of the sales being realised, or that could be realised, the sales potential of an area, purchases by the different categories of customers and the trends and developments in all these aspects. Also can determine how successful the sales operations are, whether any changes are needed to the sales force, territorial allocations, sales quota, methods, etc., because of changes in customer needs, taste, preferences, competition or technology.

(viii) *Distribution research:* to establish how a manufacturered product may be distributed through wholesalers, retailers, other 'middlemen' to the ultimate customer or user and with a better service, counter competition. For Tourism and Hotels, it can indicate the most efficient way of distributing information about the services (tours, etc.) to potential customers. In both cases, can indicate how distribution costs can be controlled. For goods, also establishes the number, size and location of depots, size of inventories, the mode of transport and types of 'middlemen' to be used.

(ix) *Promotional research:* helps to determine what advertising, sales promotions and public relations activities are needed, the nature and timing of them and the resultant costs. Or what can be done for a given expenditure budget. Helps with decisions on the media to be used. Used also to measure the effectiveness or success of current methods and how these should be altered to meet changing market conditions.

(x) *Effectiveness of research methods:* used when it is necessary to check the effectiveness of the marketing research methods being used, their costs and timing. Can also indicate when methods, etc., need to be changed due to changing market conditions or development of new methods.

(xi) *Pricing studies:* more detailed studies of pricing is needed from time to time, to match market and competitive developments and to check how price sensitive or elastic markets may be. Used when the intelligence needed is more complex than can be obtained through market or demand studies.

(xii) *Other studies:* it is sometimes also necessary to establish

Table 7.1 Basic marketing techniques

what packaging and merchandising methods are needed
or to determine if current methods are as effective as
they should be, or if any changes in them are advisable.

B PRODUCT MANAGEMENT
(i) *Managing existing products:* maintaining the profitability,
market shares and sales of successful, current products/
services, seeking new customers or applications,
especially any markets or customers that have been
overlooked. Watching the pricing and costs of these
products/services especially *vis-à-vis* what competitors
are doing.
(ii) *Product modification:* modifying the specification, nature
or style of the product/service to meet changing market
conditions, competition or technology, to extend the life
of the product/service. Used also to avoid cost increases
and hence price rises, or to reduce costs to permit price
reductions or increase profit margins. Necessary also if
the original concept or specification was wrong or has
not been accepted by potential customers.
(iii) *Product rationalisation:* the planned removal of a product/
service that has become obsolete, or can no longer earn
sufficient profit and modifications are not possible
because of costs or other technical reasons. This may
be brought about by changes in market conditions,
changes in customer needs, etc., or the introduction of a
new product/service by competitors.
(iv) *New product development:* because all products/services
have a finite life and have to be rationalised at some
time, if a company wishes to remain in business, it must
have a programme for seeking out new ideas and
converting these into profitable, commercial new
products or services. The work involves the assessment
of new ideas and the planning and launching of those
that appear to be the most viable with good long-term
profit prospects. Changes in technology, market
conditions, competition and customer needs also make
this a critical part of the work of product management.

(v)   *Pricing and profit management:* involves decisions on the pricing and profit strategy, policies and plans to be followed, checking the performance of each product/ service and making any changes that may be necessary. Marketing works with Finance and other departments in agreeing what the company's profit targets can or should be.

C   MARKET MANAGEMENT

(i)   *Managing existing, successful markets:* making sure that operations continue successfully in the company's selected markets, keeping track of developments in customer requirements, related technology and competition. Ensuring that the marketing activities are achieving optimal results.

(ii) *Modifying markets:* the original selection of market segments may not be proving successful, or changing market conditions may be proving adverse, then the selection of additional categories of customer may be necessary. Or as the company develops, it may be possible to add other customer groups within a market segment to the operations.

(iii) *Market rationalisation:* like products, markets have a finite life, customer needs and tastes change, demographic changes occur, people move to and from other countries. The composition of a market alters and it may no longer require the products/services on offer. If the company does not wish to change its products, it must then make a planned, phased withdrawal from what has become an unprofitable market.

(iv) *New market development:* to counter the effects of (iii) above and if a company wishes to grow, develop and survive into a long-term future, it must find, assess and develop new markets. Here it seeks new markets where its resources can be more profitably employed.

D   COMMUNICATIONS MIX

The work and responsibilities under this general heading are as follows:

Table 7.1 Basic marketing techniques

D1 Promotional activities

(i) *Advertising:* 'a paid form of promotional activity (usually) by an identified sponsor', it involves decisions on the media to be used, type, nature, size, content, timing and frequency of the advertisements required. Also the number of colours to be used and the advertising theme and message. All these influence the 'impact' of the advertising campaign.

(ii) *Sales promotions:* special activities for a limited period used at peak sales periods to obtain optimal sales or market shares, to help to launch new products/services or to support ailing ones. The activities include the preparation and distribution of brochures, leaflets, poster and point-of-sale display material as well as special price offers, free offers, competitions, tent cards, exhibitions, seminars and conferences, etc.

(iii) *Public relations (PR):* includes 'press relations' (pr) and seeks to keep public and press fully and correctly informed of the company's activities, achievements and future intentions. Involves distribution of information through press releases, etc., hopefully to obtain free editorial matter in selected media (e.g. news on new tours and other travel aspects). Open days, special lunches or dinners, exhibitions and conferences all play roles in PR.

D2 Sales management

Responsible for all activities of the sales operation. This involves:

(i) Planning the size, nature and extent of the personal selling activities and the size, location, qualifications and experience of the sales staff.

(ii) Selecting the administrative and the other methods to be used and the size, nature, experience and qualifications of the sales office staff.

(iii) Recruitment, remuneration and training of the sales staff, especially the sales force.

(iv) Devising a suitable information and monitoring system

to keep track of results v plans and so recommend any changes necessary.

D3 Packaging

The attractively designed and printed outer wrapper of consumer goods (particularly) which with the brand name helps to identify the product and attract the attention of potential customers. Work involves decisions on the design, layout, number of colours used, size and type of print, etc. For tour operators their travel brochure cover is the packaging element of their 'products'. For travel agents, the decor and layout of their sales offices can be judged thus also.

D4   Merchandising

Involves a special display of the product, in carefully selected positions in a shop, supported by attractive posters, banners, display cards, etc. and sometimes pretty girls. Meant to attract the attention of customers. For tour operators, the layout of their packages in the brochure and supporting photographs fulfil this function. With travel agents, the display of posters and brochures and friendly, cheerful staff fulfil that function.

E   PHYSICAL DISTRIBUTION MANAGEMENT

(i)   *Depots:* deciding on the number, size and location of depots and whether they should be owned, leased or rented.

(ii)   *Inventories and inventory control:* involves decisions on the size of inventories, maximum, minimum and re-ordering levels, cost control, method of storage, location of stocks, etc.

(iii)   *Channels of distribution:* which middlemen to be used (wholesalers, retailers, agents, distributors, franchisees, etc.); terms of agreement, discounts, etc.

(iv)   *Transport:* whether to use road, rail, sea, air or any combinations; size and composition of fleet, whether to own, lease, contract-hire, etc. Control of maintenance, replacement and costs.

(v)   *Administration:* all administrative matters including appropriate paperwork, insurance, heating, lighting, security, overall cost control, etc. Staff recruitment, etc.

Table 7.1   Basic marketing techniques

F   OTHER ACTIVITIES
The following may also be used in the marketing operation if
these prove necessary and beneficial:
TELEPHONE SELLING
SYSTEMS SELLING
COMMANDO MARKETING ACTIVITIES

---

tion work could also be under the sales department where these
two functions are closely related and are critical to the sustained profitability of the company. Or a company distributing
other firms' products would have distribution and the selling of
that service as its main department, with such support services
as it needs under the control of a marketing services department.

Tour operators, although they may not call it such, will have
a 'marketing department' in the traditional sense, that is one
responsible for all the marketing activities including selling. Its
market research, product research and development, advertising, sales promotion (including brochure design and production), public relations and selling should then be properly
integrated and balanced as a result. A few even give special
attention to quality control (of the components of its packages)
and have a quality control director. Travel agents on the other
hand are primarily concerned with selling the packages and
travel facilities they handle, with any supporting advertising
and promotional activities that may be necessary or advisable.

However the marketing work is organised, the aim is simple.
It should be divided into appropriate parts that allow the
persons responsible to do the work efficiently and effectively.

7.1.1   Purpose and aims

The purpose of marketing is to apply the rational and logical
use of people, money, materials and other resources to the
changing conditions of the present age to ensure profit, survival
and growth over the longest possible period. It involves the
systematic application of entrepreneurship to business situa-

tions. It must assess objectively, every factor important to the business so that decisions are based on judgement which is itself based on as much relevant knowledge as is possible or practical to obtain. The use of 'hunchplay' is doomed to failure especially as business situations become more complex and competitive and every decision becomes more far-reaching in its effects.

The aims of good marketing may be summarised as follows:

(a) provide a means of assessing, classifying and integrating relevant information – the mere accumulation of facts is not enough;

(b) provide a sound basis for studying business problems to allow correct decisions to be made which will form the basis for action;

(c) explain, predict and control the marketing processes used, not just interpreting the facts but also showing their inter-relationships;

(d) employ analytical methods to solve problems – these are based on methods drawn from economic, statistical, sociological and psychological theories;

(e) allow a derivation of a number of principles of market-. ing behaviour particular to a specific business.

Marketing principles and practice can be applied to any business large or small whether in manufacturing or service industries. However not all the activities in Table 7.1 are needed by every business. Careful selection of relevant ones is necessary. The main constraints are the needs of the business and the money and time that can be allocated to the marketing function.

Marketing's main aim may also be described as improving the profit and sales of a firm. It will not do so if the executives are ignorant of what marketing is and what the techniques can and *cannot* do. The inter-relationships and interdependence of these techniques must also be known. For example, there is little point in spending a lot of money and time on massive market research if the company is in no position to use the gathered intelligence, or if the cost exceeds any financial benefit that might accrue. However, if the research shows that further capital expenditure on a project would be fruitless, then the research is worth doing.

Marketing will fail to achieve its aims if the techniques are used blindly without thought to their relevance to the business and its objectives. The *ad hoc* use of techniques is useless. A common failure here is to do marketing research as and when the firm has the time and money to spare! It must all be part of an integrated and carefully thought through marketing plan. Finally, failure to realise the relevance, importance and cost involved in the application of marketing may lead only to the ultimate failure of the business.

Marketing encompasses a wide range of activities and requires close and regular cooperation with colleagues from the other departments of a firm. The range of this work is summarised in Table 7.2.

Table 7.2   Marketing's contributions to the management process

1   Working with colleagues from the other departments to agree a company's plans for the future, agreeing objectives and targets (profit, profitability, revenue, return on capital, future rates of growth, new investments, etc., i.e. formulating the corporate plan).

2   Evaluating the resources, skills, experience, knowledge, strengths and weaknesses of the company (especially the Marketing department) to indicate the product range and mix the company could handle (e.g. the range and mix of package tours and other travel services).

3   Identifying, assessing and selecting the markets or market segments in which the company should do business (e.g. the areas and types of customers – income or social groups – that will be the 'target markets' for the company's products).
This and the work under 2 above form the product-market management of the company. See Section 7.6 and Chapters 5 and 6 in *Mastering Marketing*.

4   Establishing in the above work the product specifications (type, nature and location of hotels and rooms; countries and resorts; mode of transport – air, road, rail, sea – and timing

and duration of journeys; excursions and other attractions and services to be offered). Also the pricing strategy, policies and prices and discounts to be followed.

5 Estimating the potential demand for the selected product-market situations and the market shares possible.

6 Identifying the promotional and selling activities that will be needed to achieve the intended profit, revenue and market shares and to stimulate and create demand, especially for new products.

7 Deciding on the methods to be used in distributing information on the package tours and other travel products to potential customers and the subsequent confirmation of bookings and distribution of tickets and other documents to the customers.

8 Selecting the middlemen (e.g. travel agents, etc.) to be used in the selling and distribution process and the associated terms of agreement with them.

9 Working closely with those responsible for advance reservations of hotel rooms, transport seats, etc., to ensure that the resultant packages are as required and can be sold.

10 Calculating, checking and controlling the costs of the above to ensure that the intended prices are possible and that the target profit, revenue and return can be achieved.

11 Monitoring the results and new information being obtained to check that the company is on course.

7.1.2 *Definition*

There are several definitions of marketing. The one currently in use by the British Institute of Marketing is: 'Marketing is the management process responsible for identifying, anticipating and satisfying customer requirements profitably.' However, marketing may be more fully described as set out in Table 7.3.

7.1.3 *Marketing tourism products*

Tourism products are in reality intangible services! Although the components of a package tour are tangible items that exist in some physical form (accommodation, transport seats) the package tour and other travel services are intangible. They

Table 7.3 The eight key points about marketing

1 Marketing is a philosophy that believes that a business and its decisions should be governed by its markets or customers and their needs rather than by its own desires. Its resources should be tailored to match market demand as closely as possible.
2 It is an orderly, systematic process of business planning, execution and control.
3 It requires an improved form of commercial organisation.
4 It employs improved methods and systems based on scientific laws drawn from economics, statistics, finance and the behavioural sciences.
5 It involves a system of commercial intelligence (information and statistics) relevant to its markets or customers, competitors and its own industry.
6 It places strong emphasis on innovation.
7 It is a method of achieving dynamic business strategy.
8 It is a form of management by objectives.

cannot be sampled, weighed or otherwise assessed before use. The special characteristics of services, as set out in Table 7.4, apply to them. These have important implications for the marketing of tourism products, especially when linked to the special characteristics of tourism as discussed in Section 3.4.

First, the forecasting of demand and the marketing planning and operations must be done more carefully and with greater precision. Overestimating demand for example, will mean that capacity will exceed the sales potential and market shares that could be realised. Underestimate demand and business and profit potential will not be fully exploited. Next, the facilities are inflexible. So a firm geared to holidays in Spain, say, on finding that its resources are not being fully used, will not be able to switch quickly to other destinations. It takes time to find the resorts, accommodation and transport needed and to make advance reservations. Further, the tour operator may not have the staff experienced in, or knowledgeable about, the new country. Time will be needed to retrain staff or recruit new people. In every case the profitability of the business will be adversely affected.

Table 7.4 Special characteristics of services

Intangibility

Services cannot be touched, weighed, seen, measured, heard or sampled. They do not exist in physical form like manufactured products ('tangible goods'). Potential buyers cannot judge quality or what they will actually get before use. Tourists for example only know what is actually provided by a package tour, regardless of descriptions in a brochure, when they actually go on that tour.

Perishability

Their utility is shortlived. They cannot usually be made ahead of the time of their demand (though packaged tours are created in advance because of the need for advance reservations of rooms, transport, seats, etc.). So they cannot be stored to meet peak demand periods as can tangible goods. (The elements of package tours can be stored through the forward reservation mechanism. However because of the rigidity of the supply components – see Section 3.4.1 – if the forecast of future demand is wrong, the tour operator will face marketing and other problems.) So the utility and potential profit margin of an unused hotel room or transport seat is lost immediately for the period of their non-use.

Standardisation

Difficult if not impossible for offerings of the same service by different suppliers. Nor can a seller guarantee consistency at all times. Potential customers have difficulty in making evaluations and hence choice and buying decisions. Because of these three points, reputation of seller plays key role in the buying decisions. (The reputation of a large well-established company like Thomson Holidays outweighs that of a small, local, newly established tour company.) Creative marketing needed to show how any service meets the needs of individual buyers.

Table 7.4 Special characteristics of services

Value

Because of the above it is difficult for potential customers to judge the 'value' before purchase and consumption of the service. With tourism products value is judged subjectively and depends on individual attitudes, prejudices, preferences and relevant knowledge.

Buyer behaviour and involvement

Thus the behaviour of individual buyers affects decisions. Sellers must also ensure that potential buyers specify clearly what they want and that these statements are interpreted correctly (e.g. what does the prospective tourist mean by a 'quiet holiday'? Some may want to laze on a beach all day. Others may want to get away from children or escape from their normal lives by visiting historical sites, art galleries, museums, concerts, etc.).

Heterogeneity

Services are usually designed around the specialised needs of individuals or firms (e.g. insurance policies, business travel) hence their heterogeneity. However some services are capable of standardisation (tour operators sell a standard set of holidays to all) but customers' individualised needs still result in heterogeneity.

Inseparability

For many services production and consumption occur at the same time.

Ownership (lack of)

Use of a service facility does not mean that ownership of it passes to the user. Hotel rooms, transport seats, etc. are only hired for a specific period. They remain the property of the proprietors.

In situ *nature of the business*

The service company must have all the necessary resources in place before business can begin. Insurance companies must have all its specialists and other staff *in situ* before it can offer insurance cover. In some countries they must also satisfy the authorities that they have the necessary financial guarantees. Tour operators and travel agents must also do the same and make the necessary advance reservations.

Then, since buying decisions are usually based on subjective views and greatly influenced by personal traits and attitudes, knowledge of human behaviour and motivations is necessary. Finally, greater care is necessary in the selection of marketing techniques to be used and their adaptation to the needs of the business.

Potential tourists have to form their judgements on indirect information from friends, travel brochures and articles in newspapers and magazines. Even if they have visited a resort, because of the long time periods between purchases (twelve months or more) and the fact that their needs and attitudes can change, they lack assurance that they have made the right decision. Uncertainty prevails! Thus tour operators and travel agents must not only present what is on offer clearly but also understand how different types of customers will interpret the information. This is why greater attention is being given to the psychological aspects of leisure and tourism.

The important questions that need answering include those identifying the aspirations of tourists regarding their holidays and recreation. Then there is the tourists' awareness of the choices available, how they become aware of these, what criteria they use to assess them, how they weigh these in arriving at their decisions and the information they need to reach correct decisions? Once they have selected their holidays, what processes do they use to evaluate their experience and what role does experience play in reaching future decisions? Finally, what is remembered and ignored in evaluating the experience, what criteria are used and does membership of a social or work group influence these points? Those wishing to study the psychological aspects of buying decisions in tourism should read the books on this subject.

Apart from these points, the marketing requirements of tour operators and travel agents, as well as carriers, are very similar to that for other industries. The firm must identify the products (package tours and other travel facilities) required by the different types of customers forming the target markets. It must estimate the total demand for each product, the pattern of that demand (value, time of year when required, any seasonality and fluctuations in demand), the competitors active in the field, their prices and market shares and thus the prices and market shares possible for the firm. Executives should also find out what elements comprise the packages offered by competitors (resorts, accommodation, types of rooms, carriers, aircraft used, timing and duration of flights), all of which should be obvious from a study of other firms' brochures. This information will guide the executives on the 'specifications' for their own products and the unique or special aspects that could be included to make their packages more competitive – have greater appeal to potential customers. In other words, all this intelligence will indicate the product-market opportunities open to the firm.

Having established the above, the firm must then consider how their products could be best marketed to their selected target markets. This involves decisions on the methods to be used (advertising, sales promotion, PR), the media needed, the theme and message of the promotional campaign, its timing, frequency of use and permitted expenditures (these aspects are covered in the next chapter on 'Communications Mix'). Finally they must decide how the information required by consumers should be distributed and the system required to handle reservations and the issue of tickets. For management control purposes there should be some information feedback procedure showing how the product offerings are being accepted, why some customers prefer competitors' products, how customers arrive at their decisions and the changes occurring in all market conditions as well as the points mentioned above.

7.1.4 *Marketing business travel facilities*

Marketing these facilities is considered easier than marketing other tourism products. The purpose of a visit and the choice of destination are known. These decisions are based on rational factors – the needs of the business – and not on impulse. So also are the timing and duration of each trip and, on most occasions, the route selected. Regarding the last however, irrational aspects can creep in as, for example, when executives avoid a carrier at all costs because they do not like their service, or take a longer route to avoid visiting a country whose political policies are not acceptable to the executive! On these two points personal prejudice may override the true facts.

The travel agent must know what are the best and most economical routes and the most efficient carriers operating on them. Fares must be competitive and the flight schedules should fit the timetables the executives have to keep. The only 'market research' that is needed is visits to the firms to identify their needs. Then close contact is necessary between the agent and the carriers and hotel groups that might be used.

However many executives almost kill themselves by travelling in the wrong direction or by trying to do too much in a short time. They would welcome advice on routes and schedules. For example, is it better to fly clockwise or anticlockwise around Africa? Is it better to get over the trying climates first, while the executive is fresh, or leave them to the last when the traveller has acclimatised to the changing conditions? Where can rest days be best fitted into the schedule? The important questions that should be considered are listed in Table 7.5.

7.1.5 Marketing for tourist boards

The marketing requirements of tourist boards, of whatever name, vary from that of the travel trade because these bodies are not trying to make actual sales. Their aim is to influence more people to visit their regions. They wish to improve the knowledge of would-be tourists about the country or region for which they are responsible.

They are concerned with promoting interest in the attractions of the region, creating an identifiable image and increasing acceptance of the area as a good holiday zone. They should also ensure that the infra- and superstructure is adequate for the volume of tourist traffic they are trying to create. Theirs is a 'door opening' exercise. It is up to the tour operators and travel agents to build on this and sell their products to those that have been the targets for the tourist boards' marketing effort.

Some market research may be necessary to identify which countries would be the best tourist-generating areas, the types

Table 7.5 Important questions when planning business trips

---

1 What is the company's policy/practice for:
   (a) standard of accommodation?
   (b) standard of transport?
   (c) costs?
   (d) rest days on the trip?
2 What is the purpose of the trip and hence the length of stopovers required?
   (a) negotiate a new deal?
   (b) routine call on established agents?
   (c) rejuvenate a flagging market/agent/subsidiary?
   (d) showing the flag or exploratory?
3 Does the programme allow for:
   (a) the physical capacity/competence of the executive?
   (b) emergencies and other delays?
   (c) changes in transport schedules?
   (d) rest periods? should they be arranged daily (an hour or two) after each stage, or other convenient point?
4 Is sufficient time allowed for:
   (a) rest and recuperation?
   (b) preparation of paperwork, reports, etc.?
   (c) preparation for the next leg?
   (d) improving awareness of the business situation?
5 What accommodation is required:
   (a) hotel (standard), rented accommodation?
   (b) staying with friends or relatives?
6 What transportation is required for:
   (a) main legs and local trips at stopover?
   (b) to and from terminals?
   (c) any carriers to be avoided or preferred?
7 What health precautions are necessary:
   (a) with prior inoculations, etc.?
   (b) by taking the necessary medication, pills, etc., on the trip?
   (c) by avoiding contaminated food, water, etc.?
8 What can be done to minimise 'jet lag'?
9 What personal ailments have to be considered?
10 Any other special requirements (food, etc.)?

---

of consumers involved and their profiles regarding holiday requirements. The tourist boards should also conduct research to provide essential basic facts of relevance to the travel trade but is too extensive for the financial resources of individual firms in the travel trade. Then there is the collation and presentation of the immigration and emigration statistics collected by government departments and their agencies. These are useful aids to successful planning of tourism marketing.

Then the tourist boards should organise and coordinate the advertising and public relations programmes of the trade. Their own campaigns will be of a more generalised nature (for example, 'Come to beautiful . . .') or promoting festivals and cultural activities. It may also be necessary to organise familiarisation or educational visits by travel agents in the selected tourist-generating areas. These campaigns should keep in mind the interests and susceptibilities of the target consumers. If they are interested in history, this aspect of the region should be promoted prominently. If there is an ethnic link, as between Britain and Australia, New Zealand and North America, this can feature in campaigns in the last three zones. Market research and consumer studies will reveal these and other relevant facts. They will show in which prospective markets potential demand is great enough to offer a sufficient volume of business. If the potential demand is greater than the resources of the region in mind, the target markets to be exploited have to be chosen carefully.

Since the industry is composed of a large number of independent organisations (accommodation, carriers and the providers of support services) there is need for the marketing effort to be closely coordinated. The tourist boards are best placed to play this role and be the lynchpin of the industry. In this they must also keep an eye on changes and developments taking place and alert their partners to these trends.

7.2 The marketing mix

The meaning of the word 'mix' in marketing is explained in the 'Glossary of Terms' (Appendix B). It refers to how much of each technique should be used and when, how and where they

will be employed. It is used in the future tense when referring
to plans for a specific future period of time, or in the past tense
when referring to previous activities.

7.3 Marketing research

It will be appreciated from the foregoing that all businesses
require considerable, relevant intelligence if the resultant
marketing activity is to prove successful. The activities under
this heading were listed in Section A of Table 7.1. Of course,
not all these studies are necessary at one time. If they are the
company is in serious trouble! The trick is to select those that
provide the relevant and critical intelligence needed to resolve
the problem under study.

In marketing, 'intelligence' includes 'data' (the statistical
facts of the situation) and 'information' (descriptive material)
that gives the rationale of what is happening and explains the
purpose of the data. In theory the range of intelligence needed
for tourism purposes is immense, as shown in Table 7.6. How
much of this can be researched depends on the budget possible.
Happily, much of it can be constructed from experience over
several years, published official statistics and the records of the
firm.

The results of any research should help the firm to understand the nature and structure of domestic and international
markets so that tourists' needs and the resources of the resort
can be better matched to optimise profit, sales and customer
satisfaction. They help to choose the right target markets,
destinations, attractions and facilities and the promotional
activities necessary. For tour operators they indicate what the
components of the packages should be.

The methods that can be employed range from *desk research*
involving the study of published (secondary) intelligence and
field research to uncover new (primary) intelligence. In the latter
case the most often used methods are sample surveys which use
a carefully selected fraction of a total population to study the
characteristics of that population, motivation research which
identifies the motives behind human behaviour, especially their
buying decisions, and models. The last are simplified represen-

Table 7.6 Range of intelligence needs for tourism management

A On tourists/travellers

1 *Opinions and attitudes* (on image of destinations/countries; tourist products available; competitors and their offerings; prices; product quality and service standards; promotional and selling activities; distribution channels most used and most effective; past experience of tour operator/travel agent).

2 *Travel behaviour and motivations* (main motivations for travel/touring; travel pattern – in groups, pairs, singly, by families, etc.; expensive, median or cheap journeys/holidays; destinations and holiday activities; type and location of accommodation; mode of transport used or required; timing and duration of visits; other attractions required or expected; services at hotels. Actual reactions to prices, destinations and tourist products. Response to marketing effort. Estimated changes in all the above.)

B On markets

1 *Characteristics and trends/developments* (size, major segments, location, demographic details. Market shares and development. Trends by market segments and type of product and method of distribution.)

2 *Distribution* (roles of tour operators, travel agents, NTOs and tourist information centres especially abroad. Effect of centralised, computerised reservation systems. Effect of direct selling and selling via clubs, universities, factories, trade unions, etc. In-shop counters in departmental stores and supermarkets. Effect of sales of holiday homes apartment-hotels, time-sharing facilities, etc.)

C On products

1 *Natural resources* (scenery, climate, flora and fauna, suitability for sporting events, e.g. skiing, golf, etc. Protection of the environment. Anti-pollution needs or regulations.)

**Table 7.6   Range of intelligence needs for tourism
management**—*(continued)*

---

   2   *Infrastructure* (roads, rail, telecommunications, electricity,
       gas and water supplies, banks, hospitals, chemists, other
       shops, food stores, police, courts, garages, bookshops, etc.)
   3   *Superstructure* (hotels, pensions and other accommodation,
       holiday and sports complexes, marinas, restaurants, taverns,
       travel agents, car rental facilities, information offices,
       organisations supplying excursions, etc. Cinemas, theatres.)
   4   *Cultural heritage* (historical monuments, handicraft centres,
       museums, art galleries, ruins and other relics of past
       civilisation or culture, folklore shows, etc.)
   5   *Local lifestyle and customs.*
   6   *Access and transport facilities* (airports, ports, railway systems,
       rivers, lakes, etc.)

D   ON COMPETITION
   1   Competitors' marketing strategies, policies and products.
   2   Prices.
   3   Promotional activities, sales and distribution methods.

E   ON MARKET OR ENVIRONMENTAL FACTORS
   1   *Economic* (stability; types of consumers, their buyer
       behaviour, income patterns and purchasing power;
       geographical markets; motivations; employment levels.)
   2   *Social/ethical aspects* (population, life styles, education, age
       patterns, social and ethical attitudes, standards, behaviour.
       Cultural background. Whether urban or rural structure.
       Family size and spending habits. Social institutions. Travel
       and holiday tendencies.)
   3   *Political/legal matters* (political attitudes. Government
       involvement in tourism. Laws, regulations, controls.
       Taxation. Foreign exchange rates.)
   4   Changes and developments in all the above.

---

tations of real situations or phenomena. Marketing research investigates product-market situations to permit the formulation of sound marketing strategies and policies which will achieve marketing objectives (profit, revenue, market shares and growth) that have been set. The objectives are dependent on the characteristics of the market (total demand, competition, ruling market prices, etc.) and the ability of the firm's products to meet customers' needs. Marketing research can also indicate what experienced staff and control systems are required.

7.3.1 Marketing research for tourist boards
Because of the nature of the work of these boards, their marketing research needs vary from that needed by the rest of the industry. These are set out in Table 7.7. Much of this intelligence should be available from official or quasi-official sources and their own records. Thus research will be required occasionally to keep the facts up to date.

7.3.2 Sources of information
The main sources of information and data are listed in Table 7.8.

7.4 Marketing strategy and policy

Marketing strategy specifies the long-term goals and objectives of a business, identifying opportunities and the scope of activities needed to realise them. It is a broad statement of the aims to be achieved over the broad front of the business for the longest possible period of time. Marketing policies and plans will depend on what strategy has been agreed. Policies, therefore, are shorter-term action programmes concerned with the detailed application of effort and the control of the operations. If the resultant operations are to be successful, strategy and policy must integrate all the activities of research, product and market management, pricing, the communications mix and distribution. While policies should be altered to match changes in economic, market and competitive situations, strategy is normally changed only when some major change has taken

Table 7.7   Research needs of NTOs

A   TRAVEL
   1   *Existing:* number of arrivals and departures; distribution
       over the year.
   2   *Future:* trends and developments in numbers, types of
       tourists and distribution.

B   CHARACTERISTICS
   1   *Of visitors:* social groups; income groups; status; age;
       sex; family status; educational and other background.
   2   *Of visits:* origin of trip (tourist-generating areas); duration;
       mode of travel; accommodation used/required; activities;
       attractions, etc.
   3   *Motivations:* purpose of trip (holidays, business, visits to
       relatives/friends; conferences, etc.) Factors influencing
       decisions to travel; image of and attitudes to destinations;
       behaviour.
   4   *Satisfactions:* climate, scenery, attractions; facilities provided
       (accommodation, transport; shops, utilities, etc.) attitude to
       local residents.

C   DESTINATIONS
   1   *Facilities:* what has to be provided for planning and
       development (infrastructure, superstructure, quality, costs
       acceptable).
   2   *Marketability:* what can be used to market and promote
       destinations; best method and timing of this.

D   MARKETING
   1   *Markets:* existing/developed; potential/underdeveloped and
       underdeveloped.
   2   *Channels:* for promotions (advertising) and publicity (trade
       press, etc.).
   3   *Competition:* other destinations, locations, attractions, etc.
   4   *Forecasting:* of changes; projection of trends.
   5   *Impact:* of tourism on the economy, environment, society.
   6   *Role:* of NTOs, travel trade, hotels, carriers, etc.

Table 7.8 Major sources of intelligence

A	CUSTOMERS	Current; potential from current markets and those to be developed.
B	THE INDUSTRY	Tour operators; travel agents; hotels and other accommodation units; carriers; NTOs at home and overseas.
C	COMPETITORS	At home and overseas.
D	TRADE ASSOCIATIONS	At home and overseas (travel trade and those of hotels, carriers, etc.).
E	OFFICIAL STATISTICS	Government sources.
F	PUBLICATIONS	Trade and government; specialist media.
G	OTHER	Relevant publications by universities, banks, chambers of commerce, international bodies (e.g. United Nations agencies, WTO and similar travel/trade associations, EEC, etc.).
H	THE FIRM	Internal records (bills, invoices, quotations).

place in the business environment. Figure 7.1 indicates the process.

For tour operators and travel agents the choice of strategy can range from decisions to develop new growth sectors (e.g. holidays in the USA, Southeast Asia and Australia) where potential long-term demand is good, to decisions to specialise in holidays for which the company has established a good image. These could include skiing and golfing holidays, cultural holidays with academics as lecturer-guides and so on.

Another strategy could centre around vigorous new product policies such as offering packages for Seville's Holy Week or for outstanding arts festivals, literary events and concerts. Yet another could be based on renovated, formerly decaying regions and the promotion of them as holiday bases. Outstand-

Figure 7.1 Steps (simplified) in formulating marketing strategy

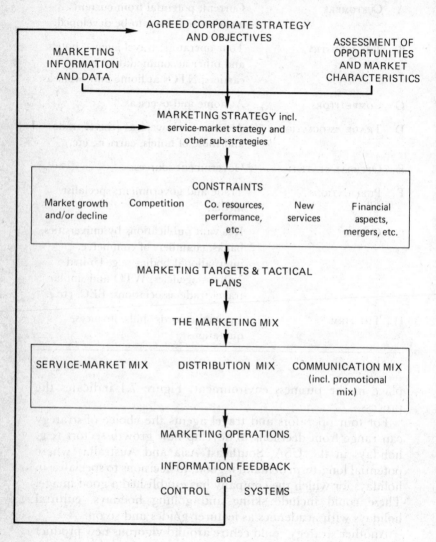

ing examples are Colonial Williamsburg, formerly derelict houses in the Dordogne and castles in Germany. Some tour operators have successfully implemented strategies that created good brand names and images for quality and reliability (e.g. Thomas Cook, American Express and Thomson Holidays).

Tourist boards have to follow a strategy aimed at improving their country's image as a tourist centre. Their objectives include increasing the number of arrivals and the expenditure of tourists, as well as increasing the length of stay at different destinations. Or they may have to persuade tourists to stay in congested resorts or towns (e.g. London) for only a few days and then move on to less congested zones (provincial holiday centres) for the rest of their vacation. Whichever of the above strategies are planned, their cost must be estimated and weighed against the resources available and the degree of risk involved.

7.5 Market strategy and policy

Market strategy and policy formulation involves decisions on all aspects of the market mix including the selection of markets or market segments to be exploited and the new markets to be developed. They must be closely related to the product and pricing strategies and policies to be followed. Usually the marketing strategy and policy set the parameters of these other activities. With long-established firms however, their market, product and other resources, knowledge and experience will indicate what products can be offered profitably to specific markets or market segments. The firm's policies will then be designed to exploit these capabilities to the full. However if long-term survival and growth are to be achieved, there must be a continuous search for new markets, products, pricing structures, communications and distribution methods. The work has been summarised in Section C of Table 7.1. How market opportunities and characteristics are identified is shown in Table 7.9.

The word 'market' is used in four distinct ways. First it can refer to the actual and potential number of customers for a tourism product or destination. Second, it can be stated as the revenue that results from customers' purchases of the tourism product. Third, it can refer to the geographical area or tourist-generating area from which the customers are drawn. Finally it can refer to the demand for a particular service or destination, for example the 'package tour market' or the market for travel to North America, the Far East or Western Europe. Care is needed in the interpretation of the sense in which the word market is being used.

Table 7.9 Identifying market opportunities and characteristics with marketing research

1 *Identifying markets and discrete market segments*
estimating total demand or market size;
identifying significant segments of total market;
measuring the coverage of the market by existing
    products or services (to deduce the new or revised/
    modified activities the company could consider).

2 *Market projections*
projections into the future (for 5, 10 or more years)
    to evaluate growth or decline of existing markets;
or changes in customer requirements, preferences, etc.;
or changes in economic, social, political, technological,
    ethical and other environmental factors which affect
    market conditions or the services being offered.

3 *Characteristics of market*
services required by customers;
function or usage of service;
essential features which the service must have;
methods used by customers in searching for services;
competitive position, including share of markets, costs/
    prices, etc. (should include projections as 2 above);
range of services to be offered;
functions critical to the success of operations offering
    services to selected markets;
commercial conditions and terms expected by
    customers;
cost/price relationship; price elasticity; possible pricing
    policy.

Identifying markets and market segments

Determining characteristics

Selecting marketing strategy. Markets and marketing operations & control and information feedback.

4 *Available market share*
estimate of market shares available;
projections of market shares as per (2) above;
company and competitors' strengths and weaknesses and how these may affect market shares;
how to modify marketing operations to improve profitability and gain increased market shares.

5 *Marketing strategy & market selection*
selection of strategy and operations (tactics) to be followed;
selection of markets and market segments to be attacked;
possible service mix to be offered;
deciding the resultant marketing plans to be implemented;
implementation and control of marketing operations incl. analysis of results being obtained, feeding new information and data into marketing planning activities and assessments.

7.5.1 Market segmentation

Except in special circumstances, for example a small specialised market where the firm has a virtual monopoly through a unique product such as foot-trekking in the Himalayas, it is no longer economically possible to serve total markets. Increased costs and competition prevent this. It is necessary to segment markets and work on a limited number of segments. Through the determination of the buying habits, patterns and preferences of different types of consumer, market segmentation attempts to split the heterogeneous (dissimilar) total market into homogeneous (similar) segments containing people with similar needs and buying habits. The market is split to give maximum heterogeneity between and maximum homogeneity within segments.

Thus consumer responses to marketing offerings should vary more between segments than within them. Besides preventing companies from doing the impossible, spreading limited resources too thinly, segmentation helps to identify opportunities quickly and clearly while permitting marketing effort to be aimed more precisely at each segment. Segments and potential customers can be more clearly identified, located and marketed more directly. Specially designed marketing mixes can be offered to them to appeal to their wants and preferences.

The variables that can be used for most businesses are listed in Table 7.10. For travel and tourism, segmentation can be by the purpose of travel as shown in Table 7.11. Market segmentation is also possible according to the stage a family has reached in its life cycle, since product and service needs and motivations change with age and family responsibilities. The

Table 7.10 Market segmentation

Variables	Possible breakdown
Socio-economic group	
Age	1–4; 5–10; 11–18; 19–34; 35–49; 50–64; 65 +
Sex	Male; femaie
Family size	1; 2; 3; 4–5; 6 and over
Income	Either by official groups (e.g. in UK, groups 1, 2, 3, 4) or by actual gross incomes.
Occupation	By official groups (1, 2, 3, etc.) or e.g. executives, professionals, clerical, sales, crafts, etc.
Education	Primary, secondary, higher; public school, university, etc.; or no. of years of formal schooling, e.g. under 7, 8, 9–11 yrs, etc.
Family life cycle	According to the age and marital status of the family (see Section 7.5.1).
Religion	Protestant, Catholic, Methodist, etc.
Nationality	British, American, German, Japanese, etc.
Social class	Either by official classifications or e.g. A, B, C1, C2, D and E.
Geographic	
Region (UK)	Southeast, East Midlands, North etc.
Area (World)	Europe, N. America, Scandinavia, etc.
Size of city	Under 5000, 5–20,000, 20–50,000, etc.
Density	Urban, suburban, rural, etc.
Climate	Northern, temperate, tropical, etc.

Personality

Compulsiveness	Compulsive, non-compulsive
Gregariousness	Extrovert, introvert
Autonomy	Independent, dependent
Attitude	Conservative, liberal, radical
Authority style	Democratic, authoritarian
Leadership style	Driver, leader, permissive leaders, follower.

Buyer behaviour

Usage rate	Non-user, light user, heavy user, etc.
Buyer class	Unaware, aware, interested, intends to try, trier, regular user
Buyer motives	Economy, status, dependability, etc.
End use	(Varies with product and service)
Brand & channel loyalty	(Classified by brands and channels used)
Price sensitivity	Indifferent, low, high, etc.
Service* sensitivity	Indifferent, low, high, etc.
Advertising sensitivity	Indifferent, low, high, etc.

*Service here = after-sales services or the way a product or service is presented, promoted or sold to customers.

various stages of the family life cycle are illustrated in Figure 7.2. It also indicates the possible level of demand for tourism for all the stages shown. Segmentation is also often based on social categories or groups. These are summarised in Figure 7.3. Segments used should be substantial, large enough to warrant the special and distinctive marketing effort needed. Obviously the segments must be capable of measurement and assessment.

7.5.2   *Selecting markets*

The selection of markets or market segments depends on several things. First is the decision on the products or services to be marketed. The potential customers must be those most likely to respond to these offerings. Hence the need for a properly balanced and integrated product-market strategy. Second is

**Table 7.11	Segmenting the travel and tourist market**

Segment	Sub-segment
Holiday tourist	fully inclusive package
	partly inclusive package
	independent traveller booked via travel agent
	independent traveller booked privately
Business traveller	booked via travel agent
	booked by employer's travel dept. or individually
	(the above could also be divided to show those who go solely for business purposes and those who tag on a short holiday at one end of such trips)
Special or common interest traveller	hobby
	cultural (art, music, etc.)
	religious
	archaeological and ancient history
	ethnic and anthropological
	flora and fauna

Source: adapted from Douglas Foster, *Mastering Marketing*, 2nd edn. (London: Macmillan, 1984) figure 5.1.

the profit, return on capital, revenue and market shares that must be obtained. Finally, the company's long-term survival and growth must be considered. All are dependent on the skills and resources of the firm. For tourism these include the skills, knowledge and experience of the staff regarding the destination countries and languages involved.

Consideration must also be given to the nature of the demand arising from the selected markets. Is it seasonal? At which times of the year do the peaks and troughs occur? Is this a regular pattern or does it vary unpredictably year on year? Or are they predictable? The solution may lie in the selection of a mix of products and market segments which peak at different

Figure 7.2 Life cycle of a family

Bachelor stage: young single people not living at home	Newly married couples young, no children	Full nest I: youngest child under six	Full nest II: youngest child six or over six	Full nest III: older married couples with dependent children	Empty nest I: older married couples no children living with them head in labour force	Empty nest II: older married couples no children living at home, head retired	Solitary survivor in labour force	Solitary survivor retired
Few financial burdens. Fashion opinion leaders. Recreation orientated. Buy: Basic kitchen equipment, basic furniture, cars, equipment for the mating game, vacations.	Better off financially than they will be in near future. Highest purchase rate and highest average purchase of durables. Buy: Cars, refrigerators, stoves, sensible and durable furniture, vacations.	Home purchasing at peak. Liquid assets low. Dissatisfied with financial position and amount of money saved. Interested in new products. Like advertised products. Buy: Washers, dryers, TV, baby food, chest rubs and cough medicine, vitamins, dolls, wagons, sleds, skates.	Financial position better. Some wives work. Less influenced by advertising. Buy larger sized packages, multiple-unit deals. Buy: Many foods, cleaning materials, bicycles, music lessons, pianos.	Financial position still better. More wives work. Some children get jobs. Hard to influence with advertising. High average purchase of durables. Buy: New more tasteful furniture, auto, travel, non-necessary appliances, boats, dental services, magazines.	Home ownership at peak. Most satisfied with financial position and money saved. Interested in travel, recreation, self-education. Make gifts and contributions. Not interested in new products. Buy: Vacations, luxuries, home improvements.	Drastic cut in income. Keep home. Buy: Medical appliances, medical care, products which aid health, sleep, and digestion.	Income still good but likely to sell home.	Same medical and product needs as the other retired groups; drastic cut in income. Special need for attention, and security.
xx	xx	x	x	0–x	xx	x	xx	0–x

Demand for tourism: 0 = none or little; x = intermittent; xx = good, regular. (Depending on income).

Figure 7.3 Classifying the consumer

GRADE	DESCRIPTION	
	General	Travel and Tourism
'A'	Top executives, administrators, professionals. Has demand for 'luxury' and quality products as well as 'normal' requirements. May be trend-setter also. High incomes – £30,000 p.a. plus.	Demand for more exotic or expensive holidays, 4 weeks or longer. Two or more holidays a year. Also independent travel with or without 'special interests'. 5* or deluxe hotels except when 'slumming'.
'B'	Middle rank executives, administrators and up-and-coming professionals. Often likes to be trend-setter. £20,000 – £30,000 p.a.; depending on family and other commitments, demand appropriately priced 'quality' products.	Demand for better grade package tours and some independent facilities depending on financial commitments. Special interest holidays. Two/three weeks vacations, often twice a year. Limited knowledge of hotels, holiday resorts.
'C1'	Junior executives and clerical, office ('white collar') workers. Earning varies but probably £10,000 p.a. or less. Heavy other financial commitments (mortgage, hire purchase, young children). Limited n.d.i. Major purchases need care.	Package holidays in middle price range; will save for special vacations; some special interest. Very limited knowledge of hotels, resorts, countries. Interested in self-betterment and learning.
'C2'	Skilled ('blue collar') factory worker, artisans and self-employed ditto. Earnings vary but can sometimes afford more luxuries than C1. Depends on interests, size of family and financial load.	Package holidays in middle- or lower-price ranges. Will sometimes spend more if special interests coincide or as an occasional treat. Interested in self-improvement; may use travel for this.
'D'	Semi-skilled and unskilled ('blue collar') workers. Limited n.d.i. and thus purchasing power for non-essentials. These purchases need careful planning; little room for extravagances.	Package tours or holidays at home at lowest prices. Prefers remaining in their normal lifestyle. No real knowledge of foreign countries, resorts, etc.
'E'	Retired executives, other pensioners and unemployed.	Depending on pension, limited holiday needs; often minimal demand. May save to visit families abroad.

times of a year to give reasonable stability to the total business. This may not always be possible because of limited resources.

Inflation must also be considered. High inflation rates tend to dampen demand. Market selection decisions in tourism are also influenced by the accommodation and carriers available, the type and size of bedrooms possible, the location of the resorts and the facilities they offer. Finally, the costs involved and thus the prices that result affect these decisions. Careful assessment and control of market selection is vital for the sustained success of the firm.

7.5.3 Pattern of demand

The main components of demand are the residents of a country, whether taking holidays abroad or at home and visitors from abroad. The demand in developed countries is usually well-established and changes gradually. In developing countries the demand by visitors from abroad can be volatile and give varying rates of growth. In both cases economic and political changes can alter the position substantially. However under stable conditions, tourism planning in developed countries is easier than for developing ones. The pattern of demand for the former varies according to the different forms of tourism involved, the climate, resort locations and topography of the host country. For developing countries it is not easy to generalise as each nation offers a wide variety of attractions – physical, historical and cultural. It is necessary to consider the economic, political, social and tourism development of each country with the attractions they offer. The climate usually determines the time of year when demand will peak and trough.

7.6 Product strategy and policy

The formulation of product strategy and policy permits decisions to be reached on the product range and mix to be used. The work involved has been summarised in Section B of Table 7.1. The basic aim is to optimise customer satisfaction. However, decisions on products cannot be made in isolation from those on markets and vice versa. So while it is unavoidable that study of product and market situations have to be carried out separately because the human brain cannot work on two problems simultaneously, decisions on them must be made jointly. For a change in the product range, for example, will alter market potential and opportunities. A change in the market mix will also alter the profit and sales potential of the products. This applies to services as well as tourism products. So to remind executives of this indivisibility of products and markets, or at least their interdependence, the phrase *product-market* strategy (and policy and plans) is used. The hyphen reminds everyone of this close relationship.

Product strategy indicates the course of action a firm will take regarding its product mix in the light of market and other relevant conditions and the objectives or targets the firm must achieve. Product policy will specify the products and their mix that are necessary to implement strategy. If product-market strategy and policy are to be dynamic, they must be modified or changed to match changes in the firm's business environment. The ability of the product range to satisfy customers' changing needs must also be reviewed regularly. Changes in competition, competitors' products, market demand and the mobility of customers (people moving to other regions) must be considered. Finally it will be necessary periodically to add new products to the mix, either to replace obsolete ones or to open up new markets (for example holidays in North America where hitherto only tours to Europe were on offer).

Therefore successful product management requires a sound understanding of market conditions. For example, buyer behaviour depends on how the lifestyle of consumers alters as their incomes change. If their net discretionary income increases they may want better holidays (three weeks in the Far East instead of two in Spain for instance). Or they may seek holidays which have an element of self-betterment. Also, executives must be aware of new product opportunities offered by changes in technology, transport, social and ethical aspects. The product management process is illustrated by Figure 7.4.

7.6.1 *Product life cycle*

All products and services have finite lives. A manufactured product should last for several, profitable years. So should a well-conceived and designed tourism product. On the other hand, a fad or fashion product (e.g. women's clothes and the colours preferred) may last for only a short time. Figure 7.5 shows the life cycle curves for (a) a product or service with

Figure 7.4 The product management process

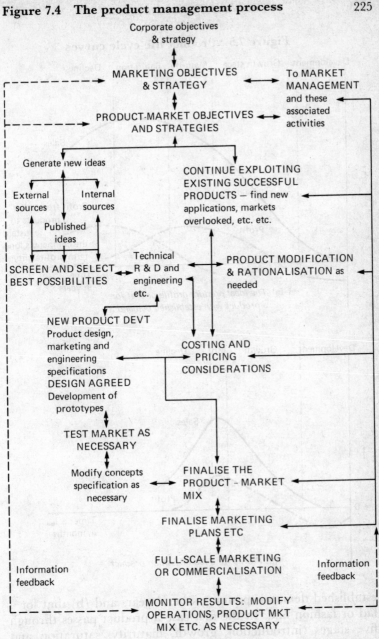

Corporate objectives
& strategy

MARKETING OBJECTIVES
& STRATEGY

To MARKET
MANAGEMENT
and these
associated
activities

PRODUCT-MARKET OBJECTIVES
AND STRATEGIES

Generate new ideas

CONTINUE EXPLOITING
EXISTING SUCCESSFUL
PRODUCTS — find new
applications, markets
overlooked, etc. etc.

External
sources

Internal
sources

Published
ideas

Technical
R & D and
engineering
etc.

PRODUCT MODIFICATION
& RATIONALISATION as
needed

SCREEN AND SELECT
BEST POSSIBILITIES

NEW PRODUCT DEVT
Product design,
marketing and
engineering
specifications
DESIGN AGREED
Development of
prototypes

COSTING AND
PRICING
CONSIDERATIONS

TEST MARKET AS
NECESSARY

Modify concepts
specification as
necessary

FINALISE THE
PRODUCT – MARKET
MIX

FINALISE MARKETING
PLANS ETC

Information
feedback

FULL-SCALE MARKETING
OR COMMERCIALISATION

Information
feedback

MONITOR RESULTS: MODIFY
OPERATIONS, PRODUCT MKT
MIX ETC. AS NECESSARY

Source: Douglas Foster, *Mastering Marketing*, 2nd edn (London: Macmillan, 1984).

Figure 7.5 Product life-cycle curves

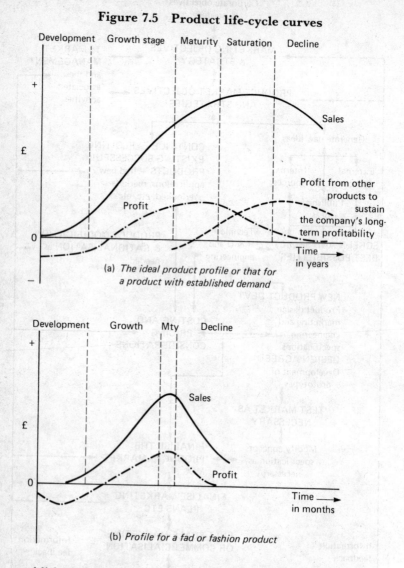

(a) *The ideal product profile or that for a product with established demand*

(b) *Profile for a fad or fashion product*

established demand spanning several years and (b) that for a fad or fashion one. In the first case a product passes through five stages (introduction, growth, maturity, saturation and decline). In the second case there are only four stages, there being no saturation period.

7.6.2 Product modification and rationalisation

When a product has entered the maturity stage serious consideration must be given to any modifications that can be made to extend its profitable life. The cost of doing this must be acceptable. That is, the resultant profit should be (considerably) more than the cost of the modification. Sometimes, if the product helps to sell other more profitable ones it may still be worth modifying it to extend its life even if the benefit above is not realised. Product modification can take several forms.

A tour operator may find that one of its packages is experiencing falling demand. The reason should be identified. It may not be simply that customers are trying other countries. They may be moving to better resorts or hotels or want better rooms and facilities. Appropriate changes to the package may improve demand. Perhaps better rooms at the same price may be all that is necessary. Even assuring customers that rooms with a sea view will be provided may be enough. A bigger modification may be to add better hotels (at the same or slightly higher prices) or include a new resort. Another could be the provision of a small car for a few days without any addition to the price for this hire. A two-centre holiday could be offered as an alternative or a 'free' excursion could be added to the package. The combinations are numerous and some were illustrated in Table 3.3.

Eventually it may not be possible to carry out any further modifications. The cost may be too high and customers may not be able to afford the higher prices. Or there may be no new alternatives that could be tried. Then the product will have to be rationalised (phased out of the product range). If this is necessary there should be a new product ready to be introduced to take its place. Incidentally, it is seldom that modifications are attempted for fad products as their lives are too short. They will be made obsolete by changes in fashion or fad (Table 7.12 summarises the process).

7.6.3 New product development

The search for, development and launching of new products is essential for the long-term survival of any business, including tourism. In the latter case, the slow rate of change in demand for tourism products disguises this necessity. With hindsight it

Table 7.12   Product modification and rationalisation

Basic steps

1   The team of executives responsible for the work meet to determine the objectives and procedures for the work.

2   They review, study and analyse the profit and revenue positions, prices/costs, competition and other market factors affecting the demand in various markets in which the company is operating. They consider also the potential, future markets the company may enter in a few years.

3   They select the products that need to be modified and which they believe could have their profitable life extended for several years through matching changes in customer needs. Cost/benefit studies are made and if satisfactory, the work of modification is initiated to a specified timetable.

4   Then those products which cannot be modified profitably for any reason are selected for rationalisation. A plan for this is prepared to phase in with the plans for the reintroduction of modified products and the launching of new products.

5   They consider the effects of these decisions on the surviving, original products – their sales and profit potential and future return – the firm's image and market standing and their competitive abilities. Future requirements for growth, stability and survival of the firm must also be considered.

6   The team makes recommendations on how, when and by whom all this work will be done, establishing plans of action and the priorities.

7   They monitor the work and the results obtained and have overall control of the work.

Important questions considered
These include:

(a)   How have the products' sales changed in relation to total demand and how have costs and price movements affected demand and the products' profit margins?

(b)   What new or substitute products have eroded the positions of current products (e.g. package tours *v* sea cruises; time sharing *v* other vacation methods, etc.)?

(c)   How have all these affected the life, profit and sales expectations of the products?

(d) Has the competitive position changed and how is it likely to change in the foreseeable future?

(e) How have the demand patterns changed in present and likely future markets?

(f) What changes in other market factors are likely and how will they affect the decisions to be taken on the firm's product range and mix?

(g) What gross profit and overhead contributions are being made by the products marked for rationalisation? How can these be balanced by the introduction of modified and new products?

(h) What will be the total cost of the modification and rationalisation programmes?

(i) Will the new/additional profit achieved by the proposed product changes more than compensate for these costs, increase the company's total profit and improve its image, market standing and competitive abilities?

Source: Modified from: Douglas Foster, *Mastering Marketing*, 2nd edn. (London: Macmillan, 1984).

is easy to see how demand for these products in the 1980s has changed from that in the 1950s and 1960s. The packages are more sophisticated and cover many more host countries at competitive prices. The growth of long-distance, activity and adventure holidays and sea cruises are just four examples. So this side of product management is vital to the tourism industry.

A number of questions must be considered, of which the following are major ones. How is demand changing with particular reference to new countries, new resorts and new types of holiday? What changes are taking place in net discretionary incomes and thus the ability to pay for more expensive and exotic holidays? How are customer expectations changing? What are the possible cost and price situations for the new possibilities? What are competitors doing, who are likely to compete and who are already in the activities contemplated? What are the political, economic, social and legal positions?

When these and subsidiary questions have been answered, ideas will emerge for detailed consideration. The mythical tour operator in the previous section may think of developing packages to Greece or North Africa. If demand is good and growing while competition is not too severe, sufficient market shares may be obtainable. However some ideas may be eliminated because the political or economic situations may be unstable or uncertain.

What is the difference between new product development and diversification? The ideas above would be new product development since the company is already active in organising package tours. All that is being changed is the resort or destination country. However if the firm went into sea cruises, especially organising its own not just selling established ones by other companies, then it would be diversification. It would be moving into an entirely new field for which it has had no previous experience and must obtain the necessary new resources and skills.

There are five basic strategies possible in the development of a product mix. These are explained briefly in Table 7.13. Table 7.14 summarises the stages in new product development.

7.7 Pricing and profit strategies and policies

Pricing strategies and policies establish the price structure, discounts and trade terms to be followed. There must be accord between them and the profit strategies and policies. They must permit the achievement of the profit targets that have been set by the company. Price and profit are themselves conditioned by product unit costs and customers' ability to pay the asking prices, their attitude to quality and whether the prices represent good value. The competitive products available and ruling market prices are other influencing factors. The gross profit and revenue generated will determine the promotional activities that can be mounted. These are discussed in the next chapter.

The general and marketing objectives are shown in Table 7.15 together with the important intelligence needed before decisions can be made. Table 7.16 shows the basic policies

Table 7.13 Developing the service mix

Terminology	Meaning for Products	Services	Example
MARKET PENETRATION	Increasing sales of existing products in existing markets	Increasing sales of current services in existing markets	Travel co. increasing sales of present operations to customer currently served.
MARKET DEVELOPMENT	Finding new markets or applications for existing products	Finding new markets or applications for current services	Travel co. developing special arrangements for business group bookings.*
PRODUCT (SERVICE) DEVELOPMENT	Seeking new products to offer to existing markets or customers	Developing new services to offer to current markets or customers	Travel co. developing, say, special interest tours to offer to existing customer categories.
DIVERSIFICATION	Finding new products to offer to new markets or customers	Developing new services to offer to new markets or customers	Travel co. breaking into say, cheap package tours, where not done hitherto, sold to new customer categories.
ACQUISITION	Buying production and/or marketing licence or, more usually, buying a company not necessarily in same business	Buying another organisation who may or may not operate in same service or market areas	A tour co. buying another operation in different tour market; or banking group buying tour co. (e.g. in UK, Midland Bank buying control of Thos. Cook Ltd)

Notes: *for its normal services; i.e. no new services developed, just special terms, etc.
'New' in this context usually means new to the company. Products/services (and customers or markets served) may not be 'new' to the industry as a whole.

Table 7.14 Practical stages in new product development

1 Prepare long-range forecasts for profit, return and sales revenue for existing product-market activities based on estimates of future customer needs, costs, prices, competition and other external factors.

2 Prepare long-range profit, return and revenue plans to meet the firm's agreed objectives.

3 Establish the 'profit, return and sales gaps' by comparing (2) with (1).

4 From this 'target' (3) which must be met by new and modified products, select the products to be modified and estimate the profit, etc., to be earned by new products. Any new market possibilities should also be considered.

5 From (4) and a provisional list of possible new products, select the new products or ideas which offer the best prospects. Determine the product-market strategy that would be needed and the markets that would be involved.

6 Finalise objectives for new products and make an audit of the company's resources and capabilities.

7 If necessary, prepare a statement of revised corporate objectives necessitated by the new product possibilities.

8 While the above is being done, new product ideas are identified, assessed and evaluated leading to the preparation of a short list of ideas for in-depth study. They should be graded in terms of immediate, intermediate and long-term development prospects.

9 A long-range plan for profit, revenue and sales is finalised.

10 Responsibility for the development is assigned and the launch plans are formulated.

11 When launched, the performance of the new products is checked and any necessary corrections or modifications are made (e.g. adjust hotel, resort or transportation used if not meeting with acceptance/approval of customers).

12 If the launch is successful, incorporate new products into firm's product range and main marketing plans and operations.

Source: Douglas Foster, *Mastering Marketing*, 2nd edn (London: Macmillan, 1984).

Table 7.15 Pricing objectives and information

General objectives

1 Optimisation of profit/profitability, both short- and long-term, without the former jeopardising the latter. Also optimisation of revenue.
2 Obtaining a specified rate of return on investment.
3 Achieving growth and long-term survival of the firm with, if possible, optimal stability of the business.
4 Minimising risk, especially of substantial loss.
5 Keeping indebtedness to reasonable limits.
6 Allowing the company to be in the forefront of its industry's innovation.

Marketing objectives

1 Maintaining/increasing market shares.
2 Gaining prestige through some form of market leadership.
3 Matching competitive prices unless offering better product when higher prices may be justified and accepted.
4 Obtaining the market penetration required of products.
5 Obtaining early cash recovery according to the demands of the corporate and marketing plans.

Basic information required

(a) Data and information on ruling market prices, terms, etc., especially prices of major competitors.
(b) Consumers' views on prices, the firm's and competitors' products. Are they sensitive to price changes? Views on price charged, frequency of price changes, etc
(c) Is the market subject to price elasticity of demand?
(d) Cost of supply components of the packages and of distributing information, etc., to enquirers and potential customers?
(e) Changes in volume sales and revenue by markets and tourist-generating areas.

SOURCE: Adapted from Douglas Foster, *Mastering Marketing*, 2nd edn (London: Macmillan, 1984).

Table 7.16 Some basic pricing policies

Skim pricing. Starting with a high price, which is reduced as competition intensifies, this policy is used when early recovery of all costs and desired total profit is needed. Should shield product from (less efficient) competitors.

Penetration pricing. A price with a lower profit margin than above for products expected to have a long life. Used when such a product must build a steadily increasing volume of business, to achieve stated market penetration. Price increases are gradually achieved. Deters competition but attracts business.

Mixed. Begins with a skim price and drops substantially to eliminate competition then uses penetration pricing to achieve longer-term market position/penetration (see Figure 7.6).

Differential pricing. Charge different prices for the same product sold to different locations, type of customer and for different uses. Not normally applicable to tourism products.

Cost-plus pricing. All costs are calculated and a margin is applied to provide necessary profit. Takes little account of current and future demand and does not take full advantage of market potential or opportunities.

Single price for all. One price charged to everyone.

Variable pricing. Similar to differential pricing. Used to regulate demand according to the supply/demand situation (e.g. if demad for a package tour exceeds a firm's reservation of hotel rooms, carrier seats, etc., a higher price may be possible than in a case when demand is less than the forward reservations made by the firm).

Price lining. Prices chosen to take into account the relationship between the items in the whole product range and not based on price estimates for individual products (e.g. if one holiday is more attractive than another, the first would have a price that gave a higher profit than for the second even if total costs were identical).

Promotional pricing. This uses a lower price than would normally be the case when, for example, launching a new product or trying to revitalise an ailing one.

Market pricing. Prices fixed according to market demand. Firm often has no control on this price (e.g. for commodities when prices can vary daily according to the amounts demanded and sold).

Source: Adapted from: Douglas Foster, *Mastering Marketing*, 2nd edn (London: Macmillan, 1984).

possible while Figure 7.6 illustrates the difference between skim, penetration and mixed pricing policies. However the best price in any situation may not be the highest nor the lowest price possible nor even the one with the largest unit profit margin. Table 7.17 illustrates this point. The highest price the market will bear is £450 per unit. It gives the largest profit margin but total revenue and profit will be low because of the limited demand at that price. Selling at cost may provide the greatest demand, which may be needed in some situations, but not the best revenue. Nor will it provide any profit. Depending on whether the profit is to be optimised or revenue maximised, the 'best price' could be £350 or £300 per package.

Consideration must also be given to decisions whether to trade 'up-market' (higher-priced packages for a limited élite of potential customers) or 'down-market' (low-priced packages for the mass market) because a high sales volume is needed for some reason or other. Then the firm's capacity must be taken into account. Can it satisfy the demand that would arise? Has it sufficient forward reservations of rooms and transport seats? If supply exceeds demand should prices be lowered? If demand exceeds supply, could or should prices be increased? Is it the company's policy to compete on price, quality or some unique aspect of the packages? Will it be necessary to introduce new products at low prices to obtain acceptance of them before raising prices to more normal levels? Are customers sensitive to prices and frequent price changes? What is the price elasticity of demand? Are there any political implications?

The reaction of competitors must also be estimated. Will they match the new product with one of their own? Would their price be higher or lower? If the firm raises or lowers prices of established packages, will competitors follow by marginal increases greater or less than the initiator's? What other

Figure 7.6 Skim, penetration and mixed pricing

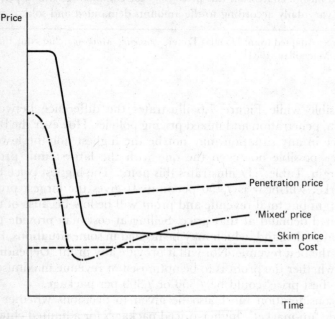

Note: At times, when trying to eliminate competitors, the 'mixed price' may be taken below costs for a while.

SOURCE: Adapted from: Douglas Foster, *Mastering Marketing*, 2nd edn (London: Macmillan, 1984).

responses are possible? What are the possible outcomes of these actions and so on?

In the case of a competitor initiating a price change should the company follow or better the change? What would be the outcome of any reaction or no reaction? In this instance it is advisable to identify the reasons for the competitor's action. If they are trying to clear accumulated stock (unsold forward reservations), it may be better to let them do so. This will prevent the ruling market price from being depressed for too long. However if the price change is likely to be permanent, aimed at altering the price situation in the market, then some response may be necessary.

Decisions on prices depend also on the firm's long-term

Table 7.17   Choosing the 'best' price

Example: A package holiday with total costs of £200 per package with a demand potential and price/volume relationship as shown below.

Possible unit sale prices (£)	Destimated demand (units)	Total revenue (£s)	Unit profit (£)	Total profit (£)
450	1000	450,000	250	250,000
400	2000	800,000	200	400,000
350	3500	1,225,000	150	525,000
300	4500	1,350,000	100	450,000
250	4800	1,200,000	50	240,000
200	5200	1,040,000	0	0

The 'best price' for profit optimisation is £350 per unit.
If for some reason the company needed to maximise revenue the 'best price' is £300 per unit.
Competition and other market factors could of course have further influences on the price actually chosen.

corporate objectives for profit, return and growth. If they wish to improve the first two, price increases with cost reductions have to be considered. If the firm wishes to increase revenue or market shares, price alterations may be needed, depending on the supply/demand and price/volume relationships of the market. Knowing the purpose of any proposed price change helps to ease what might otherwise be a complex and confusing decision.

7.7.1   Price regulation

There are three ways by which prices may be regulated. First there is *public regulation* when price decisions are taken by a government department or agency or any change requires their approval. Second is *self-regulation* where an industry or its association determines what the price should be. Finally there is *market regulation* when market demand, economic and other related market factors determine what prices can be charged. In the last instance, where a product has some unique characteristic it may be possible to charge a higher ('premium') price.

7.8 The marketing plan

The marketing plan is the principal operational and control document. It specifies what has to be done, when it has to be done, how it will be done and who has to do it. It states the objectives and targets to be obtained and requires the results to be checked against these targets and other stated standards, particularly quality and dependability. The plan also specifies the various expenditure budgets permitted and requires actual expenditure to be checked against them. Thus it measures the firm's performance so that remedial action can be taken when results are not meeting targets.

It provides a record of the reasoning behind marketing decisions and identifies strengths and weaknesses so that the marketing operation can be designed to draw on the former and avoid the latter. Steps can also be taken to overcome or remedy the weaknesses, strengthening the firm's capabilities. It provides cohesion and direction to the firm's activities and so minimises risk while enhancing long-term progress and development.

The planning process identifies where the company is in its business at the time of the planning and where it may go in some specified time (three, five or more years) if the *status quo* was maintained. It assists the corporate planning process to decide where the firm should be at the end of the planning period and indicates what development is needed and is possible. It should also indicate what alternative courses of action are possible if forecasted changes take place in the business environment. It states what marketing organisation is required and all the costs (expenditure budgets) that would be incurred in obtaining the profit and other targets that have been agreed.

For tour operators, carriers and travel agents the marketing plan will be similar to those for other businesses. There are many ways it can be written and the firm should choose one that suits their way of management. The important headings are shown in Table 7.18. Other guidelines are that the plan should have all the relevant data and only sufficient words to explain briefly the rationale and decisions. If it is necessary to report fully on, say, some market research or some important historical fact, these should be put into appendices. This avoids

Table 7.18 Contents of a marketing plan

1	*Subject*	The product-market groups or situation covered by the plan (e.g. 'Marketing Plan for 2 week all-inclusive holidays to Spain').
2	*Period*	States the timescale of the plan (e.g. 'This is a 5-year plan commencing 1/4/19..').
3	*Products*	Detailed statement of the products covered by the plan.
4	*Objectives and targets*	Specifies the profit, return, revenue, market shares and annual growth to be achieved in each year of the plan.
5	*Basic campaign plan*	Summary of what has to be done to realise (4).
6	*Sales targets*	A set of tables showing what volume sales and revenue must be achieved for each product-market situation to achieve (4) above.
7	*Market shares*	Another set of tables showing the market shares to be achieved for each product-market operation.
8	*Profit plans*	Further set of tables detailing the profit targets for each product-market activity and how this may be achieved.
9	*Pricing plans*	Tables setting out the prices, terms and discounts for different products and distributors/middlemen. Also other policy items.
10	*Product plans*	Confirms the product range to be used and the modifications and rationalisation needed, with timetables for the last two items.
11	*New product plans*	Statement of the new product ideas that will be evaluated and tested. Also list of ideas already selected for launch in the planning period in hand and the timetable for this.
12	*Sales plan*	Full details of what was summarised in (5).
13	*Promotional plan*	Full details of advertising and other promotional activities, timing of, media selected, etc.
14	*Competition*	Summary of position and how competition will be met/overcome.

Table 7.18 (cont.)   Contents of a marketing plan

15	*Distribution*	Plan showing how manufactured products, or in tourism, the information on products available, confirmation of reservations, tickets, etc., will be sent to consumers.
16	*Merchandising*	Summarises whatever merchandising activities may be planned for the period (see Chapter 8).
17	*Organisation*	Details or confirms the marketing organisation, especially the sales force, that will be used. For established companies, usually details only the changes that will be made.
18	*Training*	States the training needs of the department to give its members a chance to master new techniques and prepare them for eventual promotion.
19	*Finance*	All the above incur expenditure and will show the budgets permitted for this expenditure. All these sums are collated here and compared with the targets for profit, return and revenue. Thus cost/benefit analyses are presented here, allowing executives to make sound decisions speedily.

NOTES:

(a) For manufactured goods, the plan may have an *R&D* section also. This shows what research and development work is needed on the products from marketing's point of view. Estimates of the cost of this work are usually included in this section with indications of how much Marketing could contribute from its gross trading profit.

(b) Also, especially for consumer goods, there may be another section on *Packaging* indicating what packaging will be used and the rationale for this decision.

(c) Usual practice is to check the results being obtained against the targets of the plan at the end of each sales period, be this weekly, fortnightly, monthly, etc. However, major changes to the plan are not made until the end of the third sales period, when it should be clear whether a permanent change has occurred in the business environment and not just a temporary hiccup.

Source: Modified from Douglas Foster, *Mastering Marketing*, 2nd edn (London: Macmillan, 1984).

an over-wordy plan which might lead to incorrect decisions. The marketing planning process is shown in simplified form in Figure 7.7.

For tourist boards, marketing plans should cover the activities they will undertake as mentioned in Section 7.1.5, both for their own purposes and for joint activities with the travel trade. Major sections will specify the market research that would be done to identify suitable market segments and the consumer profiles of the people comprising them. Then the product research needed to identify the products that might be offered and their possible prices will be stated. A further section could indicate the promotional activities that would be most effective and how, when and by whom they will be undertaken. The tourist board will then be in a position to give sound advice to the industry.

7.9 Evaluating marketing effort

Many companies, especially the smaller ones, often do not identify where the customers come from and how they heard of the company and its products. The tourism industry is no exception. Thus they cannot really evaluate the true effectiveness of their marketing effort. Given their limited budgets, they cannot afford to waste funds. So they must try to measure the direct return resulting from their activities.

The firm should establish how the business is generated. Is it by a two-stage effort where the retailer creates interest and then gives the enquirer a brochure? Or does it come through direct response? The latter could be the result of an advertisement or from a brochure picked up casually from a travel agent. How much is 'off street' business by casual callers? How many customers do not book early but leave it to the last moment? What promotional activity prompted these responses? What was the conversion rate for enquiries to orders? What was the cost per sale?

When this intelligence is assembled the firm can evaluate the effectiveness of particular marketing techniques and the overall activity. The seller can then decide which is the most effective way of marketing the products for the different types

Figure 7.7 The marketing planning process

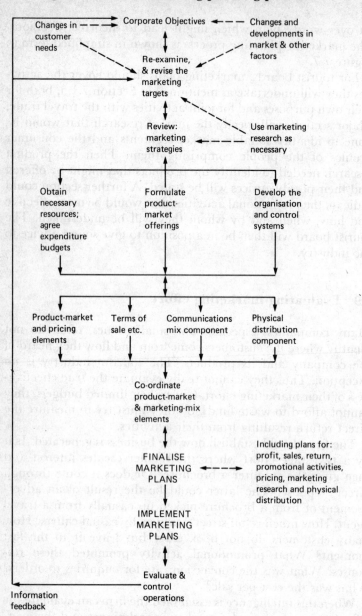

Source: Douglas Foster, *Mastering Marketing*, 2nd edn (London: Macmillan, 1984).

of business they do. As a result the marketing effort can be improved and profitability increased.

7.10 Distribution

In tourism, distribution is concerned with sending information about the products to enquirers and when bookings are made, sending confirmation of this to them. Eventually the final bill, tickets and vouchers have to be despatched. While computers, sales desk terminals and central reservation systems have made this work easier and faster, care must be taken to keep costs to reasonable limits, for whatever standard of efficiency is required.

The firm must also decide which channels of distribution they will use, and their comparative costs. Will they sell their tours direct to the consumer or through a travel agent? Will they sell through clubs, trade unions, colleges or sports organisations? Where 'middlemen' are used, the firm must decide on the commission to be paid. This must cover all the distributor's costs (staff wages, rent, rates, heating, lighting, telephone and postage) as well as leave a reasonable profit margin. In the tourism industry the basic commission is around 9 or 10 per cent but extras are given if sales exceed specified amounts and so on. Tourist boards have similar costs though their postage and telephone bills may be less. However the cost of printing posters and leaflets distributed free to the trade will be greater.

Factors determining the distribution policy required include the locations of points-of-sale, cost of distribution, effectiveness of the marketing effort, the image of the company and consumer motivations regarding tourism products. The target markets selected, where potential customers live and work, will also indicate where the points-of-sale should be. Tourist boards will decide where their tourist office abroad should be and the distribution methods to be used according to amount of tourist traffic to be generated.

The distribution system must be efficient, positive and dynamic. It should push the firm's products strongly through the distribution chain and create the right image for product and company. Otherwise it will not help to create the business nor support other marketing effort efficiently.

7.11 Intelligence flows and reservation systems

As previous sections showed, considerable intelligence has to be processed if a successful marketing operation is to be achieved. Table 7.6 listed the main items. Much of this will be collected in the course of doing business and by maintaining close contacts with the other elements of the industry. Study of published intelligence helps. If the firm is not to be swamped by the considerable flow of intelligence that results, it must identify the critical and relevant bits of it required for planning decisions and control purposes. A carefully planned intelligence retrieval system is vital. Setting up such a system is not easy and help from experienced consultants in this field may be advisable. However once established, the system is easy to keep up to date. Microcomputers have eased the problems of information retrieval and collation.

The faster acting the system, the more expensive it is to operate. So the one chosen should act only as fast as the management structure can respond to it. One that is too fast will waste money and 'lose' data during the time it is kept 'waiting' before use. Further, marketing intelligence becomes obsolescent in a short time, three or so months for a volatile industry. If the system is too slow, decisions will be delayed and customers may become disgruntled by any long wait that results. The marketing system may also become clogged by an intelligence logjam.

7.11.1 Reservation systems

Computers and microcomputers have speeded up the whole reservation system. Before them everything was done 'manually'. The customer would specify the resort, time and hotel required and the latter had to be contacted to see if any rooms were still available. If they were not, the customer would specify another hotel and the process started all over again.

Whether the contact was by letter, telephone or telex, the whole thing was time-consuming, taking several weeks to finalise matters. When centralised systems were used, the process was speeded up a little, although it could still take a week or two. With computers and their data banks, everything can be done in a minute or two, provided the computer did not break down! Figures 7.8 and 7.9 illustrate the differences in simplified form.

Figure 7.8   Do-it-yourself information and reservation 'system'

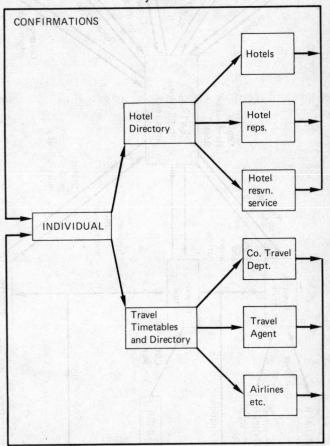

Note: Each 'channel' shown may have multiple components, i.e. more than one hotel, travel agent and transportation company may have to be contacted before a reservation is possible.

246

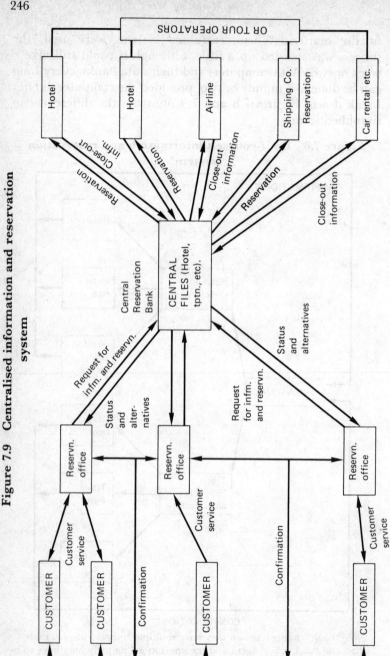

Figure 7.9 Centralised information and reservation system

7.12 Case illustrations

The following two cases may prove interesting.

7.12.1 Stardust and Camelot

No, this case does not deal with a well-known song and a very successful musical show of the 1960s. It refers to two sister companies in the mini-holiday business.

To many people in Britain, the short-break holiday is thought to be a recent development. However Stardust Mini Holidays, a division of Grand Metropolitan Hotels, celebrated its twentieth anniversary in 1982. It has pioneered marketing techniques for this type of business which have been copied in Britain and elsewhere.

The Stardust package holiday combines hotel accommodation in London with rail travel and also offers packages to Paris and Amsterdam. Camelot offers a choice of provincial and country hotels without specifying the form of transport. Between them these two operations have over a quarter of a million people a year buying their packages. Whilst at first the average stay was for two nights, by 1982 it had become over four nights. As annual holiday entitlements have increased so more people are taking the opportunity to have short-break holidays in addition to their usual annual ones. Prices are very competitive. However it has been noticed that for the country packages people seem to prefer the top two categories of hotel. It appears that customers are not going to skimp for a few pounds going to the country. This may be because they fear choosing too low a grade of hotel with all that that implies (?).

For the most part, customers appear to prefer not being regimented and seem to be following their special interests or hobbies. Generally they are reluctant to pay for more expensive packages with many inclusive 'extras'. They prefer the freedom of choice of activities which Stardust and Camelot permit through not including these unwanted items in their packages.

Over fifty staff operate the Stardust and Camelot business. While expenditure on promotional activities is around £750,000 a year, the main sales vehicle is the brochure. To many potential customers the image created by the brochure is important. Several other firms have since copied its style and layout.

A remarkable number of people now take short-break holidays probably because the industry as a whole has combined to promote the idea. Advertising expenditure on this product now amounts to several millions of pounds a year. The strength of the advertising has intensified competition against other things on which consumers spend their discretionary incomes. Opportunities for expansion exist. Provided the economy is healthy, there is no reason why people should not take two or three short-break holidays a year in addition to their main holiday. Britain is a marvellous country to explore and enjoy and more people are discovering this fact.

7.12.2   The 1980s price war

Early in November 1983 *The Times* of London reported that Enterprise Holidays, a subsidiary of British Airways, was cutting its prices for summer 1984 holidays by 6 per cent. Other price cuts already announced included Thomson Summer Sun 2 per cent, Thomson Self-catering 6 per cent, Horizon Holidays 6 per cent, Thomas Cook 4 per cent, Thomas Cook Self-catering 7 per cent and Intasun 6 per cent. Later in November Thomson and Horizon reduced their prices by a further 10 per cent. If there were further price reductions for comparable holidays by other operators, Enterprise, it was stated, would be prepared to respond to them. An executive stated that on value for money, Enterprise would not be undersold.

Brochure reprints with lower prices had already entered the tour operators' armoury of promotional weapons. The holiday price war intensified. A new twist was that consumers who had booked before price reductions were announced, also got the lower prices. In 1983 Thomson Holidays had achieved higher sales by reprinting their brochure with reduced prices. In 1984 their prices were even lower. Horizon followed.

Intasun at that time had still to produce their main brochure for summer 1984 but they have traditionally undercut Thomson and Horizon in a big battle to gain a dominant market share. Subsequently they produced an average 9 per cent cut in their prices. Enterprise, considered a middle market operator, was generally matching Thomson's lower prices and marginally undercutting Horizon. Thomson and Horizon have traditionally operated higher quality holidays. In December 1983 Global entered the fray by reducing their brochure prices by the equivalent total of more than half a million pounds. So long as demand stays at the level of the early 1980s and there is no economic recovery to boost demand, this price war is expected to continue. In March 1984 it was announced that total bookings were below expectations. Consumers' growing habit of making late bookings, in the hope of gaining bargain prices, was blamed. The trade's reported response was to cut back on its forward reservations. It warned that people who left their bookings to the last moment might not find the holidays they wanted! (For further developments in 1984–5, see Appendix A.)

Assignments

1 You are a business consultant retained by a medium-sized operator to introduce marketing into the company. How would you explain the purpose of marketing and the application of it to the business of tourism?

2 Your next assignment is in a small developing country in the Caribbean, helping to set up a national tourist organisation. How would you explain marketing's role in this case?

3 As a senior executive with a major tour operator you must recommend changes in the firm's product-market strategy and mix. How would you go about this? What market factors require study and analysis?

4 How would the application of the product life cycle assist you with decisions on (tourism) product modification and rationalisation?

5 A travel agent decides it is no longer able to sell the tours of all major operators. How can it evaluate and select the markets it should continue to serve? How will decisions here help the firm to decide which tour operators it will continue to service?

6 How should a firm's pricing policy be determined? Can this procedure be applied to (a) tour operators and (b) travel agents? How would this be done?

8

The Communications Mix

In Marketing, the 'Communications Mix' consists of advertising, sales promotions, PR (public and press relations), personal selling, merchandising and packaging, as listed in Section D of Table 7.1. The last two activities are often considered to be parts of sales promotion. They are highly specialised functions, involving special skills and are of considerable importance in helping to achieve successful selling of product or service. The first three items are also known as 'promotional activities'. The numerous methods available under this last heading are detailed in Table 8.1.

This combination of these six techniques is known as the communications mix because in their various specialist ways they are involved in communicating information to potential customers. Their aim is to provide people with sufficient, relevant intelligence to prompt them to take positive action by making enquiries, placing orders and making purchases. Other factors influence their decision processes. These include prices, net discretionary income available and the political and economic conditions of the home and host countries. However not all consumer 'needs' are converted into 'wants' and thus purchases (see Section 1.4).

Table 8.1   Some popular promotional activities

Advertising
Audio-visual sales aids
Brochures
Catalogues
Company visits
Competitions (for customers and the trade)
Design (product and packaging)
Direct mail
Directories
Financial incentives
Free gifts
Guarantees
Incentive schemes (trade and own salespersons)
Leaflets (technical and other)
Merchandising
Off-premises displays
Packaging
Point-of-sale displays
Premiums
PR (public and press relations)
Price reductions (and pricing strategy)
Special offers (price, etc.)
Telephone selling
Tent cards (hotels, restaurants, departmental stores)
Vehicle livery
Year books

Those shown in italics have been the most used.

SOURCE: Douglas Foster, *Mastering Marketing*, 2nd edn (London: Macmillan, 1984).

8.1   The buying decision

When a consumer decides to buy a product or service to obtain satisfaction of some sort (ownership, use or consumption) expenditure of money is involved. So the buying decision is taken with care and sometimes, reluctance. The amount of care displayed is dependent on the perceived degree of risk (for example, would a holiday in West Africa endanger health?). The reluctance shown depends on the amount of money that has to be spent and what proportion it is of the consumer's available assets. (For example, a person with £500 available for an annual holiday would be reluctant to buy a QE2–Concorde fly-cruise holiday to America costing several times that amount.) Caution and reluctance are the products of fear! There is the fear of being deceived or made to look foolish to one's friends. Then there is perhaps the greater fear of losing money especially if the person is afraid of poverty in old age.

8.1.1 *Tourist buying decision*

In addition to the factors discussed in Section 1.4.4, other points have to be considered.

When making ('buying') an investment the customer expects to obtain an acceptable rate of return. When buying a manufactured product the buyer expects some tangible or intangible satisfaction while spending a relatively small amount of the assets available. In deciding to buy a tourism product the consumer faces a unique situation. There is no tangible return on the investment, only some vague intangible 'satisfaction' or pleasure resulting from the holiday. The expenditure often accounts for a considerable portion of the person's free assets. The decision to buy is not taken spontaneously nor capriciously. It is usually the result of some thought and family discussion over a period of a month or more.

While the holiday tourist may be resigned to spending a relatively large sum of money and expects no economic return, the average person may be even more sensitive to the risk of being disappointed or made to look foolish. Given the many failures in the industry in recent years and the resultant problems for tourists (loss of money and holiday, being stranded abroad and so on) many now show considerable caution in their selection of holidays, tour operators and travel agents. They are aware that they are buying an illusion and will feel bitter to anyone and anything that shatters that illusion.

So several complex relationships are involved in buying decisions for tourism products. Also, it is more than just choosing one product from a large range of alternatives. Decisions entail the selection of a suitable mix of different services offered by several firms in the industry. They may also account for 10 per cent or more of a household budget. While this expenditure is for a short period of time, it often involves saving over several months. Planning ahead is needed and with the seasonality of demand, decisions on holidays have to be made some time in advance of the actual event.

The decision requires the collection and study of a considerable amount of information before it can be made. For example, the ten major German tour operators publish over four thousand catalogue pages between them. The eight major British operators produce catalogues with a total of nearly one thousand pages. Yet many customers feel that all the information is not easily obtained and is not fully understood even when it is! Then the method of presentation, phraseology and language can produce further misunderstanding or difficulties. Potential customers may also lack knowledge of the local practice, customs and lifestyles of the host countries. All these points can heighten the degree of uncertainty consumers may experience when faced with tourism decisions. Thus the communications mix must be so devised as to help potential customers overcome these problems, whether real or imagined. The basic decision process and its major elements are shown in Table 8.2.

8.1.2 Business travel decisions

The main factors influencing business travel decisions were listed in Table 3.1. These were discussed in Section 3.1.7. However it is worth restating here that these are the need for the visit, its timing and duration, the location of the people to be visited and the type of industry or customer to be seen. The decisions are in fact predetermined by these considerations. Provided the costs are within acceptable limits, business travel demand is reasonably inelastic.

However, other influencing factors can arise. If internal transport facilities are good, a wider choice of destination may be possible. For example, an executive having to visit customers in Turin or Genoa may elect to stay in Milan since the hotel and other choices there are better, or if they plan to seek new

Table 8.2   The buying decision process for tourism

A   THE BASIC PROCESS

Stage	Decisions	Considerations and influences
1 Felt need	General desire to travel – reasons for and against assessed-specific information not yet collected or assessed.	General travel motivations. When to travel? Previous experience. How much can be spent?
2 Information gathering and evaluation	Study of catalogues, advertising, consult travel agents, other specialists and friends.	Suggestions from tour operators and travel agents. Advice from friends and other experts.
3 Decisions	On destination, travel mode, accommodation, timing, duration, budget, other services and middlemen to use.	Previous experience. Image of suppliers. Advice from middlemen.
4 Buying decisions	Reservations (confirmation). Obtain currency and travellers' cheques, clothing, etc., as needed.	Bank. Shops and stores. Advice from friends and experts.

B   DECISION ELEMENTS

(a)   Where to go?   (Country, area, locality, resort)

(b)   Where to stay?   (Type of accommodation – hotel, motel, pension, guest house, camping, etc.)

(c)   How to travel?   (Air, rail, coach, car, sea or combination)

(d)   Budget?   (How much to spend on basic package? Currency and travellers cheques. Which currency? How much on excursions, etc.?)

(e) Where to book? (Tour operator or travel agent? With individual enterprises (hotel, transport, etc.?)

(f) Type of travel? (Group, individual travel? Type of service at resort – B & B, $\frac{1}{2}$-board, full-board? Excursions booked in advance? etc.)

---

business from that city. The timing of trips may not also be too critical if they are routine visits or no special event (exhibitions, conferences) are involved. Climate may also affect the timing. Company senior executives may choose to visit Caribbean, Far Eastern and Australian customers during the European winter season, especially if they plan to take a short-break holiday as well, for obvious reasons. Cost constraints may force executives to combine visits to South and East Africa, for example, when prudence may suggest that these areas be covered by separate trips. When economic times are bad, more frequent visits may be necessary as firms fight harder for available business. All these must be taken into account when a travel agent is planning the communications mix needed to win business travel accounts.

8.1.3 Timing of communications mix

The decision process for holidays usually spans a few months, even when consumers are deliberately making last minute bookings. So the activities of the communications mix must be timed to create awareness of the packages on offer, perhaps making potential customers discover their need for a specific, especially unusual, holiday before they have made their decisions about their vacations. The promotional activities should also continue for a period to heighten interest and desire for a holiday. This ensures that the operator and travel agent will achieve their target market shares.

In Britain the information-gathering stage for a summer holiday is usually January to early March. For winter holidays it is about October to December. This is when information is sought from tour operators and travel agents on what is available, the possible resorts and the accommodation, scenery, attractions and weather they would encounter. Consumers will then spend several weeks as a rule, considering the details and having family discussions on what they should do. Thus all travel-buying decisions are more complex than at first imagined. This is why the intended communications mix and the whole marketing operation needs to be carefully planned and timed for success.

The effort in these areas must be selective, according to the target markets of the firm. The promotional activities should appeal to the motivations influencing target customers and their travel behaviour patterns. They should not offend whatever socio-economic criteria the potential customers consider to be vital to their way of life or lifestyles. Intelligence on these factors may not be easily available and this is where some expensive market research may be unavoidable, to establish the consumer profiles that have to be influenced by the promotional mix.

8.2 Personal selling

Personal selling is the personal presentation of a tangible product or intangible service or idea to potential customers (business, industry or the consumer). It is supported by the promotional activities mentioned at the beginning of this chapter. This activity has to be planned on an integrated basis with the other elements of the communications mix, including merchandising and packaging where relevant, and the whole of the marketing effort. The products, prices and markets in particular determine the form or nature of the personal selling required. For example, for holidays, personal selling takes place at the travel agents and any sales office which a tour operator may have. The form of selling used by manufacturing industry is not practical. Too many potential customers are involved and the cost would be prohibitive. However, for business travel accounts, personal selling to the travel decision-makers in a firm is needed. These can range from the head of any 'travel department' that may exist to the executives themselves or their secretaries. For important trips or conferences and exhibitions the firm's directors may also have to be 'sold'.

Indirect methods may also be needed. For example, once contact and reputations have been established, direct mail, whether by letter, telex or telephone can maintain contact and interest. Well designed application or booking forms at the end of the brochure is the major 'direct mail' approach that works well with holiday tourists, especially those who are not well placed to use travel agents or who do not wish to do so. As stated elsewhere, the success of the selling effort depends on staff of operators and agents having good, accurate knowledge of all the relevant facts to do with their company's offerings.

8.2.1 Other factors influencing success in selling

Market coverage is one of these. Are sufficient markets covered and are there enough points-of-sale to cover a sufficient number of potential customers? How many are needed and where should they be located? Some should be near business and industrial centres and others in dormitory towns or suburbs. Their opening hours should be relevant. It is pointless having a sales point in a business location if it is closed between noon and 2.00 p.m. which may be the only time business people have to visit them. Table 8.3 shows the various sales outlets possible for tourism products.

Then the *buyer-seller motivations* of the various people in the distribution chain and potential customers must be considered. These are summarised and compared in Table 8.4. The seller's staff motivations will vary with their educational background, training for the job, their own career aims and their chances of promotion. They should be encouraged to have a positive and helpful attitude to enquirers and customers and be interested in the wellbeing and growth of the company.

It is very boring just to give enquirers what they request! Since most are unsure of what they really need, it is better if staff discover what is wanted and match this against what is available. Staff should ensure too that the bookings finally made represent the best available within the price. A customer will not be pleased to find out later that something better, at the same or marginally higher price, could have been obtained. It should be remembered that tourism customers are often seeking new experiences. Just selling them the same old thing, for expedience, will not guarantee a high degree of customer satisfaction. It may just lead to the loss of valuable repeat business.

Table 8.3 Tourism products – sales outlets

Tour operators	Create own packages by buying/reserving necessary supply elements. Retail through travel agents, their own offices and by direct mail (via booking form in brochure or by direct enquiries from consumers).
Direct mail companies	Tour operators who do not sell through travel agents but operate through direct selling via brochures and/or their own retail shops, i.e. being their own retailer.
Travel agents	Sell the products of tour operators at usually a fixed commission which varies in different countries. May also obtain additional commission if total sales for an operator exceeds specified targets. Major travel agents (e.g. Thomas Cook, American Express) may also sell their own package tours as well as those of other tour operators.
Via institutional outlets	The sale of tourism products, usually in some bulk to clubs, trade unions and in some countries, via banks, insurance companies, etc.
Producer-retailer	Producers of the tourism product who have integrated vertically into retailing through their own outlets having bought or built their own accommodation (e.g. Club Méditerranée).
Other mass outlets	The establishment of points-of-sale (counters or travel departments) in mass outlets such as major departmental stores, supermarkets, major bookshops, air and rail terminals, etc.
Tour operator-retailer	Producers of packages who sell them through retail outletrs and by direct mail. Examples include Wagon-Lits in France and other countries and Neckermann in Germany. Thomas Cook and American Express also fall into this category although they sell the products of other tour operators too.

Table 8.4 Buyer-seller motivations

The motivations listed below influence sellers on the extent and thoroughness of the market coverage they will undertake. E.g. a drive for greater sales volume will require coverage of many market segments. The desire for better profit margins will lead to up-market products and coverage. The customers' motivations will indicate what market coverage and product-market mix are most likely to succeed.

TOUR OPERATOR	Improved profit margins Sales volume and good repeat business Acceptable rate of return Low cost distribution Maximum attention to its products by retailers Product (supply) component reliability Products that motivate retailers to sell them and consumers to buy them Minimising risk Avoiding novelty – keep to accepted products
TRAVEL AGENT	Good profit margins Good sales volume Image: of itself and tour operators Regular product innovation Maximum range of products and service Good service from tour operators and other principals
THE CUSTOMER	Anticipation and expectation stimuli Product knowledge (own and T.Agent and T.Operator) Product variety with some new products Minimum waste of time in negotiations Help in evaluating alternatives and making decisions Competent staff which are helpful and pleasant Minimum form filling Individual attention and identification

Finally, the *image* of the product will determine where it should be sold. A luxury world cruise costing thousands of pounds is unlikely to sell well from a counter in a supermarket. On the other hand selling it through the travel department at Harrods should be effective. Apart from the image aspect, such a store can expect to number amongst its customers, many who can afford this cruise.

8.2.2 *Selling through the trade*

It is claimed, arguably, that tour operators selling through the trade (travel agents, etc.) have much to gain against those who sell direct to the consumer. The much greater resources and expertise of a nationwide network of agents should prove beneficial. This is only true if the agents take an interest in the operator's packages and put as much selling behind them as they do for other 'brands'. Alas, this does not always happen. The products of the smaller tour operator lose out against those of the larger well known firms.

The agents' attitudes can be understood if not condoned. They have a relatively small commission rate from which to generate sufficient revenue. This means they will support products in popular demand that sell in volume. They do not wish to spend time and money trying to sell items not readily accepted by consumers for any reason. The argument that using travel agents reduces the operators' total marketing costs also fails. It is only true if an operator's products gets the same sales effort as those of major firms. In recent years, the operations of direct-selling tour operators has shown that these claims need not be correct. This is yet further evidence why a successful communications mix is important.

However, when selling through the trade the tour operator must study and understand the travel agent's market. What are they really selling and to which types of customers? If the agent concentrates on short-break holidays and specialist ones to the Far East, asking them to sell standard packages to resorts in Spain or Italy may not be practical. If the agent produces his/her own leaflets, the style, layout and use of colour should be studied. The operator's brochures may then be produced in similar fashion but with sufficient variations to make them stand out from all the others. Knowing the types of consumer catered for, the operator should identify their motivations and what appeals to them. Special leaflets for different types of customer may then be considered. If this obviates the production of a bulky, expensive brochure the operator might be able to effect cost savings.

Inviting agency staff to visit the operator's office to get to know the staff who will deal with their enquiries and bookings, and to see how they operate, is also useful. Showing willingness to put themselves out to help the travel agent helps to build the support the operator needs from agents. Information packs for travel agents can lead to more effective selling through them.

8.2.3 Sales administration and control

Sales administration must control the sales effort and monitor the results being achieved. If results are deviating from the sales plans the reasons must be identified. Remedial action can be taken. So sales control must ensure that the targets for revenue, sales volume and thus profit and market shares, are being realised. Selling costs must also be controlled and kept to agreed budgets. Executives must also make sure that the market coverage is right and target markets are being contacted effectively.

Then if the conversion rate (enquiries to orders) is low the reasons must be found. Is it due to poor selling, lack of persuasiveness or knowledge on the part of the staff? Or does the product range not fit consumers' needs? Are staff trying to sell the wrong product? Or is the problem due to economic and other trading conditions? In every case remedies should be found. If none are possible, the product-market activities of the firm may have to be fully reconsidered. Perhaps it may simply be that the trends and developments taking place in the business have not been spotted, understood and compensated. The basic records required are

(a) orders booked (by number, value and type of product);
(b) cancellations (with reasons);
(c) market share estimates;
(d) rate of growth of sales (by product and in total);
(e) number of customer contacts;
(f) conversion ratio;

(g) new types of customers;
(h) sales costs (in total and appropriate sub-headings).

8.3 Promotional activities

In this section advertising, sales promotion and PR will be discussed. Elements of merchandising and packaging, as appropriate, will be considered in the light of the special, if limited, needs of the tourism industry.

8.3.1 Strategies and objectives

In most cases there are several promotional strategies which could fit the overall corporate one. However their effectiveness varies. The only way of finding the best one for a firm or a given market is to evaluate the various ones possible and test them against predetermined criteria and the objectives to be attained. To do this the firm must select its target markets (in geographical terms) and the types of consumer (market segments) to which the strategies must be applied. Obviously the key selections must be those market segments which appear to offer optimum profit and maximum sales potential for the products on offer. This will be related to the size of total demand and the strength of the competition operating in them. The final selection of strategies and markets can then be made. By concentrating on such markets, promotional expenditure will be used more effectively.

As mentioned in Section 7.5 it is not possible to operate in every market. The same applies to promotional matters. Costs make it necessary to concentrate promotional activities in the major markets that provide a firm with the bulk of its business. The smaller markets will have to be left to their own devices, provided they do not offer opportunities to major competitors to gain advantages over the firm. Business from these lesser markets, either as an indirect result of the company's major advertising campaign or reputation, is an unexpected (?) bonus. However in some small markets business that might otherwise have been gained may be lost. This opportunity foregone in order to attack better alternatives is the 'opportunity cost' of that decision. Of course the aim must be to keep this opportunity cost as low as possible.

Other criteria to be taken into account include the market standing of the firm, how it wishes to develop this and the product-market expansion or other changes necessary for long-term growth, survival and stability. The objectives of promotional strategy will vary as indicated in Table 8.5.

8.3.2 Advertising

Advertising has been defined as a paid form of non-personal presentation (of a product or service) by an identified sponsor. It uses paid space in media (newspaper, magazines, posters and direct mail) and paid media time (commercial television and radio) to get its message across to the target markets. It has three aims. First, it tells potential customers of the existence of the product (or service) and the benefits that should accrue from its possession or use. Second, it reminds customers of its continued existence to obtain repeat business. Third, it seeks to regain lost customers who may have switched to other suppliers for rational or irrational reasons, and to gain new accounts. For tourism, advertising is aimed at the public to create awareness of the travel offers available, or a resort and its attractions, to influence their buying decisions. Advertisements may be classified as shown in Table 8.6. Their various purposes are shown in Table 8.7.

Selecting the right media for a target market is important if the campaign is to be successful. It cannot be left to eager amateurs. The assistance and advice of experts (from advertising agencies) are necessary. A typical advertising agency organisation is shown in Figure 8.1. The media available in Britain are listed in Table 8.8, which also defines two phrases often used, 'above-the-line' and 'below-the-line' advertising. Table 8.9 lists the major points to be considered when selecting media. Other factors influencing the *impact* of an advertisement include the size of the advertisement, the timing and frequency of the inserts, the theme and message (or copy) and the number of colours used. These and other aspects are discussed more fully in the author's book *Mastering Marketing*.

The timing of the campaign is important. It should not be

Table 8.5 Promotional objectives for different targets

1 *The travel trade*
   (a) Develop or correct the image of the country/resort as a desirable vacation destination.
   (b) Provide comprehensive information and sales aids.
   (c) Assist tour operators and travel agents in the sales development of the various packages.

2 *Potential visitors*
   (a) Create awareness of the range of opportunities and the region's attractions.
   (b) Motivate consumers to seek further information about travel opportunities from the travel trade.
   (c) Inform consumers of the programmes and offers available.
   (d) Develop and improve the country/resort image as a desirable holiday base.

3 *Visitors*
   (a) Inform visitors of the information centres and other assistance available from all those enterprises involved in the travel and tourism business.
   (b) Counteract unfavourable reactions to service deficiencies by providing systems to deal with complaints, criticisms and suggestions and inform visitors of the effort of the industry to control and improve the quality of the tourism services.

4 *The media*
   (a) Ensure that the relevant publications carry newsworthy information on tourist development plans, the availability of new and expanded services and the activities of the NTO.
   (b) Assist the news media (travel sections of newspapers, magazines) to give accounts of travel opportunities and attractions available.

Table 8.6 Classification of advertisements

By appeal	Factual
	Emotional
By content	Product advertising
	Institutional advertising
By demand influence	Primary (main) product level
	Selective brand level
By geographical spread	National
	Regional
	Local
By intended effect	Direct action
	Delayed action
By sponsor	Tour operator (= manufacturer/ wholesaler)
	Travel agent (= retailer)
	Other
	Jointly by two sponsors
By target market	Whichever social group
	Package tour vacationist
	Independent traveller
	Business traveller
	Purpose of travel (vacation, etc.)

SOURCE: Adapted from: Douglas Foster, *Mastering Marketing*, 2nd edn (London: Macmillan, 1984).

launched too far in advance of the time when the buying decisions are made. Nor should it be started too close to that time! In the first instance, the message might be forgotten. In the latter case, many customers might have already made their decisions. In both instances the advertising expenditure may be wasted. Decisions on timing require knowledge of when the peak buying periods are, the level of competition faced and the time taken by consumers to make their decisions.

Table 8.7   Common purposes of advertising

Announce
* Location of stockists: to support dealers and encourage selling-out of stock.
* New product/ service: announcing new brands, insurance, holidays, unit trusts etc.
  New pack: pack identification at points-of-sale is important.
* Modification: to product or service to revive sales.
* Price changes: to keep customers fully informed.

Assist
  The sales force: by providing back-up support of their effort.
* The stockists: critical when dealing with supermarkets and chain stores to get dealer support; helps stockists to move goods down the line; persuades them to hold stocks.

Attract
* Enquiries: so as not to miss any opportunities.
* New business: to expand markets and increase profit.
  Return of lost accounts: to reverse negative sales trends.

Challenge
* Competition: to hold market shares, etc.; to reduce impact of new/substitute products etc.

Educate
* Customers and stockists: to explain anything that needs it.

Expand
* Markets to new buyers: to ensure full exploitation of all opportunities for a product/service.
  Stockist network: (or develop)   find new stockists to improve market coverage.
  Direct sales: to reduce distribution costs and increase market shares.

Make
* Special offers: to counter competition, off-peak demand; to increase sales, launch new product.

Maintain
* Sales: to hold market shares etc. (usually by reminding customers about the product).

Test
* A market: checking response before a national launch.
* A medium: for effectiveness, readership etc.

---

* Relevant for tourism but for 'stockist' read 'Travel Agent'.

SOURCE: Adapted from: Douglas Foster, *Mastering Marketing*, 2nd edn (London: Macmillan, 1984).

In Britain, decisions on the annual (summer) holiday are usually made by Easter though in recent years, there has been an increase in late bookings (in June or July) in the hope of securing special reduced prices. Consumers begin to think seriously about this around mid-January when they have recovered from the orgy of Christmas and the worry about the rates, taxes and other major expenditures that fall due in the New Year. So the main campaign should run from January to April with perhaps a few opening, reminder shots in early December and if necessary, a less intensive programme from May to June to catch the latecomers. If sales need boosting at the last minute, short campaigns highlighting special offers could be used in July or August. It all depends on the money available but it is always wise to place some of the funds in a 'contingency budget' for special uses like these if results are not matching targets.

Advertising for winter holidays usually begins in October though there is a tendency to start in September, depending on the strength of the competition. The campaign can be continued, in varying intensity, until February or even March. The brochures for the summer season are usually available or mailed out in December or January but may be available in travel agents' offices by September. Winter season leaflets and brochures come out in October but sometimes, confusingly, in September. With the intense competition in 1983 and 1984, some tour operators issued special, short brochures with guaranteed lower prices for some resorts to attract early bookings.

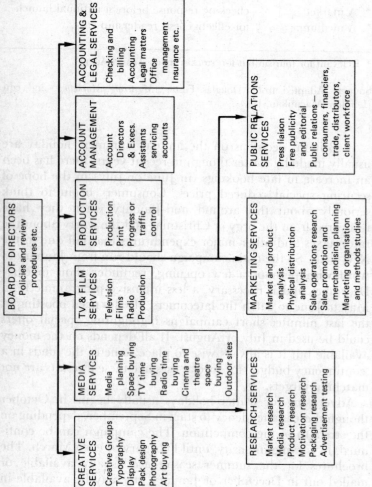

Figure 8.1   Typical advertising agency organisation

BOARD OF DIRECTORS
Policies and review
procedures etc.

CREATIVE
SERVICES
Creative Groups
Typography
Display
Pack design
Photography
Art buying

MEDIA
SERVICES
Media
planning
Space buying
TV time
buying
Radio time
buying
Cinema and
theatre
space
buying
Outdoor sites

TV & FILM
SERVICES
Television
Films
Radio
Production

PRODUCTION
SERVICES
Production
Print
Progress or
traffic
control

ACCOUNT
MANAGEMENT
Account
Directors
& Execs.
Assistants
servicing
accounts

ACCOUNTING &
LEGAL SERVICES
Checking and
billing
Accounting .
Legal matters
Office
management
Insurance etc.

RESEARCH SERVICES
Market research
Media research
Product research
Motivation research
Packaging research
Advertisement testing

MARKETING SERVICES
Market and product
analysis
Physical distribution
analysis
Sales operations research
Sales promotion and
merchandising planning
Marketing organisation
and methods studies

PUBLIC RELATIONS
SERVICES
Press liaison
Free publicity
and editorial
Public relations –
consumers, financiers,
trade, distributors,
client workforce

SOURCE: Douglas Foster, *Mastering Marketing*, 2nd edn (London: Macmillan, 1984).

Table 8.8 Media available

Newspapers
National/regional/local: weekday and Sunday editions.

Technical press
Technical magazines and 'newspapers'.

Magazines
General (of general interest to readers, e.g. women's magazines
etc.) and special interest (e.g. sport, recreation, house and
furnishings, hobbies etc.)

Commercial television

Commercial radio

Poster sites
Outdoors generally, at transport termini etc.

Display cards
On transport* (e.g. in trains, buses); in hotels and restaurants.

Cinema and theatres
In programmes and displays during intervals.

Direct mail

*Sometimes referred to, in America, as 'Transit Advertising'.

Above-the-line advertising: This is where advertisements are placed in
media which, having 'recognised' the agency, pay the latter a
commission on the purchase of space, sites and air time. These media
are the press, commercial TV and radio, transport organisations and
(some) cinemas. They provide the bulk of an agency's income.

Below-the-line advertising involves media that do not normally pay a
commission or fee to the advertising agency. The latter must add a
percentage to cover handling charges, profit etc. The fee can also be
based on the time spent on making use of these media. The media
here include merchandising, exhibitions, direct mail, printers,
package designers, film makers, producers of display material.

SOURCE: Douglas Foster, *Mastering Marketing*, 2nd edn (London: Macmillan, 1984).

Table 8.9   Media selection: points to consider

CIRCULATION

Normally means the audited net sale per issue, i.e. the number of copies sold. Advertising rates vary according to audited net sales. Usually the number of free copies distributed has been subtracted from the total copies issued. (For *exhibitions*, certified attendance figures are the equivalent. However, what is more important here is the quality and calibre of the people attending rather than the total attendance figures.)

READERSHIP

The total number of people who see or read the publication which is usually greater than the number of purchases, i.e. the circulation. This is the better figure to work to when considering the media to use and the cost effectiveness of advertisements. *Quality aspect:* refers to the type of people seeing or reading the publication (income, age, sex, social grading etc.). National Readership Surveys usually give these details but have to rely on publishers' statements especially for the lesser publications. *Quantity aspect:* refers to the fact that readership can be from three to fifteen or more times greater than the circulation figure.

PROFILE

This refers to the proportional breakdown of the readership by social or income groups. Useful when matching media selection to market segments.

PRIMARY OR SUPPORT MEDIA

Refers to whether the media gives an initial, powerful impact by reason of its coverage etc. (e.g. *The Economist,* leading women's magazines, *Radio Times,* Sunday papers etc.) or plays a supporting or secondary role (e.g. local press, direct mail, window bills and displays etc.)

PRODUCT LIFE CYCLE

The stage a product has reached in its life cycle can also be a guide to the media that should be used. There are two aspects.
Staircase effect: This refers to established products whose life cycle is extended, or takes off from the maturity stage as new uses, markets or applications are found for it. Various plastic products were examples.

Leapfrog effect: Products with a long life may not suffer any real decline in sales by do encounter periodic market challenges which are often met by product modifications, repackaging, restyling and merchandising. In these cases it is necessary to leapfrog the new challenge by such developments. The choice of media will then depend on the nature and scope of the challenge and how best this can be countered or overcome.

PENETRATION
The degree of market penetration achieved will depend on a blend of creativity in the design of the advertisement and the effectiveness of the media used (assuming the product has the right attributes). How well media assist successful penetration of any market is important and must therefore guide executives in their selection of media.

SOURCE: Douglas Foster, *Mastering Marketing*, 2nd edn (London: Macmillan, 1984).

8.3.3 , *Sales promotions*
While advertising aims at a steady long-term improvement in sales with the growth held when the campaign ends, sales promotions are short-term activities. They seek to boost sales at peak demand periods to ensure the firm obtains its market share and are used to help launch a new product or support an ailing or modified one. These sales gains are not usually maintained when the sales promotion ends and sales volume may in fact drop below previous levels. This is because promotions aim to advance sales that may normally be made at some later time. Thus they just bunch up the sales rather than achieve a real, permanent increase in total annual sales.

For the tourism industry the main sales promotions are the brochure, leaflets, point-of-sale display, and direct mail material. Brochures are normally bulky, expensive items which are really catalogues of the packages available. They need careful planning of the layout, number of colours and quality of the paper used. They should echo the theme and message of the advertising and other promotional material if an integrated and effective total campaign is to result.

Sales letters are useful to tour operators when trying to increase the interest of travel agents and potential customers in their products. Travel agents can also use them effectively on potential customers, particularly people who have been customers in previous years. They can be quickly organised and selectively targeted to customer groups and improve the flexibility that can be injected into the promotional activity. The response rate can be quickly checked, allowing better control. From the experience gained, subsequent mailings can be improved.

In tourism, *point-of-sale advertising* involves the planned display of this material in the offices and windows of travel agents and other points-of-sale. It uses posters, floor and counter displays, banners, related wall decorations (for example, pictures of the country or resort being promoted) literature racks for leaflets and brochures and of the aircraft or airlines used. It is in fact a form of merchandising.

Merchandising devised originally for mass market goods like foodstuffs and drink, involved displaying the product in the right location in a shop, on carefully selected shelf positions in sufficient quantity to attract the attention of customers. Well presented, attractive young ladies are usually used by these displays to call the customer's attention to the product. It is a highly skilled activity, using the same materials as mentioned under point-of-sale advertising. Merchandising is particularly effective with products bought on impulse.

It is effective with tourism products also, despite the fact that they are not normally bought on impulse. They increase the effect of other related promotional activities. However, with tourism, merchandising can be a subtle way of clinching a decision in the minds of enquirers. There is nothing like attractive pictures of a resort to convince would-be holiday-makers they should go there for their next holiday!

Packaging is normally the attractive outer wrapper of a product designed to attract the eye of the consumer. It identifies the product and its uses. It should not be confused with packing, the inner wrapper and other material designed to protect the product from damage or contamination in handling and storage. For tourism products, the outer cover and internal layout of brochures and leaflets represent the 'packaging' of the items. Through an attractive style and presentation, consumers can be persuaded to handle and look at the brochures and leaflets. Often this is the final persuasive move on the part of sellers which leads to a favourable buying decision by customers. The basic aim of packaging is thus achieved.

Competitions can also be used in tourism to increase the interest and support of customers and the trade. Trade competitions usually award prizes to the travel agent that sells more than a stated quantity of a tour package or other travel facility. For consumers the prizes can range from free holidays for two or special reduced prices for the winners.

8.3.4 Public and press relations (PR and pr)

Activities here range from a press release to newspapers and travel magazines to create consumer interest in a holiday, resort or country, to familiarisation trips organised by tour operators or tourist boards for travel agents. These trips may also be organised by tourist boards for the travel trade. They include also special seminars and other functions to promote a new destination. One such was the wine and cheese parties organised by British Airways some time ago to launch the then new resort of the Seychelles. They used colour sound film and slides with commentary at conferences and seminars for members of the travel trade and consumers. These were supported by a number of press releases to the national and local press, television and radio.

PR has been defined as deliberate, planned and sustained efforts to establish and maintain mutual understanding between a firm and its various publics, customers, financiers, investors, employees as well as the media. In tourism it is also used to educate the customers and travel trade on the products and services available, in particular new ones, and to improve their knowledge of other countries, peoples, cultures, resorts and destinations. PR activities are an essential part of a company's communications mix and should be included in their integrated plans for this.

8.3.5 Promotional objectives
The individual activities in the communications mix have their

own objectives and aims but these have to stem from and support the firm's overall promotional objectives. These can be summarised as making their products, company and reputation as widely known as possible and to present messages that are true and honest. They have also to try to keep customer expectations in balance with the realities of the situation they will find. This is particularly important in tourism where customers may fantasise on the holidays they have booked and be disappointed by the reality. They will be disillusioned and no matter how unfair their original fantasy, they can blame the tour operator!

If expectations greatly exceed reality, repeat business will be lost and customers may avoid the operator concerned for all future holidays, even ones that have no relevance to the package that disappointed them. They may make adverse comments to friends and relatives and damage the operator's business further. If customer satisfaction is at a low level, repeat buying may be minimal. However, if reality is better than expectations, satisfaction will be at a high level and the business will prosper through word-of-mouth recommendations and repeat business.

8.4   Travel writers

Travel writers and correspondents of newspapers and magazines play an important part in promoting (and killing off!) tourism products and destinations. It is important to gain their support and assistance but to achieve this, careful consideration must be given to the style and type of articles they write or publish. The articles released must be written in the style favoured by the publication or correspondent. It should also be of the required length. If published articles tend to be 500 words long, ones of 1000 or more will usually end in the wastepaper basket even if it was excellent enough to win the Pulitzer Prize for literature. Journalists do not have the time, nor the inclination, to rewrite someone else's effort.

Other points to remember include the fact that travel correspondents seek interesting stories that will catch readers' attention and hold their interest. What may excite the executives of the travel firm may just bore the publication and its readers. For example an article that eulogises a safari lodge because it has all 'mod cons' creates little interest. This is taken for granted. It may turn off those who are seeking less sophisticated facilities. However, if the safari park abounds with leopards or other rare animals or birds, an article on this should create considerable interest. This could provide a good opening hook on which to hang the rest of the release. Or if some new and unique holiday is featured (say flying to Nairobi by Concorde or combining a stay on Bali with a cruise to other Indonesian islands) then the article could be acceptable.

Another point concerns the market for which the release is intended. If the holiday being featured is not suitable for the publication's readers, a release on it may be ignored. For example, an article featuring inexpensive holidays, with limited accommodation facilities but offering deserted sandy beaches and lots of sunshine, would be appropriate for a paper read by the younger age groups. Those on expensive and exotic tours may be better placed in prestige publications.

Free holidays, business lunches and dinners are ways by which a good relationship could be developed between the travel firm and travel writers. However these can be overdone. Free trips are effective if part of a familiarisation programme. Too many lunches and dinners can dull the senses and may become just a free meal ticket without producing the required editorial. It must be remembered that other travel firms may be plying the poor travel writer with such blandishments and not doing the latter's health or life expectancy any good at all!

8.5 Presentations

Presentations are useful promotional activities. They permit a more fullsome exposition of what has otherwise to be compressed in brochures or leaflets because of space and cost limitations. The message can be altered to suit the specific interests or problems of the audience. When the audience is restricted to one or two types of customer or firm, the message can be tailored more precisely to appeal to them. An hotel organisation can use presentations to show tour operators and travel agents what facilities they can and do offer. Airlines can promote their services, routes and aircraft. The possibilities are endless. The work under this heading requires a good knowledge of target markets, audiences and innovative abilities.

8.6   Promotional budgets

Expenditure budgets for promotional purposes include personal selling costs and, like these, should be based on what the activities have to achieve in the current and future years. They should be adequate for the tasks to be done. Any skimping would just be wasting money. Activities would have to be scaled down, possibly to such an extent that their objectives cannot be realised. Nor should the budgets be based on some percentage of *last year's sales*. Last year has gone by and events then are of no real relevance to what the firm must achieve now and in the future. Any percentage should be applied to the sales revenue that has been targeted.

However there are other ways of arriving at a budget. First, the work that has to be done successfully is considered. The activities needed should be selected and the extent and coverage should be estimated. Then from past experience and knowledge of current cost levels, the estimated cost can be calculated and the budget fixed accordingly. If at a later date it is found that the objectives can be achieved without spending the entire budget, appropriate reductions can be made. If the original estimate understated the true cost, effort should be made to find the additional funds required. Given that the margins in tourism are not generous, great care is needed in planning promotional work and thus its budget.

In the cost estimates the figures normally used as guides are the total cost of each advertisement and the cost per reader or viewer. However the impact or effect of one advertisement is pretty negligible and several insertions or broadcasts are necessary to influence potential customers. Past experience should show how many times a message has to be exposed to obtain the desired result and the budget should allow for this.

8.7 Planning promotions

The planning of promotional (and other marketing) activities in the tourism industry, while much improved in recent years, still needs a more systematic approach. Some hotel executives express their aim as keeping promotional and marketing expenditures as low as possible! Executives of smaller organisations complain about the lack of funds. Many still argue that marketing and promotional work is the responsibility of someone else, a government department, tourist boards and others. They seem to think it is solely the responsibility of tourist boards to bring customers to their door. They do not appear to realise that an integrated and cooperative effort by all members of the industry is vital if a high degree of success is to be achieved.

Some countries are better at organising and maintaining successful, integrated promotions and marketing. The USA, Australia, New Zealand, Germany and Singapore are five examples. Other countries (Britain and Malaysia) are improving their efforts. For smaller places like the Pacific Islands, the efforts of Air New Zealand and Qantas make up any shortfall due to lack of funds. They provide useful information about the islands as well as their own timetables and services to them.

8.7.1 Methods

Several methods of planning promotional activities are available. First there is the *optimisation approach* which analyses the functional relationships between the decision variables that apply and the 'estimated outcomes' for alternative plans. A quantitative model is used for existing demand and supply variables, their possible changes during the planning period and the promotional inputs. These inputs are varied and a computer is used to show when the optimum combination and level of arrivals and sales are achieved. The model is more complex than this simplified explanation might suggest!

Second is the *empirical approach*. This relies on experience, tradition and subjective judgements. Market research and intelligence are used mainly to confirm initial hypotheses and assumptions. It is a popular method because it is simple to use and provides estimates quickly. It applies some general rules and principles to the process. These range from concentrating all effort on major markets to the optimisation of the communications mix according to the money available.

These two assumptions are considered by some experts to be too generalised for the selection of a course of action from several alternatives and as guides to new or unusual markets or in highly competitive situations and conditions of change. There is not sufficient experience to be certain of sound subjective judgements. Promotional decisions, when money is limited, must be taken with exactitude. They cannot be done in an *ad hoc*, aimless or chaotic manner. There is no guarantee that all relevant problems have been clearly defined, stated or assessed. Nor do they consider critically or objectively all the possible courses of action and their outcomes. What may be appropriate for one market or destination need not be so for others. For example, an appeal based on the availability of quiet, almost deserted beaches may be correct for say, Malaysia, but is unconvincing for busy, well patronised Spanish resorts.

Finally, there is the *heuristic approach*. Here a strategy or rule of thumb is used aimed at simplifying the choices and so the search for a reasonable solution. By establishing the objectives and targets for the promotional campaign the number of choices is reduced and only those that are compatible with the targets are used. Decisions are taken in stages.

First, broad strategic decisions are taken on the markets in which to promote the firm's products, the aims of the promotion and the resources needed for a successful campaign. Next, operational decisions are made about the promotional activities that are available and which will be used, how they should be combined into an integrated campaign and the resources allocated to each (deciding the promotional mix). How the results will be evaluated is also decided here. The final stage defines the action programmes and covers decisions on content, timing, frequency, colours and media to be used.

The inherent danger lies in the heuristic decision taken in the first stage. For example, take a tour operator whose main group of holiday packages is bought by social groups C1 and C2 (85 per cent of the total business) and some B and D people (sharing the remaining 15 per cent). It may decide to limit promotional activities to the C1s and C2s, expecting to pick up the rest of its business from the remaining two groups as before. This assumes that the *status quo* of the demand situation will remain for the period of the plan, probably three or four years. This can be a dangerous assumption especially in uncertain economic times. It ignores the fact that prudence might be forcing the B group to consider cheaper holidays formerly accepted mainly by the Cs. Also the Ds might be improving their wage position and taking greater interest in more expensive holidays. Whenever heuristic decisions are necessary, the bias and risks involved should be known. Compensation can be made for them. If they are too substantial then the promotional and other marketing decisions will have to be reconsidered.

Promotional plans should be consistent with the other marketing and corporate plans and objectives. They should be able to draw on sufficient resources, including the skills and experience of the firm's staff. They should not damage the company's reputation, rather enhance it, nor its customer goodwill. The plans should also be flexible in that they allow for changes to be made quickly and efficiently when market and other conditions change. Finally, a very good promotional plan that takes too long to make and is thereby launched too late is worse than having no plan at all!

8.8   More case illustrations

The following are relevant to the study of the communications mix.

8.8.1   *The birth of an international airline*
In 1955 Lufthansa, now the airline of West Germany, began operations again with flights across the Atlantic. Its promotional and marketing problems lay in how to carve out a useful share for itself in the lucrative and well-served North Atlantic market. It had also to promote West Germany as a desirable holiday destination even though it did not have an obvious tourist capital like London, Paris or Rome. Germany was then not considered a holiday playground. The devastation of the

war years and tough times of the immediate postwar era did not help. The airline had also to overcome other unfavourable images left over from the war.

In the mid-1960s a touring lecture programme was used in America to promote Germany as having various holiday destinations. In 1968 the 'Vacation Germany' campaign was launched. It used four colour advertisements in major national magazines, various special tour packages, sales promotions and PR activities. In 1970 the theme was changed to 'Think twice about Germany'. This campaign added television advertisements in New York and Chicago to its activities. Tourist traffic from America increased by about 20 per cent. However market research showed that only a quarter of the people crossing the Atlantic were tourists, the remainder being business executives and first-generation Americans of German descent. Only a very few tourists used Germany as their gateway to Europe, London, Paris and Lisbon being preferred. If they did visit Germany they used other modes of transport which did not benefit Lufthansa.

So the promotional strategy was changed. The new one emphasised Frankfurt as the gateway to Romantic Europe and Munich as a gateway to the Alps. Lufthansa also began cooperating with tour operators on packages starting at these gateways. Specialised tours covering stays at castles, wine-tasting and folk festivals were added to this product range. Special events such as the Berlin Beer Festival and the Oberammergau Passion Play were also exploited.

Then, since 80 per cent of the business was booked through travel agents, familiarisation tours for the agents, films and other audio-visual presentations were organised for selected groups of customers and travel agents. Specific market segments were approached. For example, teachers of German in America were tempted with study tours. Lutherans were offered special packages for the 300th anniversay of Luther's birth. The conference market was approached by mailings and visits by sales persons to the decision-makers. Comparisons were made between the cost of holding conferences in Germany, including the travel cost, with that in America. The German tourist authority was also involved in motivating and pre-selling Americans on the idea of visiting Germany and in research on what motivated Americans to visit any country. As a result of all this and with the growth of industrial actvity, Lufthansa became a major international carrier, with a strong position in the Transatlantic trade for both business travel and vacations.

8.8.2 *The mighty atom!*

In the 1960s and 1970s the number of tourist arrivals in Hong Kong increased substantially. During the period 1961 to 1970 the average growth rate was over 16 per cent. Tourist expenditure rose by some 19 per cent to US $300 million. The image of Hong Kong as one of the world's most exciting places helped but the work of the Hong Kong Tourist Association (HKTA), created in 1967, played a major role.

During this period the HKTA's total budget amounted to an average of one-half of one per cent of the annual expenditure by tourists. Three-quarters of this was allocated to promotional work in the field or in support of it. About 45 per cent of this latter sum, on average, was spent on overseas information offices, 35 per cent went on promotional activities and the remaining 20 per cent on producing the necessary promotional material and other support activities. Because of the high cost of a direct approach to consumers, HKTA decided to boost indirect methods. These included using carriers, tour operators and travel agents to sell Hong Kong whilst providing them with promotional material and activities relevant to the packages being offered.

In addition, the press relations side of PR was built up, establishing useful contacts with the media. Particular attention was given to travel writers and correspondents. Films and audio-visual presentations were also concentrated on the travel trade. Finally, a general information service for the public and trade was maintained through HKTA's offices.

Their marketing research concentrated on visitor surveys. These included consumer profile and motivation studies, as well as product development and improvement and pricing research. Others covered the effectiveness of the promotional and marketing activities. From these there emerged important points for decisions on future marketing strategy.

First, the all-in prices of packages for Hong Kong had to be maintained at very competitive levels. Some adjustments had to be made to meet changing market conditions. Second, the established attractions would lose their appeal in time and steps had to be taken to develop others. Third, market coverage would have to be expanded to new, larger markets or market segments. Fourth, direct selling would have to be increased over the years as would more advertising to potential customers. Market segments overlooked in earlier years would have to be developed. Finally, future projects would have to be less labour intensive. Labour is in short supply and is in growing demand for manufacturing industries.

It will be interesting to note how the tourism traffic to Hong Kong may alter once Britain hands back Hong Kong to China in 1997.

8.8.3 A legal surprise

A few years ago an established British tour operator, in its brochure, featured a weekly beach barbecue evening at one of its resorts. Besides listing this event as an attraction they showed colour photographs of a magnificent, large sandy beach and imposing barbecue area, good beach furniture and a very appetising spread of food. On the strength of this two brothers booked themselves and their families for a two-week holiday at the resort.

As they subsequently claimed during the court case they brought against the tour operator, the reality was a shock! The beach where the barbecue was held was small, littered with stones, rocks and old rubbish. The beach furniture was broken or badly damaged. The food was limited and of poor quality, some of it apparently uneatable. There were many flies and a plague of other insects, including biting ones. They claimed back the cost of the tour or at least demanded some compensation for the grave disappointment they claimed to have suffered.

The tour operator's lawyer in refuting the claim, stated that the pictures were not intended to show precisely what customers would get at that resort or hotel. He said they were intended simply to show the sort of things that were usually presented at resorts along the coast. To the surprise of the two brothers, the judge accepted this view and found in favour of the tour operator. Further, the brothers were ordered to pay a substantial sum to cover the operator's legal costs. *Caveat emptor!*

Assignments

1 What activities normally comprise the communications mix? Why is it important to understand their roles and to plan them in an integrated manner? How may this help in marketing tourism products?

2 How does the choice of target markets and market segments influence decisions on the type, nature and extent of the communications mix required?

3 You are a junior executive with the tourist board of a developing, independent East African country. It offers many attractions to tourists including safari parks, superb lodges, abundant wildlife and flora. You have to prepare an outline marketing and promotional plan that will increase the tourist traffic, while keeping total numbers within bounds that will not damage the environment or ecology. Prepare such a plan.

4 What role does personal selling play in developing tourism to a major, developed country? How are the standard activities adapted for this purpose?

5 You are the marketing manager of a national airline with substantial transatlantic business. The company wishes to develop its traffic to Southeast Asia and Australia to comparable proportions. It has the approval of IATA and the appropriate governments. What promotional campaign would you recommend?

9

Finance and Organisation

In this chapter consideration will be given to the financing of, and organisations in the tourism industry, in particular national tourist organisations (NTO).

The extent and success of the industry in any country depends on how well it is organised, given the great variety of (mainly) independent organisations comprising it and whether the necessary finance is available at acceptable terms. This finance is needed not only by the supply components of the industry (accommodation or hotels, carriers, etc.), the travel trade (tour operators, travel agents) but also by destinations. The last require funds to develop the necessary infra- and superstructures and absorb the greater amount of what can be termed 'tourism finance'.

In other industries, provided they have the finance, they can often struggle along with poor or inadequate organisations – consider the many badly organised businesses that still survive! In tourism getting the organisation right is going to be a critical factor of future years as competition grows. Making sure the operation is adequately financed will be the other critical factor. Not surprisingly, finance and sound organisation are interdependent when sustained success of the industry, over the long term, is required. Intensifying competition will increase the interdependence.

9.1 Financing tourism projects

In considering this subject it is necessary to study the implications for both the macro- and micro-aspects of the different aims of the public and private sectors involved in a project. The difficulties met in obtaining finance, especially for projects in the developing countries, and the use of grants and other assistance from host governments, also require careful consideration. The public and private sectors pursue different goals. The first is seeking increased foreign currency earnings, economic development and the increased revenues that can be obtained directly and indirectly from tourism (see Sections 1.2 and 1.3). These are of special importance to developing nations. The private sector is primarily interested in making a profit and securing acceptable returns on the money they invest in a project. It is also interested in the amount of that profit that can be remitted to the home countries of the private enterprises.

The scale of a project influences the degree of involvement by the public and private sectors. If it is a large one requiring considerable development of the infra- and superstructures of the region, the public sector has to play a major role. With smaller projects, for example the building of an hotel or marina, the private sector plays the major role. The public sector may only be involved if grants or other assistance are given. This will be when the host government considers a project as important to the realisation of its own economic aims. Further, while the private sector is dependent on being able to make a profit to survive and grow, the public sector is assured of future income through the fiscal revenues it will receive as a result of the development.

9.1.1 *Public sector criteria*

Because of the different aims, the financial criteria used by the public and private sectors to evaluate projects are different. The important criteria for the public sector are the improved level of employment that would result, increased income from taxation and other dues such as import duties and the improvement in the infra- and superstructures. The last two improve the amenities provided for both tourists and local residents.

The first improves the potential earnings of residents. The others increase the government's ability to boost economic development.

Regarding employment it should be realised that the once-and-for-all cost of creating a job in tourism is about £7000 at 1984 rates. This is less than that for creating a job in agriculture and considerably less than that for manufacturing industry. In addition, the cost of supporting an unemployed person can be high. In Britain in the early 1980s the cost varied from £5000 to £6000 *a year*. In other countries, especially developing ones, all the indicated figures should be lower.

Nonetheless much is to be gained by the host government, economically and politically, if it can bring about a substantial reduction in unemployment, relatively quickly. However, if there is too much dependence on imported labour, this 'gain' will be eroded. On the other hand, the various multipliers and their effects can enhance the benefits gained. Also, since not all development is on a grandiose scale needing vast capital investment, improvement in the employment position is possible quite quickly. The greater the number of modest projects developed, the greater will be this improvement.

Government income is enhanced by increased revenues from sales taxes (or VAT), payroll taxes, taxes on profits, excise duties (especially on alcohol and tobacco products), import duties, income tax from a growing number of employed persons, property taxes and even tax on profits remitted abroad. All these are soon increased as tourism development progresses, especially if many modest projects are involved. Even when a host government invests in the projects either directly or by grants, it is usual for the payback period to be relatively short. With the economic multiplier effect this period can be a mere two or three years, much shorter than for other capital projects.

The tourism industry is also an important source for additional foreign currency earnings for the host country. This is even if the gain for developing nations in particular, may have been overstated by not taking into account the amounts spent by tourists with international carriers and hotel groups. Much of the expenditure may be made in the tourists' home countries when they book and pay for their package holidays, or remitted by these organisations as profit to their home bases. There are other causes of drain on the gross foreign earnings potential. They include the servicing (interest payments) on foreign investment, whether this was loan or equity capital, management fees charged and remitted abroad, need for imported skilled labour to supplement local labour and the cost of importing goods which the host country cannot provide. Nonetheless the potential for earning foreign currency through tourism, especially for developing nations, is worth consideration. Some countries, put off by these drainages, may kill this potential by severely restricting or preventing foreign investment and so preventing the tourism development they need. However, many countries make a careful study of the advantages and disadvantages and accept that even a reduced net gain is better than none.

The improvement of the infrastructure and superstructure is attractive to host countries, not only for the direct benefits that will accrue but also because of the improved base this provides for the development of industries not related to tourism. Better roads and transport systems, electricity supply, telephone service, sewerage, public health services and so on attract business enterprises to an area. The wet weather facilities, car parks, sports centres, shops and improved local transport expected by tourists increase and improve the amenities available to local residents and make the area an attractive one in which to live and work. This is a further attraction for new business enterprises unrelated to tourism.

Public sector executives should carefully consider all these points before approving new projects and investing in them. Most do. However more thought is also being given to the possibility of increased pollution due to substantial growth in tourist traffic flows because of the development. While uncontrolled pollution is destructive, it is possible to limit or prevent it. This costs money and the investment in pollution control will have to be offset against all the other benefits that would arise, not least of which is the long-term preservation and conservation of the area.

9.1.2 *Private sector criteria*

While the prime criterion for the private investor is the ability of a project to contribute suitable and increasing profit over the longest possible time, or some predetermined period, other criteria are involved. First, there is the project's anticipated ability to meet a predetermined repayment schedule or pay-back period. Second is the need to attain, hold and improve the return (rate of interest or profitability) on the capital invested. Third is the ability of the project to make prompt payment, or servicing, of loans and grants from the public sector. Finally, the anticipated cash flow and discounted cash flow return are other points of interest to the equity investor.

9.1.3 *Some other reasons for development*

Besides the essentially financial reasons mentioned in the last two sections, there are others. First, besides seeking immediate gain in terms of profit, the developer will be interested in achieving long-term appreciation of land. Building an hotel is another method of increasing the value of surrounding prop-erty, in most cases. The increased flow of people to the hotel will increase the potential earning capacity of other enterprises in the vicinity. A few developments arise because the deve-lopers enjoy doing this. They gain considerable pleasure from being seen as successful entrepreneurs!

Governments may have as their reasons also, various politi-cal considerations such as helping an economically stunted area of the country, paying off political debts through granting aid to a region or trying to redistribute wealth or improve the earning potential of local residents and labour. Some resorts or hotels are built to express national pride. Having one or two major units, rather than a number of small hotels with limited facilities, does improve the international reputation of the region. The development of a tourist resort may also require the building of an international airport which may be seen as further enhancement of prestige.

9.1.4 *Choice*

In most cases the government and developers must decide if they should support developments serving the luxury trade or low-cost sectors of the tourism business. The former brings into the resort sophisticated, affluent people who can spend in a week what local residents may take a year to earn. This can cause resentment in the latter. However a luxury hotel catering for the rich becomes an important national symbol, even if it accentuates the gulf between the 'haves' and 'have-nots'.

Low-cost development, sometimes called 'social tourism', involves the development of camp sites, cabins and other cheap accommodation units, often in national parks and other areas of scenic beauty. They appeal not only to the low-budget vacationist but also to those wishing to avoid the sophistication of traditional resorts or those who wish to commune with nature. The natural attractions of the sites and do-it-yourself activities (lake swimming, hiking, boating, fishing and so on) are the things that appeal in these cases. However if development is carelessly done and controlled, the scenic beauty of the region can be ruined by litter and ecological damage. Some countries oppose these low-cost developments for these reasons and the fact that they attract visitors whose spending in the area is by necessity or design, minimal. Some planners maintain that low-cost tourism does little for the host region and it is not easy to move, later, to the luxury market. The country becomes known for its 'cheap tourism' and the more affluent may avoid it for this reason.

9.1.5 Why projects fail

Projects fail financially and aesthetically if little market research and area planning is done. In the first instance potential demand may be inadequate so a tourist project without a market, like any other venture, will fail. Facilities built without thought to market feasibility can fail to achieve financial viability. Those that have not been carefully planned and controlled, taking into account the whole region, become just a tourist jungle or trap. Often they will just be garish, without beauty or attractiveness, especially if proper landscaping has been omitted. No one profits, not even the tourist.

9.2 Sources of funds

There are several sources of finance for tourism projects. These are governments, the industry, commercial and merchant banks, other investors such as insurance companies and pension funds, the tourist organisations and the tourists. *Government financing* can be at national, regional and local levels. Most governments are aware of the net economic benefits that can accrue directly and indirectly to the region being developed and the country as a whole. Properly planned and controlled, taking the needs and aspirations of the local population into account, tourism projects can enhance the wellbeing and standard of life of local residents.

Governments are also involved in investment (loans and grants) in major projects beyond the purse of private industry or where they think it is advisable for many reasons. Sometimes the private sector is reluctant to become involved until certain guarantees and support is forthcoming from the government. Cooperation by the government in financing such projects can increase the confidence of the private sector in them. Financial assistance from governments is more readily forthcoming in designated development areas whether in general terms or specifically for tourism purposes. Primary interest may be in the improvement of the superstructure of the region but can also be in assistance with the development of the infrastructure. Tax concessions or 'holidays' also feature in such support, as do low-interest loans for working capital and equipment purchases.

Commercial banks are usually interested in major, long-term or venture capital forms of investment but may consider fixed-term loans for even small amounts (£30,000 or less) which may be used for the purchase of essential equipment or as working capital. Repayment is usually by monthly instalments that cover principal and interest. *Merchant banks* which may or may not be subsidiaries of commercial banks, are usually interested in ventures offering several years of profitable potential. Substantial funds can be obtained from this source but merchant banks seek a quick turnround of funds. Their preference is mainly for loans over three or four years which make 500 per cent over the period. They may also take a share of the equity and representation on the board if this is possible. However besides providing venture capital, they will also offer fixed-term loans without equity participation, to firms they consider suitable.

Finance houses provide medium-term funds. They usually

favour their existing customers and require security for a loan, such as a mortgage on that part of a project they are funding (for example, an hotel, marina or sports complex). *Pension funds* sometimes provide venture capital provided this is in excess of about £100,000. Their terms are similar to those of merchant banks. *Insurance companies* as yet not very active in providing venture capital, may offer medium-term funds secured against an appropriate mortgage, at competitive terms.

Finance corporations such as the Industrial and Commercial Finance Corporation (ICFC) and Finance Corporation for Industry (FCI) are other sources. However they are usually interested in major projects of national importance though the former will also provide medium-term loans. The ICFC is not government owned and would expect to earn commercial rates of return. Loans of £5000 to £1 million are possible on various terms, depending on the project. Usually the interest charged is 2 per cent higher than current debenture rates, so that the cost is similar to that of a mortgage from other sources. Other organisations that could provide funds include the Council for Small Industries in Rural Areas, Small Business Capital Fund Ltd and such as the Highlands and Islands Development Board.

Finance from the *tourism industry* involves investment by firms active in tourism. The extent of their investment will depend on the extent of their involvement in the project. For example, a major international hotel group could provide substantial finance for the development of a tourist complex. *National tourist organisations* may also provide limited funds. Here it is often the case of, say, the national organisation making grants to a regional office. They may also contribute to the cost of marketing research and promotional campaigns in cooperation with other members of the industry. *Tourists* themselves are relatively limited providers of funds. They contribute through the various tourist taxes they pay. In some instances special visitor taxes and other levies may be imposed.

In seeking long-term capital, funds may be drawn from both domestic and foreign sources. By 'domestic' is meant that funds are raised in the home countries of the major participants in a project and in the host country where the project is to be located. 'Foreign' means any other countries whose governments, banks, financiers and other private sector companies may be interested in making investments for commercial reasons. Developing countries, especially those short of capital, will depend heavily on foreign sources and assistance from international bodies (such as an appropriate agency of the UN) or foreign government finance.

9.2.1   Short-term finance

Besides the sources mentioned in the preceding section, short-term finance can be obtained by other means. First there are *bank overdrafts*. They are not loans but facilities, allowing cheques to be drawn to predetermined limits. Interest is calculated on a day-to-day basis on the amount overdrawn at the moment. A flexible form of short-term finance, an over-draft is legally repayable on demand. Interest is charged at some rate above bank base rate depending on the standing of the borrower. A relatively cheap form of finance, it is helpful when emergencies arise.

Some *suppliers* of consumables (e.g. brewery companies) may also provide short-term loans for the extension and develop-ment of accommodation and restaurants at their customers' premises. The size and terms of the loan are determined by the credit rating of the customer.

9.2.2   Other methods

Other methods of financing projects include sale and leaseback arrangements and franchising. Both help to reduce the amount of capital the developer will have to find.

Sale and leaseback involves selling the buildings to an insurance company, pension fund or bank and then leasing them back at an agreed percentage charge or fee. This raises 100 per cent of the capital needed instead of about 50 to 75 per cent normal for mortgage arrangements. If a buy-back clause is included in the contract the method can be used as a continuing source of funds. The drawbacks are first, the borrower's further borrow-ing potential may be reduced. Second, it can prove expensive in the long term if general interest rates fall during the life of the leaseback. However if interest rates rise and the terms of the arrangement are fixed, the method in fact produces a cheaper form of financing. Thus careful consideration should be given to the possible future trends in interest rates.

With *franchising* the organisation selling the franchise (the franchisor) permits the buyer (franchisee) to use the former's expertise, skills and sometimes their name, in exchange for an initial payment followed by annual fees based on turnover or revenue or some other basis. The franchisee provides all or some of the capital needed. This approach has been used by hotels, the most wellknown being, perhaps, Holiday Inns. There are advantages for both parties. For the franchisor, not having to find all the capital, the main gain is that projects can be developed more quickly. Also with hotels, the management and running of them is the responsibility of the franchisee, relieving the franchisor of this chore. For the franchisee, it is easier to raise capital if the project is tied in with the tried and proven system of the franchisor and if the capital investment is shared. The last reduces the amount of money both parties have to find. This also reduces the inherent risks. The important ingredient for success is the availability of a standard product or service which has wide recognition amongst customers for dependability, known standards, value and so on (see also Section 4.2.1).

9.3 Investment appraisal

In appraising the viability of projects, their anticipated life must be carefully assessed as must the effect of inflation on demand and the return that could be obtained. Thought should also be given to what modifications could be made to the project should customer needs and expectations change over the projected life of the project.

9.3.1 *Appraisal methods*

Of the various methods possible, estimating the *payback period* (number of years that would be taken before the net income received equals the total capital outlay) is a good screening process. This is especially so when the cash flow situation is critical or when the inherent risks appear to be high. In these situations a rapid recovery of capital is necessary. Usually a minimum payback period is set and this guides investment decisions. Often, all projects which fail to meet this standard are rejected.

The disadvantages include not taking into consideration the economic life of the project and the earnings that would be achieved after the end of the set payback period. Nor is any account taken of the timing of these earnings. This is important since those early in the life of a project are worth more than those made later, especially if inflation is high or rising. Normally also, the impact of taxation is ignored and since different payback periods can be set for different projects, it is impossible to find a sound basis for comparing competing possibilities. Finally, assumptions are made that no profit is earned until the total capital outlay has been recovered.

Another method uses the *average rate of return,* on the original capital invested, that is forecast for the project. The average income over the expected life of the project, less depreciation but before tax, is calculated as a percentage of the total capital invested. The disadvantages are that no account is taken of the impact of taxation nor the timing of the earnings. Neither is consideration given to the recovery of capital over the life of the project. Thus this method understates the return and overstates the capital employed.

Using the *average rate of return on the average capital invested* is similar to the above but relates income to the average capital employed. It allows for the recovery of capital at an even rate over the life of the project and overstates the return. It has also the other disadvantages of the previous method.

The most used method today is *discounted cash flow.* This is based on the principle that the value of money earned at some future time is of less value than that earned at earlier times. Cash flows rather than profit are used. The figures should be net of taxes but non-cash costs such as depreciation should be added back to the cash flow. It is used in two ways. First there is the internal rate of return method when the rate of interest used represents the true (internal) rate of return over the life of the project. Second is the net present value method which estimates the net gain over the capital invested. The advantages of these methods include the fact that the timing of the earnings is taken into account as are tax allowances and payments, the full life of the project, the value of the residual assets and the full recovery of the capital outlay over the expected life of the project (see also Section 1.5.2, Project Appraisal).

9.4 Organisations

The trading members of the tourism industry (the 'Travel Trade') have been described in Chapter 2. This section will consider the various tourist boards and organisations active in the industry.

9.4.1 National tourist organisations

Most countries now have some form of national tourist organisation (NTO). These range from the British pattern of 'Tourist Boards' to departments within a government ministry, Tourist Development Corporations (mainly in developing countries) and a Ministry of Tourism (as in Spain). Their basic aims, functions and responsibilities are similar though their method of operation may vary in detail. In this section the British pattern and the basic approach will be discussed. There are however certain influences in each country which determine the nature of the NTO they have. In some countries, including Britain in 1984, thought is being given to reorganisations which it is claimed will improve the efficient working of the boards.

The first and most important factors influencing the choice of organisation are the *political and related economic systems*. In countries like the USA, Austria, Germany and Switzerland with federal government systems, the tourist organisation is based on a national authority with considerable devolution to organisations at state or local level. (In Britain, the British Tourist Authority – BTA – fulfils the national role, with devolution to the regional or area boards.) In most countries the national organisation coordinates the work of the NTO system, aiming for a high level of cooperation between the lower level units. The latter are expected to fulfil the requirements of national policies that are in force for tourism.

In the USA the Department of Commerce, via its US Travel

Service, carries out the national role but the detailed work is the responsibility of state organisations (guided by the policy of each state) and specialist or sectoral bodies such as the National Parks and National Forest departments. For Russia, Eastern bloc countries and China, tourism is controlled by the central government. Many developing nations also have central control through a tourist development organisation but the prime consideration is economy. With limited resources the governments are concerned with optimising the use of available resources to reduce wastage.

With the individual states of the USA, tourism development and promotion may be organised through a State Highways department, Department of Industry, or Commerce, or Economics. A few make them the responsibility of a Department of Parks and Recreation. Several of these are independent offices reporting directly to the state governor. In New Zealand, the main tourism arm is the Tourist Hotel Corporation of New Zealand. This operates major hotels, air, rail and shipping lines and the main tour agency business. In addition the corporation maintains the national parks in which their hotels are located, for example Mt Cook National Park.

A second significant influence is the importance of tourism and its development to the national economy. Where they are major contributors to foreign exchange earnings and/or play important roles in providing business to other industries and related activities (such as transport) a more centralised system is used. This is particularly applicable to developing countries with few opportunities or natural resources to permit major development of other sectors of the economy.

However, Italy has a dual Ministry of Tourism and Entertainment. Besides being responsible for tourism development and operations, it looks after historical monuments, museums, theatres and other important forms of entertainment. Spain also has a dual ministry responsible for tourism and the media. Where voluntary cooperative national tourist bodies exist, tourism is not rated as highly in the economy. Austria and Switzerland are the exceptions to this rule.

A third influence is the stage of development achieved by tourism. In countries with a well-developed tourism industry (e.g. the USA, Britain and other developed nations like Austria, Germany and Switzerland) it is usual to have a more flexible, decentralised organisation evolved over several decades. Where tourism is a new development but capable of considerable expansion, governments may take a strong, direct interest. Examples of the latter are to be found on the Mediterranean coast, such as Spain, Italy, Greece, Tunisia and Egypt. (All the foregoing are just some examples of the variations that can occur.)

9.4.2 The hierarchy of tourism organisations

Thus a hierarchical approach has evolved. In countries with a two- or three-tier structure, the government should define at national level, the role of tourism in the national and regional levels and therefore the objectives that must be achieved. Ideally the objectives should include quantified targets for such things as the number of tourists or tourist-visits needed per annum and the total tourist receipts that are required. If accommodation or other major resources are in short supply, the policy should also state the maximum number of tourists permitted in the resort at any given period.

The policy should state how the objectives will be realised, the fiscal and administrative procedures to be followed and the roles to be played by public and private sector organisations in the tourism business. A national government's task is to plan and facilitate the development of tourism and its infrastructure and to provide the finance and resources that cannot otherwise be obtained.

9.4.3 National boards

At national level, NTOs set guidelines and objectives based on government requirements, by mutual agreement with all interested parties. In the UK this work is done, under the approval of the government, by the BTA and the English, Scottish and Wales Tourist Boards (respectively: ETB, STB and WTB). Prior to 1969 these were non-statutory bodies without power to ensure action. However statutory bodies existed more or less independently for Northern Ireland, the Isle of Man and the Channel Islands. The BTA was originally a voluntary cooperative association of organisations in the travel and tourism industry who wished to promote travel to and in Britain.

In 1969 the Development of Tourism Act was passed and the four major boards (BTA, ETB, STB, WTB) became statutory bodies together with the Northern Island Tourist Board (NITB). The BTA promotes Britain as a tourist country as a whole and currently is the only one empowered to carry out promotional activities abroad. It is charged with the task of increasing the number of visitors to the country. The other three boards are concerned with the marketing of the tourist attractions in their regions. Their promotional work is concentrated in this country, anything needed abroad is done through the BTA. All four organisations try to ease congestion in popular areas (e.g. London) by trying to persuade visitors to go to other interesting provincial areas and obtain more business in the off-peak winter season. The BTA and ETB are responsible to the Department of Trade. The STB is responsible to the Secretary of State for Scotland and the WTB reports to the Secretary of State for Wales. Obviously a degree of coordination and cooperation over advertisements and promotions abroad is required when activities in major tourist-generating areas (markets) are necessary.

Other countries have similar arrangements. In the USA there is the US Travel Service (USTS) and India has its Government Tourist Development Corporation (TDC), to mention just two. In Spain, because private enterprise has well-(over-?) developed the Mediterranean resorts, the Ministry has concentrated its more recent activities on promoting the central and northwestern parts of the country. The range of work of NTOs is given in Table 9.1.

Table 9.1   Responsibilities of an NTO

'MANAGEMENT' FUNCTIONS
(In conjunction with regional and local offices and other relevant participants in tourism – accommodation units, transportation and other supporting services)

Planning
(a)   Product-market research and agreement on tourism products and target markets.
(b)   Agreeing on infrastructure and superstructure needs and their provision.

(c) Agreeing personnel needs, training requirements and actions required of cooperating enterprises.

(d) Agreeing advertising and other promotional needs, resultant plans and timing and how the necessary funds will be raised. Also coordinating the national promotional plan with the individual ones of the various participants (e.g. hotels, transport companies, etc.).

(e) Selecting the attractions, entertainments, etc. to be offered at the resorts and helping to select appropriate organisations.

Marketing

(a) Accepting responsibility for the implementation of the agreed international advertising and promotional campaigns concerned with promoting the nation as a tourist destination and its attractions (historic, cultural, social, etc.).

(b) Producing and distributing appropriate literature.

(c) Commissioning the agreed, necessary marketing research studies and undertaking the necessary demand forecasts.

(d) Undertaking any approved public relations activities.

(e) Providing information centres at agreed sites.

Financial aspects

(a) Contributing funds from government sources as agreed in planning.

(b) Advising the private sector of the industry on capital development.

(c) Approving, directing and controlling government aid programmes for tourism projects.

Control activities

(a) Licensing and controlling sectors of the industry that require this.

(b) Coordinating and implementing agreed regulations on pricing.

(c) Coordinating the marketing activities of the private and public sector of the tourism industry.

(d) Arranging conferences and meetings on tourism matters.

(e) Acting as the link and adviser for trade and professional, regional and local tourism boards and related enterprises.

An early problem with NTOs was the fact that they were designed to suit the bureaucratic system of a country. They took on the aspect of a ministry or secretariat, department or committee. Initially the staff were drawn from the civil service. They had little experience or knowledge of the tourism business. They were more interested in administrating the system they had been told to operate rather than to help the industry be more successful and profitable. The lack of positive results reflected this situation. Happily this is all changing and more and more people with knowledge of tourism and its needs are joining the boards.

There is growing awareness of the need to mobilise and coordinate the necessary resources and activities and managerial and technical skills for greater efficiency and effectiveness. With the recruitment of more people with knowledge and experience of tourism, better results are being obtained in Britain. However the degree of success depends on the willingness of enterprises and executives, in the supply elements of the industry, to respond positively to a coordinated operation. This often means sacrificing some personal goals to achieve collective ones for the mutual benefit of all participants. In the end too, the success of an NTO will depend on the support it gets from its government.

9.4.4 Regional tourist boards

Regional tourist boards (RTBs) cover specific regions of a country, for example in Britain, England, Scotland, Wales and Northern Ireland. Their work is similar to that of the NTO as mentioned in the previous section. The RTOs currently in existence in Britain are shown in Table 9.2. However in 1984 the government expressed its intention to do away with the English Tourist Board to a greater extent. Other changes may also be possible. In other countries, RTOs may be based on states (USA and West Germany), provinces (Austria), regions (France) and cantons (Switzerland). In New Zealand, because of the geographical position, the split is between the north and south islands. A region may become a separate, main destinational area for foreign tourists and replace individual resorts for domestic holidaymakers if touring by car or coach is

Table 9.2   Regional tourist boards in Britain

ENGLAND
  Cumbria
  East Anglia
  East Midlands
  Heart of England
  Isle of Wight
  London Visitor and Convention Bureau (formerly London Tourist
  Board)
  Northumbria
  South-east England
  Southern
  Thames and Chilterns
  Yorkshire and Humberside

SCOTLAND
  Borders
  Central
  Dumfries and Galloway
  Fife
  Grampian
  Highlands & Islands
  Lothian
  Strathclyde
  Tayside

WALES
  North Wales
  Mid-Wales
  South Wales

(The Northern Ireland Tourist Board covers that territory on its own, i.e.
there is no regional structure as above.)

At the end of 1983 the Government announced its intention to rationalise
this Board structure.

envisaged. Thus they form a basis for the creation of composite
tourism products to selected markets.

  They coordinate tourism strategy for their region with their
local authorities. RTOs can form a network of organisations
coordinated at national level and represent regional interests at

that level. They should also coordinate local tourist organisations in their regions, encouraging the development of facilities and promote the region by use of suitable marketing and literature.

Generally there are benefits to be gained by setting regional boundaries to coincide with administrative ones, or that group together territories that offer a common image to potential tourists. They should represent areas having common interests that can be developed and promoted successfully. There is also some advantage to be gained by basing tourist regions on economic planning ones so that tourism can help to stimulate economic development in them.

9.4.5   Local tourist organisations

This is the bottom layer of the tier. Local tourist organisations promote an individual town or district, for example Scarborough, the Lake District and Yorkshire Dales. They are the oldest form of tourist organisations. They are usually based on and are supported by the local authority of their town or district. They recognise the significance of tourism to their locality and usually cooperate with the appropriate RTO and the NTO. They provide a strong base for the development and coordination of local tourist interests.

9.4.6   Basic aims of tourist boards

To summarise therefore, tourist boards aim to achieve a high rate of tourist satisfaction within the resources available, coordination of the various activities involved and provision of facilities that allow successful implementation of tourism strategies. In addition, they carry out the necessary research programmes which help to indicate what modified and new tourism products are needed. They provide also the basic data required for planning purposes. They should increase the awareness of the industry of tourism prospects to appropriate markets and maintain adequate and constant communications not only with members of the industry but also the selected tourist-generating areas.

9.4.7   Other organisations in the industry

The tourism and other trade associations active in the industry were discussed in Section 2.4.5 and listed in Table 2.4. There is need here to mention only the other organisations that arise when governments have major involvements in the industry.

In this case various statutory, official and quasi-official bodies will be active. These include wages councils which set minimum wages and other terms of employment. (In Britain, the Conservative government of the early 1980s has tried to eliminate its role in these two areas.) Then there may be economic development organisations to assist in and control all forms of development including tourism. Also training boards and councils may exist to specify the amount of training and the levels of skills needed by different industries to improve their efficiency of operation. The extent of the activities of such bodies will depend on government policy, whether they see it as vital for the national economy for such activities to be directly controlled by government or whether they should be left to a free enterprise (or private sector) system.

9.5 Future possibilities

As stated in earlier chapters, the simple economic benefits of tourism are increasingly being weighed against the social costs of the activity. In particular, damage and destruction of the environment, ecology and residents' ways of life are causing increasing concern. So the first major change might be that tourism executives will have to give greater consideration to these social costs and seek ways of minimising them while promoting the development of tourism. Governments may also take a bigger hand here, rather than simply promote the growth of tourism. Obviously some governments will carry this responsibility more fully than others. However even those who believe in 'free enterprise' or 'market forces' will realise, sooner or later, that they cannot let free enterprise rip, as they see the social costs increasing to dangerous proportions. It should be obvious that the destruction of the world's ecology and environment can lead eventually to the destruction of all life on earth. Some regulation, or even compulsion, will be necessary if firms are hellbent on making money and show little (short-sighted) interest in the damage they may be doing to many regions.

However care is needed to ensure that conservation policies adopted do not go against their original purpose. For example, the restrictions on the shooting of elephants, coupled with unbridled safari tourism, drove ever larger herds into ever smaller regions. Wild animals do not like large numbers of minibuses crashing and roaring through their habitat. They will retreat further into the bush. As tourism increases the amount of bush that is free from tourists decreases. The amount of food – vegetation – becomes limited and the animals will strip the area bare in a desperate attempt to stay alive. The effect is the reduction of these zones to near desert conditions unable to sustain any animal life. The human residents will also suffer. Thus sensible national and international policies are needed. Only national governments working closely through international agencies such as the World Wildlife Fund and the United Nations Organisation, can achieve them.

The more governments become involved in regulating tourism, the more the industry feels the need to influence official policies and decisions. To this end in 1975 the International Union of Official Travel Organisations (IUOTO), a non-governmental association, was replaced by the World Tourism Organisation (WTO). This is an inter-governmental body responsible for all aspects of tourism. It is recognised by the United Nations Organisation and is the official voice of tourism in discussions with governments. How effective it will be in the future will depend on the willingness of governments to accept its advice. This advice should be based on a balanced view of all aspects of tourism. It should consider not only the interests of the industry and local residents at resorts but also those of the animals and other wildlife and the protection of the environment as a whole. Without this the very things that create tourist attractions will be destroyed. While over 100 countries are members of WTO, several important ones and some developing into important tourist centres have yet to join.

In the thirty years the EEC has been in existence its main objectives of freedom of movement of labour and peoples across national boundaries, also finance and investment, have helped the development of tourism. However there has been only a limited amount of integration and cooperation as far as tourism is concerned. Although cooperation has developed between NTOs, several members consider that tourism matters can be handled adequately by existing committees dealing with general economic and transport matters of the Community. Others would like to develop EEC policies for holiday and leisure activities including legislation on and regulation of accommodation, travel services and the staggering of industrial and school holidays.

Meanwhile in Britain in the early 1980s the government showed signs of wishing to limit government involvement though they remain interested in the rationalisation of existing regional and area tourist bodies. On 22 November 1983 the British government announced in the House of Commons, major changes in the structure of the BTA and the ETB. The changes it was hoped would be effected by March 1985 and included the appointment of a joint Chairman for both boards and the creation of common services. From January 1985 they shared some common services (publishing, information, PR, research, finance, training and administration). The statement also outlined proposals for improving hotel standards, new computerised reservation systems, new training initiatives, the revitalisation of traditional resorts and launching a 'hard sell' of London as one of the world's greatest tourist attractions. These moves towards closer coordination, clearer objectives and better use of resources should benefit the industry. However the main task of realising the full potential of tourism is to be left to the industry itself. The government's aim was stated as the realisation of a more aggressive and effective tourism industry.

The wide-ranging government review on which these proposals were based, highlighted the concern that had been expressed on the plight of several traditional resorts which had failed to invest in modern facilities in order to compete with the standards of overseas resorts. The ETB agreed to work with the Department of the Environment, the Civic Trust and others to identify how assistance could be concentrated to give new life to rundown urban areas which may have tourism potential.

The ETB, Civic Trust and British Rail will also study ways by which the tourism potential of historic railway stations could be developed to make them attractive places in their own right for tourists and local residents to visit and use. Other considerations include improved signposting on major roads for tourist attractions off them, Sunday opening, changes in the licensing laws and improvement in facilities to enhance the impression given to visitors at air and seaports. However the review also stated that compulsory registration of hotels would lead to unnecessary bureaucracy and expense. The tourist boards and interested parties were to examine ways of strengthening the voluntary registration scheme to make it more effective against units with inadequate standards and facilities.

In general there should be a change of emphasis. Conservation will not be the sole important consideration. There may be growing interest in managing tourist flows to destinations while balancing this with the need to promote development so that new and existing investments in accommodation, transport and other services will give acceptable returns for all involved in tourism, including the tourists.

In December 1983 the British Restrictive Practices Court reported that package tour customers must continue to be protected from untrained, inexperienced and incompetent staff. The quality of travel agents' staff should be subject to compulsory minimum standards to be imposed and policed by ABTA. The Chairman of the Court stated that the purchaser of a foreign package tour was entering into one of the most substantial transactions of the family budget. The tourist had difficulty in finding out whether the travel agency staff were offering the most suitable product, knew what they were talking about or where really able to get the expected services. In an earlier judgement it gave approval to the 'closed shop' system among ABTA members. It ruled then that maintaining protection for the travelling public was more important than objections to the exclusive trading system.

9.5.1   *Future demand*

Assuming that the major world recession of the late 1970s and early 1980s will be overcome, the general view is that there will be more leisure time for most people. It does not follow that this will be used automatically for more holidays away from home. It will depend on the net discretionary income of the consumer. The British Home Tourist Surveys show that only one in five of the population take more than one holiday a year, although the demand for weekend breaks at home and abroad has grown. The increase in population of the developed nations, who also have the greatest propensity for taking holidays away from home, should bring about a 'natural' increase in consumers able and willing to go on holiday. Also, as stated earlier, increased car ownership should show a growth in demand for motoring holidays.

However, since developed countries have already achieved a high propensity to purchase holidays, very substantial growth seems unlikely. It is the developing countries that offer interesting possibilities assuming improvement in net discretionary income is achieved. If they can resolve their economic and fiscal problems, Mexico and Brazil could be just two nations which could experience increased demand for holidays abroad. The advent of lower air fares and other cost-cutting operations could give impetus to efforts to convert those who do not take holidays abroad to do so.

Finally, the development of new, exotic resorts and holiday centres should stimulate demand though they may just take vacationists away from old established destinations. Then there are the political aspects. Tourists are concerned about the political implications only when they feel they may be unwilling targets for injury, insult or contempt. Reduce these risks and many countries could experience growth in tourist traffic flows.

Assignments

1   What sources of capital are available to tourism developers? What factors need careful study before decisions are made on raising venture capital?

2   Discuss the different criteria used by the public and private sectors when having to make a decision on a new tourism project.

3   How may a new project be appraised for viability?

4   What is the role of a national tourist organisation? How do regional and local offices fit into the overall picture?

5   Taking into account current economic and market conditions, how do you see the pattern of tourism changing over the next five or ten years?

Appendix A

Abridged History of Travel and Tourism

Although the Greeks and the Romans, being great traders, had to travel extensively for their times in pursuit of trade as their empires expanded, tourism as we know it today is a recent occurrence. The word *tourism* itself did not enter the English language until the early nineteenth century, although merchants throughout history have had to travel to trade with other nations. Their journeys were arduous and hazardous since there were inadequate roads and modes of transport and much banditry.

Good transport facilities are essential for all forms of travel (trade, business, vacations). The growth of travel and later tourism, over recent centuries, depended on improvements in transport systems. The developments that had the greatest impact on travel range from stage- and mail-coaches to inshore and deep water shipping, the railways and more recently, the aeroplane and motor vehicles. Other contributory factors were the increased interest in health spas and seaside resorts. Later inland scenic and sporting centres played major roles in the expansion of demand for vacational travel and ultimately, modern tourism.

Before the Industrial Revolution, travel was mainly for pilgrimage, business and official purposes. By the end of the sixteenth century, private travel mainly for educational reasons began to develop. Later, curiosity about the way people of other parts of the world lived gave further impetus to the demand for private travel. Foreign travel became part of the aristocrat's education.

Domestic travel for pleasure or health developed in the eighteenth century with the growth of seaside resorts and spas. The latter had been well established during the days of the Roman Empire but declined in popularity in the intervening centuries, though they never fell completely out of favour. During the eighteenth century travel was the prerogative of the landed gentry and élite. They travelled for educational and official purposes. The majority of people, however, usually travelled only to their local village or nearest towns. For them, travelling for leisure, as it is understood today, did not occur. The élite did not perceive the difference between travelling for work purposes and leisure since they did not see themselves as working people nor that their normal activities required any respite for rest and leisure. If they needed a rest then staying in their manors and enjoying their land and its facilities was all that was necessary. The life of the gentry was elegant, relaxed and not as hectic as today so they had no need for leisure. For the peasant, life was all hard work. They needed leisure time but could not afford it!

The Industrial Revolution led to a big increase in the size of the country's population and considerable migration of people from the country to the new industrial towns, centres offering hope of increased earnings. New households were created and their higher earnings from work in industry increased each household's purchasing power. Consumer demand was stimulated and the range of goods and services demanded also grew steadily. As mass production developed and the population continued to increase, demand continued to rise and the range of products bought also increased further. The intensive nature of work in industry, plus workers' growing ability to pay for leisure activities, saw demand for this develop.

However for leisure travel the provisions of good transport and accommodation services was not enough. Their costs had to be within consumers' budgets or else their propensity to buy leisure activities was frustrated by their inability to pay for it.

Before the nineteenth century transport systems could not meet this requirement. Accommodation facilities were also restricted once the monasteries, traditional providers of shelter for travellers, were dissolved by Henry VIII. It was not until inns and ale houses started to provide sleeping facilities for travellers that travel of all kinds developed.

Two separate groups emerged in society as a result of the Industrial Revolution. There was the ever growing urban population, initially centred on the towns and cities of the Midlands and North and the financiers and bankers whose wealth was not founded on large landholdings. The urban society obtained its wealth from hard work in the new industries. They were the chief users of the railway systems which were emerging and they used them also for the popular excursions they ran. Their journeys for trading purposes shifted from being mainly to Northwestern Europe and Mediterranean countries to take in North America after the War of Independence. It was not coincidence that led Thomas Cook to set the foundations of his business in the Midlands, nor the great railway companies to originate from Northern cities. For the financiers, as soon as the development of railways made travel easier, their demand for travel began to grow. The increase in the North American trade also led to the emergence of transatlantic passenger shipping and the Great Western Railway Company.

Prior to the railways, travel was by very inadequate roads, poorly maintained and intended for local traffic. They were maintained by local funds. With the increase in trade and traffic this placed intolerable burdens on existing roads. Rather than create a national road authority, the development of better roads was by use of turnpikes (tollgates) which raised funds for the building and maintenance of the roads. Whilst most turnpikes have long disappeared, remnants of the approach exist today with most roads left as the responsibility of local or county authorities but major trunk roads and motorways are the concern of the central government.

Turnpikes were essentially private business ventures. Capital was raised by local landowners and other trustees who were allowed to charge tolls for the use of their roads. The turnpike system has found favour again in the USA and may be one way of transferring the heavy cost of providing roads and bridges from the taxpayer to the actual users. It is also an unfortunate fact that the provision of better roads generates more traffic than the system can handle, a fact that is still with us today.

The improvement in the road system led to growing demand for stage- and mail-coach services. In the seventeenth and eighteenth centuries they were unable to exceed speeds of four or five miles an hour. They covered short-distance journeys of about thirty miles a day. The services were rudimentary and seasonal. In 1669 for example, Oxford and London were connected by a daily summer service and a two-day one in winter.

As business increased so did the demand for a faster, better and safer mail service. Mounted postboys were gradually replaced by mail coaches which carried a small number of passengers as well as armed guards to protect the mail. At the end of each stage, the horses were changed by innkeepers who had been appointed contractors to the Post Office. The contracts were sought after, not only for the fees paid by the Post Office but also for the custom (for bed and food) of the passengers. As the postal system expanded, the number of staging inns increased. Customers were assured of clean and comfortable accommodation where they could stay overnight, *en route* to their destinations. Further, other, often larger, inns were built at destinations where travellers could stay for as long as their business required. Eventually by the mid-nineteenth century the larger, modern hotels familiar today began to replace inns at destinations.

With the development of the coal-fired steam-driven railway system, travel became more universal and was not confined to just the wealthy or élite. The Liverpool and Manchester Railway opened in 1830 and by 1845 the railway linked many major towns to London. By 1881 over 600 million passengers were carried over some 7000 miles of line, owned and operated by about 100 railway companies. The Midland Railway was the first to introduce cheap third-class carriages but it was on the London to Brighton line, in the 1880s, that the luxury Pullman cars (an American concept) were first introduced. The idea was also taken up by the Midland Railway.

As the railway traffic grew there emerged, at first, inns and then hotels at major stops and final destinations. These provided a suitable range of accommodation for railway travellers. These facilitated not only travel for business purposes but also for visits to relatives and friends and for leisure purposes to spa towns, seaside resorts and other developing holiday towns.

Until the mid-eighteenth century, cross Channel shipping services were not owned by the railway companies. By the 1860s they had opened their own services to Belgium and France. Later, services were extended to Ireland. The development of inns and hotels at ports such as Dover, Southampton, Folkestone and Liverpool resulted from the increased demand for this traffic.

The need for improved services to America led to the development of the large ocean liner and other deep-water shipping. Awards of contracts to carry the Royal Mail, in effect a subsidy, helped. The opening of the Suez Canal in 1869 and the transfer of the East India Company out of private hands, boosted the development of long-distance deep-water shipping to the East. The shortened route to India and China stimulated trade and passenger traffic.

The luxury and glamour of ocean travel was reserved for the wealthy European and American but this would not have been possible without the large volume of traffic in cheap and rather rudimentary steerage accommodation. However it was the descendants of these migrants (who formed the bulk of steerage passengers) who created the growing demand for transatlantic travel in the first half of the twentieth century. The Peninsular and Oriental Steam Navigation Company (now P & O) began their operations to India and the Far East in 1838.

The heyday of rail travel ended for the most part with the development of the motor vehicle. Charabancs (large coaches) were preferred for trips to the seaside, though rail travel to continental destinations continued. With the development of the aeroplane and then passenger airlines, the demise of the railways as the main carriers occurred, especially for long-distance journeys. Increase in the ownership of private motor cars in turn caused a decline in the use of railways for domestic journeys. Cars provided greater comfort and flexibility. They also opened up inland scenic centres for holidays which previously, not being on a railway route, were difficult to reach.

After the Second World War the development of such inland resorts increased.

The heyday of the ocean liner was before the First World War. While between the two world wars the liner continued to be in demand especially for the longer journeys (e.g. to the Far East and Australasia) it was the development of the intercontinental airliner after the Second World War that spelt the demise of this mode of transport. Transatlantic and other long-distance travellers transferred their allegiance to the major airlines, because they provided faster transit times and at first, cheaper fares. At first also the state airlines were successful.

It was the private airlines (that is not state owned) offering charter services that really permitted the development of modern package tourism. It was Vladimir Reitz, in 1950, who experimented with package tours by air to Corsica. By being able to fill every seat on the chartered plane, he reduced the unit cost and the overall price to the public. By the 1960s, mass-market package tours had become a norm of the annual holiday business. Eventually national airlines also began offering charter and other competitive block-booking facilities to tour operators. Some airlines, for example British Airways with their subsidiary British Air Tours – likely to be sold off in 1985 in the privatisation of British Airways – even became directly involved in the package tour business. While Britain pioneered holidays to the Mediterranean Coast, it was not long before other European countries followed and began competing for accommodation at these resorts.

The growing use of the private car for long-distance motoring holidays led to the development of motels, really a modern version of the staging inn. Shipping companies, seeing the demise of their traditional passenger business, either concentrated on freight or in some cases used their passenger liners for cruising. While ships built for long-distance, fast sea voyages were not really suitable for this purpose – operating costs were high and their deep draught made some tourist stops impossible – they created interest in sea cruise holidays, particularly their luxurious connotations. P & O also went into the Channel and Irish Sea ferry business. More recently, ships purpose-built for cruising were introduced by Greek, Scandinavian and other lines, and are being developed by British and American companies. The latest editions, in 1983–4, were the *Sea Princess* and *Royal Princess*, smaller but super-luxury ships. Now Cunard and others have introduced the fly-cruise holiday. Apart from the attractiveness of this, especially if *Concorde* is the aircraft used, the saving in travelling time one way appears beneficial to many holidaymakers.

In Britain in 1984 it was announced that the British government intended to make an 'assault' on high air fares in Europe and the restrictive practices of European state airlines. The latter were believed to be contrary to British interests and in flagrant contravention of the Treaty of Rome (which formed the EEC). The government estimated that air travellers in Europe were paying up to 40 per cent more than they should. The proposals called for a common market in aviation with the airlines of any EEC country allowed to enter any European internal route without restrictions. This would create a new style of competition in fares, number and timing of flights and quality of service, all up to now controlled by governments under bilateral agreements. This would extend to Europe the competition seen increasingly on British domestic routes, which the government considers good for the traveller and the airline. Britain's interest in such a move may be due to the fact that British business executives have further to go to reach the heartland of the EEC. If the move is successful, it should stimulate demand for both business travel and general tourism.

A separate report at the same time (April 1984) in the London *Financial Times* highlighted the growth in demand for package tours and travel facilities by long-haul luxury coaches. Coach traffic through Dover has grown by 675 per cent in the decade to 1984, while that of private cars had risen by only 74 per cent. In 1983 while four and a half million people travelled to Europe in their own cars, five and a half million preferred the chauffeur-driven comfort of modern coaches. Growth has been in three areas. First was the express inter-city routes (London–Paris, London–Milan, Paris–Madrid, etc.). Second was the shuttle services where a company charters a coach rather than an aircraft and third, the traditional coach tour. Europe's express coach system has developed over the last six years as a result of the liberalisation of regulations and rules. The system relies on reciprocal arrangements between countries. For example, a coach operator in Belgium would get a full licence for the route to Italy only if Belgium granted a similar licence for the same route to an Italian company. Both companies are allowed to pick up and set down passengers on each other's territory and usually establish a joint timetable. This has produced a complicated network of routes. Leading British companies in the business include Wallace Arnold, National Express and Frank Harris.

The Greeks and Spaniards see the system benefiting the major tourist-generating areas like Britain and Germany, since these nationals would probably prefer to ride the flag. In 1983 the cost of these coaches ranged from £75,000 for the basic model to £125,000 or more for those with video and other luxury fitments. The practical limit of operation is to destinations taking twenty-two hours or less to reach, since under EEC rules this length of journey can be covered by two drivers. While travelling by coach has become fashionable and saves on costs, the economic recession had by 1983 slowed down growth in demand. A surplus of capacity may result for a while given that most operators have expanded their capacities considerably.

In 1984 the magazine of the London *Sunday Times* also highlighted more recent trends and developments in tourism. At that time, depending on the route and stopovers selected, RTW (round the world) tickets cost from £699 to £1276 each, economy class. The comprehensive write-up also featured the growing interest in seats on charter rather than scheduled flights, which offer considerable cost savings because of the much cheaper fares available for the former. However, availability and cost vary considerably depending on destinations and time of travel. In all instances they represented worthwhile savings on APEX and other scheduled cheap fares. Sea cruises by liners were also subjected to competition from voyages by cargo and banana boats. Since the last two often carried only twelve passengers in almost equal comfort to cruise liners, their attraction from many people wishing to escape crowds and too much sophistication was enhanced.

The wide-ranging self-catering facilities in Europe (especially in Austria, Germany, Switzerland, France, Italy and

Yugoslavia and especially use of the *Gites de France*) were proving popular with families or those wishing to break away from sophisticated or traditional hotels. The price range was considerable. For example in 1984 for the high season, a ten-person chalet at Crans-Montana in Switzerland cost £710 a week; a four-person apartment in Montreux overlooking Lake Geneva cost £200 a week. Living expenses were of course additional to these sums.

In all events, the changes in consumer holiday habits over the next five or ten years promise to be interesting. Motivations for holidays are changing. Improvement in the economic situation could enhance these changes and even boost destinations further afield, such as North America, Australia, New Zealand and the Far East.

1984–5

The end of 1984 and the beginning of 1985 was a traumatic period for the travel and tourism industry which suffered severe cases of the jitters then. This was despite the fact that the industry is large, with turnover exceeding £2,000 million, with some 700 companies used by more than 50 per cent of all Britons travelling abroad for whatever purpose. Until 1985, despite uncertain Sterling exchange rates and the economic recession of recent years, the industry has maintained reasonable growth. Estimates at the end of 1984 indicated that, notwithstanding all this, the industry could be handling a total of 9 million customers, though if Sterling reached parity with the US dollar (£1 = $1) the cost of holidays in the USA would rise substantially and result in a big reduction in the number of holidays taken there. The more substantial growth was experienced by the smaller, specialist tour operators.

However towards the end of 1984, because of increasing costs and falling Sterling exchange rates, prices for package tours in the Summer 1985 season were expected to rise by 20 per cent, though the actual increases would vary from country to country. The 20 per cent increase was expected for Spanish holidays since hotel tariffs there had risen by 18 per cent and the Sterling rate against the peseta had fallen by 16 per cent in

1984. Airline costs had also risen. However holidays in Portugal and Italy were expected to cost only 12 per cent more with Greek holidays 14 per cent up, Yugoslavia up 11 per cent and Maltese holidays up by only 6 per cent of their 1984 prices. Horizon Holidays forecast that its 1985 prices would average an increase of 20 per cent, with several at 23 per cent and Thomson, Intasun and Cosmos expected similar increases. Further, tour operators who had 'no surcharge' guarantees in the early 1980s, withdrew these for the Summer 1985 season but some stated that any increase would be limited to 10 per cent provided 'increased costs were not due to any government action' – the sting in the tail of such 'guarantees'!

By December 1984 these reports on price increases brought about a rush of bookings for winter holidays both before and after the normally dull booking period around Christmas. On the other hand, advance bookings for Summer 1985 were reported as being between 30 and 40 per cent down on the same period of the previous year. There was also the belief that more holidaymakers would rediscover their own country for holidays and that many hotels and resorts in the UK would be fully booked by early 1985.

At the same time the Civil Aviation Authority announced its intention to increase the entrance fee for all wishing to enter or continue in the package tour industry, together with a tightening up of the procedures for keeping a watch on its licence-holders. The increased 'fee' would be in the nature of a higher bond which tour operators would have to lodge or have guaranteed by a third party. Twenty tour companies of various sizes collapsed in the latter part of 1984, including Budget Holidays, which was believed to have had a shortfall of £12 million in its indebtedness to creditors. Although it probably ranked only fiftieth in the tour operator league table, it managed to end up owing the Thomson airline subsidiary, Britannia, nearly £2 million.

By the end of 1984 and the beginning of 1985, the jitters in the industry saw a revival of price reductions and associated offers. Horizon limited the increases in its prices overall to 19 per cent. In January 1985, Global Tours, a subsidiary of Great Universal Stores, cut £1 million off its 1985 tour prices. About 50 000 holidays would give savings up to £70 per person. Also

at that time some operators reintroduced no surcharge guarantees (Blue Sky, Flair and Olympic being the first) and more
were expected to follow before the peak summer season got
under way. Other price reductions were also likely.

The travel agents, concerned at the shortfall at the end of
1984, in bookings for Summer 1985, also entered the fray with
special offers. Lunn-Poly, part of the International Thomson
Organisation, offered a £15 cut in the prices of holidays
booked through them provided the customers also bought
Lunn-Poly holiday insurance. Thomas Cook responded by
saying it would match any final Lunn-Poly price on strictly
comparable holidays and would not link this to insurance
purchases. Pickford Travel also promised to match such offers
'on the informal basis at branch level' and Hogg Robinson
made a similar offer. By January 1985 Pickford's had come up
with an offer of a £10 discount on the total cost of holidays for
two persons and the chance to win a £100 competition. Most
of these agents also had a number of other offers or guarantees
including money-back guarantees should a tour operator fail
financially and so threaten the holidays of those who had
booked with it. Table A.1 shows the estimated change in
demand for 1985.

Table A.1   Estimated change in demand pattern for 1985 (UK)

| Country | Package holidays: % share | |
	1984	1985
1. Spain	51	Down to 32
2. Greece	13	Up to 21
3. Yugoslavia	4	Up to 9
4. Italy	7	Same 7
5. Portugal	3	Up to 6
6. Cyprus	1	Up to 2
7. France	Less than 1	Up to 2
8. Tunisia	Less than 1	Up to 2
9. Others	About 21	Down to 19

Total demand for Summer 1985 is now expected to be down by at least 10
per cent on 1984.
Source: *The Sunday Times*, 3 February 1985.

Another development at the end of 1984 was the bid by Intasun, Britain's second largest tour operator, for Comfort Hotels. The bid failed when the latter accepted the offer by Ladbrookes, a property, hotels and bookmaking combine. In January 1985 P & O sold its Anglo-French cross Channel services to European Ferries (for £12.5 million) who already own Townsend Thoresen and Sealink services, operated with Continental companies. This came during a period of intense change for all ferry operators. However, P & O intend to spend over £40 million on a new ferry for the Hull-Rotterdam service of North Sea Ferries. At about the same time P & O merged with Sterling Guarantee Trust.

Finally in January 1985, *Which?* magazine published a report on package holiday operators in which five leading names received low ratings in a customer survey.

Appendix B

Short Glossary of Terms

ABC	Advance Booking Charter; also airline, shipping and railway guides/timetables
Abbonnement	Continental rail ticket permitting unlimited travel within specified zone
above-the-line	Commission paying media (expenditure in)
ABTA	Association of British Travel Agents
advertising	Paid form of promotional activity, usually by an identified sponsor
Agent	Organisation or individual appointed to sell some other company's products or services (e.g. travel agents selling tour operators' package holidays)
AIP	Agency Investigation Panel of IATA – responsible for agency appointments and administrative matters in a country
air/sea interchange	Agreement between shipping and air carriers covering acceptance of each other's tickets, granting roundtrip rebates and where applicable, enabling a complete trip to be taken using both types of transport
AP	American Plan – full board or pension: accommodation, full breakfast, lunch and dinner at the stated rate for the room (*see also* MAP)

APN	Advance Passenger Notice
ASTA	American Society of Travel Agents
ATA	Air Transport Association (USA)
ATC	Air traffic control; Australian Tourist Commission; Air Traffic Conference (USA)
ATOL	Air Travel Organisation Licence
attitude research	An investigation of people's attitudes by personal interview or group discussion
BAA	British Airport Authority
below-the-line	Media that do not pay commission to advertising agencies (expenditure in)
Bermuda Plan	Accommodation and full breakfast included in the quoted room rate
bias	Distortion of intelligence by known or unknown factors or as a result of research methods used (for unknown or unrealised reasons)
brand or market leader	Product with the greatest share of a market
brand name	Distinctive name by which a product or group of products is identified
brief	Summary of objectives and instructions governing the creation of a marketing research exercise or advertising campaign
brochure	Stitched booklet often with a prestige connotation
budget	Estimate of expenditure for a stated period of time and purpose. Not to be confused with target (*which see*)
buying motives	Motives which create a desire to buy a product or service
CAA	Civil Aviation Authority
CAB	Civil Aeronautics Board (USA)
cabotage	Travel that is within or between territories of the same sovereign nation

captive market	Purchasers who have to buy a particular product or service because there are no other practical alternatives
carrier	Transportation company
catalogue	Describes and details, with or without illustrations, a range of products or services (*see also* brochure)
circulation	Total number of distributed and bought copies of a publication (excluding copies distributed free for promotional or other purposes)
check list	related questions to verify all that must be known, investigated or done
coarse screening	Initial (rough) check, at an early stage, on viability of a new idea
column mm	Area in a publication: the number of columns used multiplied by the depth in millimetres
competition	*Direct competition:* rival products or services (identical or similar) sold in a market. *Indirect competition:* alternative or dissimilar products or services on offer (e.g. sea cruise versus package tours to a land resort) that can reduce demand for the original offering
continental breakfast	Rolls, butter, preserves usually with coffee or tea
Continental Plan	Accommodation and continental breakfast included in quoted room rate
copy	Text of a publication or advertisement
copy platform	Main theme of an advertisement
customer need	In the broadest sense, potential customer's requirements which have to be satisfied
declining market	Market for a product or service whose total demand is falling

demand	Demand required of, or number of customers for, a product or service
direct mail	Mailed literature to selected prospects
diversification	When company enters an entirely new field of activity which it has not tackled before (e.g. tour operator buying accommodation units). Involves the introduction of new products or service usually to new markets or customers. The products need not be 'new' to the industry.
downgraded passenger	A passenger who travelled in a lower class of service than that to which he or she was entitled
economy class	Second-class travel with less space per passenger at fares much cheaper than first class. Also called *tourist class* if kept exclusively for package tour groups who in effect pay very low fares as part of the package price. Individuals paying the full fare may then have their own *cabin class* or equivalent, with more space and improved or slightly better services.
editorial publicity or 'free editorial'	Editorial matter describing a product, service or activity without charge to the initiating organisation
elapsed time	Time taken to travel between two points including any time change
English breakfast	Breakfast consisting of cereal, main (cooked) dish, toast, preserves and beverages
ETA and ETD	Estimated time of arrival and estimated time of departure
European plan (EP)	Accommodation only covered by quoted room rate

F	First class
FAA	Federal Aviation Administration (USA)
fare construction point	Point in an air fare computation where one fare ends and another starts
feasibility study	Study which ascertains whether a proposed course of action is possible
feedback	Intelligence (usually on sales and customer reactions) passed back to the company and used to update plans and intelligence
field selling	Direct selling by salespersons in the market to all prospects
franchise	Grant to retailer or operator of sole selling or operational rights within a specified area
gateway	Main city of access for any country where travellers go through customs and immigration formalities and on which international fares are calculated
growth market	Market in which demand for a product or service is increasing
handout	Cheap leaflet for handing out at exhibitions, conventions or by travel agents
IATA	International Air Transport Association. The governing body for world airlines. Establishes fares or fare levels, rules and regulations concerning carriage by air
ICAO	International Civil Aviation Organisation. International governmental body responsible for safety standards, communications and so on
inclusive tour (IT)	Inclusive tour is an advertised journey, including travel, accommodation, certain meals (usually the three main ones) and possibly other activities, arranged and promoted by a tour operator, which is paid for in full prior to departure

image	How customers view a firm and its products
impact	The effectiveness of an advertising or other campaign and the selling message
infrastructure	Roads, parking areas, railway lines, airport runways, utilities (such as drainage, sewage disposal, water supply, electricity and other power supply). Necessary for intensive human living activity within an area. Must be adequate to serve tourists and local residents. Its development should precede development of the superstructure (*which see*)
ITA	Institute of Travel Agents
ITX	Inclusive tour fares on which tour costs are based
key factors	Essential elements of a situation that affect the achievement of specific goals
key prospects	Important potential customers or buyers in a market who have substantial purchasing power
leaflet	Printed paper, folded to form four pages; may be stitched or stapled together if more pages required (*see also* brochure)
local press	In the UK, local newspapers covering a borough, rural district or similar area
mailing list	Classified list of names and addresses used for mail shots. Often compiled from membership lists of clubs, trade and professional associations/institutes, local council rates list, etc.
mailing shot	A single mailing operation
MAP	Modified American Plan. Accommodation, full breakfast and either lunch or dinner included in the stated room rate
margin	Difference between total cost of a product and its market price, i.e. the profit before tax

| medium/media | channel/channels of communication |
| MIX | Planned mixture of all elements of a specific marketing operation for optimal effect or greatest effect at minimum cost |

market mix: selection of markets and the volume of business attained/to be attained in each of them.

marketing mix: all the various marketing operations and the amounts of them that will, be or have been, used, where and when they will be, or were, used, etc.

product mix: selection of all products and the quantities of each to be/have been sold to give the best return for given resources and capabilities.

product-market mix: selection of the products and markets and their combination or permutation to give optimal return in any given resource and capabilities situation.

sales mix: the quantities of different products sold or to be sold and the incidence and timing of these sales

national press	In the UK, daily and Sunday papers with mass circulation throughout the country (many countries do not have a national press in this sense)
no-show	A person who fails to take up previously confirmed reservations for travel and/or accommodation
off-line	Countries or towns through which a carrier does not operate nor have traffic rights to pick up passengers
on-line	Countries or towns where a carrier has the right to pick up passengers
open-date ticket	A ticket that has been paid for but the actual date and time of the flights have yet to be declared by the passenger

open-jaw	A return journey with different originating and terminating ports. The latter need not be declared at the time of purchase of the ticket
opinion leaders	People who because of their status, position, etc., are considered to influence the views and decisions of others
PATA	Pacific Area Travel Association
penetration	Normally refers to the market share or extent by which market potential has been realised
pilot study	Short study carried out before main research to test accuracy of assumptions, etc.
point-of-sale	Place where sale or purchase occurs (American = point-of-purchase)
PTA	Prepaid ticket advice: notification by any means of communication that a person in one city has paid for the transportation of one or more people in another town or city. The journey need not involve the place where the fare was paid
price/demand price/volume relationship	Relationship between the price of a product and the demand for it
price sensitivity	Consumers' sensitivity to different prices and price changes
'product plus'	Unique property or characteristic of a product
product screening	Process whereby new or modified products are evaluated against company or marketing objectives, future potential and other critical factors
publicity	Process of securing attention and imparting a message
purchasing influences	All the factors which affect a (favourable) buying decision

RTW	Round the world
'skew'	The bias given to data, or way it has been distorted by bias either accidentally or deliberately injected into any study/research
size	A characteristic of a market or market segment, usually expressed in quantitative terms
standby fare	A low fare for people prepared to wait till the last minute to obtain any unoccupied seats
static market	One of relatively unchanging size, i.e. not subject to growth, decline or any fluctuations in demand
stopover	Deliberate interruption of journey, agreed in advance by the carrier, between point of origin and point of destination
superstructure	Hotels and other accommodation, restaurants, shopping facilities, entertainment services and structures (cinemas, theatres, museums, art galleries, concert halls) and traffic terminals. Dividing line between this and infrastructure not distinct but is fundamental to planning of new resorts, etc.
target	Quantity or thing to be achieved by specific activities, e.g. sales target. Not to be confused with budget (*which see*)
TC-1	IATA Traffic Conference Area 1 (North and South America and adjacent islands; Greenland, Bermuda, West Indies, islands of the Caribbean and the Hawaiian Islands)
TC-2	IATA Traffic Conference Area 2 (Europe, European USSR, adjacent islands, Azores, Africa and islands, Asia lying west of and including Iran, Ascension Island)
TC-3	IATA Traffic Conference Area 3 (all Asia

	east of Iran and islands; all of East Indies, Australia, New Zealand adjacent islands; islands of the Pacific Ocean excluding those in TC-1
tour-based fare	Creative roundtrip air or sea fare used by tour operators as basis of promoting an inclusive tour on which they qualify for overriding commission if they provide promotional literature in specified amounts
tour broker	Individual or company not owning transport or other facility who charters space, etc., to supply ground arrangements needed for package tour commissioned by a tour wholesaler
tour conductor	Individual in charge of or who personally escorts a group of passengers for all or part of the journey
unique selling proposition	(USP) A special benefit or property offered to customers that is unique to the product or service
upgraded passenger	A passenger who travelled in a class higher than that paid for
UATP	Universal Air Travel Plan – IATA credit card facility
visa	Authority permitting entry into a country
vouchers	Documents issued by wholesalers/tour operators for accommodation, meals, etc. The value of these are then debited back to the wholesaler
Y	Economy class

Bibliography

Abridged list of related books

Archer, B. H., *Demand Forecasting in Tourism* (Bangor, University of Wales Press, 1976).

Beaver, A., *Mind your own travel business* (2 vols) (Edgware, Beaver Travel Ltd, 1979).

Beaver, A., *Retail travel practice*, Wharton G. (ed.) (Edgware, Landtours Ltd, 1975).

Burkart, A. and Medlick, S., *Tourism – past, present and future*, 2nd edn (London, Heinemann, 1982).

Curran, P., *Principles and procedures of tour management* (Boston, CBI, 1978).

Eyre, E. C., *Mastering basic management* (Basingstoke, Macmillan Press Ltd, 1983).

Foster, Douglas, *Mastering marketing*, 2nd edn (Basingstoke, Macmillan Press Ltd, 1983).

Harvey, J., *Mastering economics*, 2nd edn (Basingstoke, Macmillan Press Ltd, 1984).

Holloway, J. C., *The business of tourism* (Plymouth, Macdonald and Evans, 1983).

Kaiser, C. and Helber, L. E., *Tourism planning and development* (London, Heinemann, 1978).

Medlik, S., *The business of hotels* (London, Heinemann, 1980).

Nelson-Jones, J. and Stewart, P., A practical guide to package holiday law and contracts (London: Fourmat Publishing, 1985).

Organisation for Economic Cooperation and Development *International tourism and tourism policy in OECD member countries* (Paris, OECD Annual).

Pearce, D., *Tourism development* (London, Longman, 1981).

Schmoll, G. A., *Tourism promotion* (London, TIP, 1977).

World Tourism Organisation *World tourism statistics* (Madrid, WTO Annual).

Index